TRADE SECRET LAW
IN A NUTSHELL

By

SHARON K. SANDEEN
Professor of Law,
Hamline University

ELIZABETH A. ROWE
UF Research Foundation Professor of Law,
University of Florida

WEST®

Mat #41269521

10/10/13

Nutshell Series, In a Nutshell and the Nutshell Logo are trademarks registered in the U.S. Patent and Trademark Office.

© 2013 LEG, Inc. d/b/a West Academic Publishing

      610 Opperman Drive
      St. Paul, MN 55123
      1-800-313-9378

West, West Academic Publishing, and West Academic are trademarks of West Publishing Corporation, used under license.

Printed in the United States of America

ISBN: 978–0–314–28116–6

In memory of my parents.
S.K.S.

To Fred, Jonathan, and Victoria.
E.A.R.

PREFACE

Statistics about the amount and value of intellectual property owned by U.S. and foreign companies tend to be overstated and unverifiable. However, there is no escaping the fact that every company probably owns one or more trade secrets, even if they do not know it. In fact, although patent, copyright, and trademark law get most of the attention when intellectual property rights are discussed, arguably it is trade secret law that does most of the work protecting the valuable intangible assets of companies, particularly small and mid-sized businesses. This is because the type of information that can be protected by trade secret law is very broad and companies are inclined to keep at least a portion of their operations private.

Because a wide array of information can be protected if it meets the requirements of trade secret law, it is important for businesses and their attorneys to understand how to identify and protect valuable trade secrets. Conversely, due to the high costs of trade secret litigation, it is also imperative for businesses to understand the limits of trade secret protection. For important public policy reasons, not every bit of information that a business creates or holds is deserving of trade secret protection.

In this book, you will learn the details of trade secret law both under common law and the Uniform Trade Secrets Act. Topics covered include: (1) the

scope of trade secret protection; (2) the requirements for establishing trade secret rights (3) the
legal and policy limitations of trade secret protection; (4) the essential elements of a claim for trade
secret misappropriation; (5) major defenses; and (6)
available remedies.

Because there are many practical aspects to trade
secret protection, the book is one-part legal, and
one-part practical. In addition to explaining the
black-letter law governing trade secrets, it provides
practical advice on how to protect trade secrets and
an overview of many of the subtle issues that can
arise in trade secret misappropriation cases. It is
designed to provide useful information to attorneys,
law students, and business professionals alike. It
can also serve as a companion to our casebook, *Cases and Materials on Trade Secret Law* (West 2012).

As of the date of publication of this book, nearly
all states (47) have adopted the Uniform Trade Secrets Act (the UTSA) and North Carolina has enacted a statute that is similar to the UTSA. Accordingly, this book focuses on trade secret doctrine as defined by the UTSA. However, given the size and influence of the two states that have yet to adopt the
UTSA (Massachusetts and New York), applicable
provisions of the Restatement (First) of Torts and
the Restatement (Third) of Unfair Competition are
discussed where appropriate. Of course, the laws of
each individual state should be researched as necessary to determine whether and to what extent they
deviate from the basic principles that are detailed
herein. Generally, those differences often relate to

the definition of a trade secret and the scope of available remedies for trade secret misappropriation.

SHARON K. SANDEEN
ELIZABETH A. ROWE

June 2013

ACKNOWLEDGMENTS

We have many people and several organizations to thank for assisting us with the publication of this book. We are particularly grateful to the American Law Institute and the Uniform Law Commission for allowing us to reprint portions of their copyrighted works.

Throughout the book you will find excerpts from the Restatement (First) of Torts (Copyright 1939 by the American Law Institute) and the Restatement (Third) of Unfair Competition (Copyright 1995 by the American Law Institute). These materials are reprinted with permission of The American Law Institute. All right reserved.

The Uniform Law Commission (also known as the National Conference of Commissioners of Uniform State Laws) not only allowed us to quote extensively from the Uniform Trade Secrets Act (UTSA), but gave us permission to include the entirety of the UTSA (as amended in 1985), with commentary, in Appendix A to this book.

Professor Sandeen wishes to thank her research assistants, particularly Jessica Alm and Holly Danielson, for their excellent work on the final review and cite-checking for this book. Credit also goes to a long-list of research assistants who helped with trade secret research throughout the years, including most recently, Lauren Dwyer, Jameelah Haadee, Mike Ryan, and Michael Mangold.

Professor Rowe wishes to acknowledge and thank her many current and former law students who have continued to motivate her study of trade secret law. She is grateful to Matthew Morrow for his research assistance on this book, as well as previous trade secret research assistants, including most recently, Jonathan Blocker, Jessica DaFonte, Derek Fahey, Constance Jones, Seth Jones, Daniel Mahfood, Alicia Phillip, Abood Shebib, Robyn Shelton, Adrianna Swedowski, and Mi Zhou, whose contributions are indirectly reflected herein. Thanks also to the University of Florida Levin College of law for its generous research support.

INTRODUCTION

Like other areas of law, trade secret law has evolved over a long period of time and while it is important to understand the current state of the law, it is also important to know its historic origins and the theories and policies that underlie trade secret doctrine. An understanding of the evolution of trade secret law is particularly important because there is a tendency in trade secret cases for attorneys and judges to cling to "old" principles of law which, arguably, were modified and refined by the enactment of the Uniform Trade Secrets Act (the UTSA).

With the foregoing in mind, this book begins in Chapter 1 with an examination of the theories, origin, and evolution of trade secret law. An important insight that emerges from this examination is that there is an ongoing debate among scholars whether trade secret doctrine is anchored in property theory or principles of unfair competition law. This debate has naturally led to questions about which approach better protects the interests of society and trade secret owners.

As is noted throughout this book, whether one views trade secrets as a form of property or not can affect how trade secret law is applied. Generally, those who desire more absolute protection for information tend to favor the property view, while those who see the potential anti-competitive effects of strong trade secret rights tend to favor the unfair competition view. There is an emotional appeal to both points of view. Thus, as a practical matter, the plaintiffs in a trade secret misappropriation case will not hesitate to assert either or both arguments if it will help their case.

Although for rhetorical or philosophical reasons a litigant may choose to emphasize either the property or unfair competition views of trade secret law, in reality trade secret doctrine includes aspects of both. This is because there are two essential requirements of a trade secret misappropriation claim. First, the information to be protected must be a trade secret (a form of intangible property). Second, the trade secrets must have been misappropriated (a form of unfair competition).

Chapters 2 and 3 explore the definition of a trade secret and the requirements for trade secret protection. Pursuant to the UTSA, there are three requirements. First, the information in question must be secret; in trade secret parlance it must not be "generally known" or "readily ascertainable." Second, the information must have "independent economic value" because it is secret. Third, for information to be protected as a trade secret it must be the subject of efforts that are reasonable under the circumstances to protect its secrecy.

Chapters 4 through 6 focus on lawsuits for trade secret misappropriation. In Chapter 4, the essential elements of a trade secret misappropriation claim are explored, including a careful examination of the possible types of misappropriation. This includes misappropriation by improper means and misappropriation by breach of a duty of confidentiality. Chapter 5 looks at trade secret litigation from the perspective of the defendant, detailing the major defenses and strategies to be pursued. The remedies that are available for trade secret misappropriation are discussed in Chapter 6.

Because most trade secret misappropriation cases arise in the employment context, Chapter 7 focuses on a number of special employment-related issues, including the value and enforceability of non-compete and non-disclosure agreements. The question of the ownership of trade secrets is also discussed.

The book concludes in Chapters 8, 9, and 10 with an examination of three important trade secret issues: (1) the protection of trade secrets in dealings with the government; (2) the protection of trade secrets outside of the United States; and (3) potential criminal liability for trade secret misappropriation and related crimes.

ABOUT THE AUTHORS

Sharon K. Sandeen is a Professor of Law at Hamline University School of Law in Saint Paul, Minnesota where she teaches a variety of intellectual property courses, including trade secret law. Prior to starting her teaching career, she practiced law in California for over fifteen years where she specialized in IP litigation, protection, and counseling. Professor Sandeen received an LL.M. from the University of California, Berkeley School of Law (Boalt Hall), a Juris Doctorate from the University of Pacific, McGeorge School of Law, and a Bachelor of Arts degree from the University of California, Berkeley. She is a Fellow of the American Bar Foundation and a member of the California Bar.

Elizabeth A. Rowe is a Professor of Law at the University of Florida Levin College of Law and the Director of the Program in Intellectual Property Law. She teaches Trade Secret Law, Corporate Espionage, Trademark Law, and Patent Law. Professor Rowe is currently the holder of the University of Florida Research Foundation Professorship as well as the Feldman Gale Term Professorship in Intellectual Property Law. She is a former litigation partner at Hale and Dorr (now WilmerHale) in Boston where her practice focused largely on trade secret litigation and employment litigation. She received her Juris Doctorate, *cum laude*, from Harvard Law School, and her Master of Arts and Bachelor of Arts degrees from the University of Florida. She is a member of the Massachusetts Bar.

OUTLINE

TABLE OF CASES

References are to Pages

TABLE OF STATUTES

References are to Pages

TABLE OF AUTHORITIES

References are to Pages

TABLE OF AUTHORITIES

TRADE SECRET LAW

IN A NUTSHELL

CHAPTER 1

THE THEORIES, ORIGIN, AND EVOLUTION OF TRADE SECRET LAW

§ 1.1 THE COMMON LAW DEVELOPMENT OF TRADE SECRET LAW

Trade secret law in the United States emerged in the middle of the 19th Century; its development generally coinciding with the Industrial Revolution. Like other unfair competition and business torts that were developing at the time, including trademark infringement, the development of trade secret principles arose from cases that were brought to resolve disputes between competitors. The classic case involved a claim by one business owner that the defendant was about to disclose or wrongfully use "his" secret process, method, or formula. *See Vickery v. Welch*, 36 Mass. 523 (1837) (involving a process for making chocolate) and *Peabody v. Norfolk*, 98 Mass. 452 (1868) (involving a process for making gunny cloth). Often, these complaints arose after a valued employee (or, in an earlier time, a valued apprentice) left the employ of one company and began work for a competitor.

With little case law and no statutes at their disposal, attorneys in early trade secret cases relied upon a variety of theories and claims for relief, including tort law, contract law, agency law, the law of trusts, and principles of equity. Some claims stressed the asserted property nature of trade secrets while others stressed the unfair competition aspects of trade secret misappropriation. *Compare Cincinnati Bell Foundry Co. v. Dodds*, 1887 WL 469 (1887) *with Allen-Qually Co. v. Shellmar Products, Co.* 31 F. 2d. 293 (1920). Other litigants relied principally on the existence of express or implied duties of confidentiality and couched their claims in breach of contract terms. *See Peabody v. Norfolk,* 98 Mass. 452.

From the mid-1860s through 1988 when the Uniform Trade Secrets Act (the UTSA) was adopted by most states, trade secret law in the United States was primarily governed by common law. In keeping with the purpose of the *Restatement* series, this common law first found organized expression in the *Restatement (First) of Torts* (hereinafter the *Restatement of Torts*).

§ 1.2   THE *RESTATEMENT OF TORTS*

By the mid-1930s, enough trade secret principles had developed so that in 1939 the American Law Institute could "restate" the law of trade secrecy in three sections of the *Restatement of Torts*: sections 757, 758, and 759. Although not very lengthy or detailed, section 757 generally describes the primary tortious activity (or wrong) of a trade secret claim as the disclosure of another's trade secret (1) when the discovery of the trade secret was by improper means, (2) the disclosure was made in breach of a duty of confidentiality, or (3) the disclosure was by a third party (not the original misappropriator) who had knowledge that the trade secret was improperly acquired by another. Rest. (First) of Torts, § 757 (1939).

Section 758 of the *Restatement of Torts* addresses situations where the misappropriated trade secret falls into the hands of a third-party who does not have knowledge of the original misappropriation. The third-party may become liable for trade secret misappropriation if he is put on timely notice of the earlier misappropriation. Section 758 states that notice is timely if it is given before the third party "in good faith paid value for the secret" or otherwise "changed his position." Restatement (First) of Torts, § 758.

Section 759 of the *Restatement of Torts* seems out of place when compared to modern conceptions of trade secret law because it deals with business information, generally, and not just trade secret information. It recognizes a cause of action where one improperly acquires business information with the specific purpose of "advancing a rival business interest." Restatement (First) of Torts, § 759. Compared to Section 757, it was not highly litigated and the cause of action that it describes was not carried forward into the UTSA or the *Restatement (Third) of Unfair Competition* (hereinafter the *Restatement of Unfair Competition*), discussed *infra*. It does, however, highlight a recurring issue of trade secret law, namely, whether any theories of liability exist to protect business information that does not qualify for trade secret protection. *See infra* § 2.8.7.

§ 1.3 THE PURPOSES OF TRADE SECRET LAW

As with the evolution of trade secret law general-ly, the stated purposes of trade secret law have evolved through the years. In the early years, the primary purpose was the preservation of commer-cial ethics. Referring to former employees who started a competing business using plaintiff's trade secrets, one court noted, "[t]his is not legitimate competition, which it is always the policy of the law to foster and encourage, but it is *contra bonos mores,* and constitutes a breach of trust, which a court of law, and much less a court of equity, should not tol-erate." *Eastman Co. v. Reichenbach,* 20 N.Y.S. 110, 116 (Sup. Ct. 1892), *aff'd sub nom. Eastman Kodak Co. v. Reichenbach,* 29 N.Y.S. 1143 (Sup. Ct. 1894). This is why the tort of trade secret misappropriation is classified as a form of unfair competition, as evi-denced by its inclusion in the *Restatement of Unfair Competition.*

As corporate and business interest in intellectual property increased and trade secrets began to be seen as a form of intellectual property, another pur-pose of trade secret law was identified; namely, to encourage invention and innovation. *See Kewanee Oil Co. v. Bicron Corp.,* 416 U.S. 470, 481–482 (1974) ("Trade secret law will encourage invention in areas where patent law does not reach, and will prompt the independent innovator to proceed with the discovery and exploitation of his invention.") The incentive rationale and utilitarian view of trade secrecy is consistent with the principal rationales for patent and copyright law and is based upon eco-

nomic theory and assumptions about what moti-
vates individuals to invent and create. Trade secret
law is said to supplement patent law and provide a
means of internalizing the benefits of innovation.
See David D. Friedman, William M. Landes, &
Richard A. Posner, *Some Economics of Trade Secret
Law*, 5 J. Econ. Persp. 61 (1991).

Without intellectual property protection, the theory goes, individuals will be disinclined to create
and invent because of the public goods problem
which results when a good is non-excludable and
non-rivalrous. This can happen, for instance, when
creations and inventions are publicly disclosed or
shared, thereby allowing others to copy the creations and inventions at little or no cost. Since trade
secrets are, by definition, kept from the public, the
public goods problem usually arises with respect to
trade secrets when there is a need to share the secrets with others.

According to the "Arrow information paradox,"
economic actors need information to make decisions
that are consistent with their economic self-interest.
Kenneth J. Arrow, *Essays in the Theory of Risk
Bearing* (No. Holland Pub. Co. 1971). The paradox
with respect to trade secrets is that the holders of
secrets are disinclined to share the very information
that is needed for a potential buyer or licensee to
determine if it wants to purchase or license the information. Trade secret law specifies the circumstances under which disclosures can be made without loss of trade secrecy. As noted in *Some Economics of Trade Secret Law,* trade secret law also makes

it possible for businesses to protect their secrets without wasteful or inefficient expense.

The foregoing leads to the third, but seemingly illogical, purpose of trade secret law. It emerged out of *Kewanee* when the Supreme Court had to explain how state trade secret law did not interfere with the disclosure purpose of patent law. The court concluded that trade secret law does not conflict with the disclosure goals of U.S. patent law because it facilitates the sharing of information, albeit on a smaller scale. *See Kewanee Oil Co. v. Bicron Corp.*, 416 U.S. at 484–486 (commenting that the abolition of trade secret law would result in the hoarding rather than the dissemination of knowledge). This is due to a concept of trade secret law known as "relative secrecy." Pursuant to this concept, explained in greater detail in § 3.1, trade secrets do not have to be kept absolutely secret to be protected but can be shared pursuant to an express or implied duty of confidentiality.

§ 1.4   THE PROPERTY/NOT PROPERTY DEBATE OF TRADE SECRET THEORY

Since the emergence of trade secret law in the United States in the mid-1800s, there has been an enduring debate among lawyers, judges, and legal scholars about whether and when trade secrets should be considered a form of property. Comment a. to the *Restatement of Torts*, section 757, reads:

> The suggestion that one has a right to exclude others from the use of his trade secret because he has a right of property in the idea has been

frequently advanced and rejected. The theory that has prevailed is that the protection is afforded only by a general duty of good faith and that the liability rests upon breach of this duty; . . . Apart from breach of contract, abuse of confidence or impropriety in the means of procurement, trade secrets may be copied as freely as devices or processes which are not secret.

Rest. (First) of Torts, § 757, cmt. a.

Fueling the debate about whether trade secrets are property is an oft-cited passage from *E. I. Du Pont De Nemours Powder Co. v. Masland*, 244 U.S. 100 (1917) in which Justice Holmes wrote:

Whether the plaintiffs have any valuable secret or not the defendant knows the facts, whatever they are, through a special confidence that he accepted. The property may be denied, but the confidence cannot be. Therefore the starting point for the present matter is not property or due process of law, but that the defendant stood in confidential relations with the plaintiffs, or one of them.

Justice Holmes' reluctance in 1917 to categorize trade secrets as a form of property may have reflected his personal views concerning the scope and nature of property rights, but it was also consistent with the prevalent view of the time. The modern case that is frequently cited for the proposition that trade secrets are private property, *Ruckelshaus v. Monsanto Co*, 46 U.S. 986 (1984), reflects a different point of view.

In *Ruckelshaus* the Supreme Court considered whether certain provisions of the Federal Insecticide, Fungicide, and Rodenticide Act (FIFRA) were unconstitutional. Monsanto argued that the provisions of the law that required it to disclose certain information and data were unconstitutional because they amounted to a taking of property without just compensation in violation of the Fifth Amendment to the U.S. Constitution. In finding a property interest in Monsanto's data, the Court explained:

> Although this Court never has squarely addressed the question whether a person can have a property interest in a trade secret, which is admittedly intangible, the Court has found other kinds of intangible interests to be property for purposes of the Fifth Amendment's Takings Clause.

The court went on to note, however, that Monsanto's Takings claim was based upon the wording of the applicable statute which created an "investment-backed expectation" that the information that Monsanto submitted to the government would be protected from disclosure for a period of fifteen years. 46 U.S. at 1005. Thus, the case does not stand for the general proposition that all government requests for trade secret information or other data constitute a taking of private property.

As indicated by commentary to Section 39 of the *Restatement of Unfair Competition,* although the property/not property debate continues, it has had little practical effect on trade secret doctrine.

> The cases generally require that the plaintiff establish both the existence of a trade secret under the principles described in this Section and the fact of misconduct by the defendant under the rules stated in § 40. Many cases acknowledge that the primary issue is the propriety of the defendant's conduct as a means of competition.

Rest. (Third) of Unfair Competition, § 39, cmt. b (1995).

In practice, whether trade secrets are characterized as property often depends upon the facts of a case and the perceived power of the property rhetoric. It also depends upon whether trade secret law is perceived as a means to punish and prevent wrongful behavior or to protect property rights. Often, assertions of "unfair competition" or unfairness hold greater sway with judges and juries. Moreover, although the rhetoric of property rights may suggest that all forms of property are the same, this is not the case. Even when trade secrets are categorized as a form of property, the limited scope and fleeting nature of that property right must be taken into account when applying the law. As one commentator has noted, trade secret rights are in a special category of property rights known as "intellectual property rights" which have both similar and different features than real and personal property rights. *See* Mark Lemley, *The Surprising Virtue of Treating Trade Secrets as IP Rights*, 61 Stan. L. Rev. 311 (2008).

Ultimately, the real value of a property characterization may lie in the ancillary effects of such a
characterization. As explained in *Milgrim on Trade
Secrets,* "different legal consequences might flow
from the [property] characterization, including potentially different statute of limitations, admissibil-
ity of evidence principles and remedies." Roger
Milgrim and Eric Bensen, *Milgrim on Trade Secrets*,
§ 3.01 (2012) (hereinafter *Milgrim on Trade Secrets*). Whether trade secrets are characterized as
property may also affect the application of defenses,
including the First Amendment defense (discussed
in § 5.9) and the application of principles of free
competition.

In summary, because trade secrets can be bought,
sold, licensed, and used as security for a loan, they
will often be treated as a form of property. *See
Ruckelshaus v. Monsanto Co.* 467 U.S. 986, 1002–
04. However, like other forms of intellectual property rights, trade secrets are not an absolute form of
property and the intangible nature of "information"
sometimes makes a property characterization inapt.
See Alderson v. U.S., 718 F. Supp. 2d 1186 (9th Cir.
2010) (finding that information that was provided to
the government pursuant to the False Claims Act
was not property for purposes of federal income tax
purposes). Additionally, from a practical point of
view, the characterization of trade secrets as property is not always necessary or in the best interest
of trade secret owners.

§ 1.5   THE UNIFORM TRADE
SECRETS ACT

While the common law of trade secrecy developed in the U.S. for over one hundred years, a variety of events and forces transpired in the middle-part of the Twentieth Century to convince members of the practicing bar that a uniform trade secret law was advisable. *See* Sharon K., Sandeen, *The Evolution of Trade Secret Law and Why Courts Commit Error When They Do Not Follow the Uniform Trade Secrets Act*, 33 Hamline L. Rev. 493 (2010). First, the U.S. Supreme Court's decision in the famous case of *Erie Railroad Co. v. Tompkins*, 304 U.S. 64 (1938) caused a vacuum in the law of unfair competition because the development of a body of federal common law (except with respect to the application of federal statutes) was no longer possible. In order to fill this vacuum, interested attorneys and policymakers advocated for a number of uniform laws, including the UTSA. *See* Unif. Trade Secrets Act (amended 1985), reprinted in Appendix A.

Second, the Supreme Court's decisions in the companion cases known as *Sears/Compco* raised serious doubts about the ability of states to regulate acts of unfair competition when such state laws conflicted with U.S. patent law. *See Sears, Roebuck & Co. v. Stiffel Co*, 376 U.S. 225 (1964) and *Compco Corp. v. Day-brite Lighting, Inc.*, 376 U.S. 234 (1964). While, as it turned out, the *Sears/Compco* cases did not preclude all state unfair competition laws, they did signal that such laws must be carefully drafted and circumscribed to avoid conflicts with federal law. The lengthy and multi-stakeholder process that is used to draft uniform laws was one way to ensure that state unfair competition laws would not be drafted in a manner that unduly conflicted with federal law.

The third factor leading to the drafting and adoption of the UTSA was a desire to improve trade secret law as it had developed at common law. Many businesses and their attorneys were concerned about the incomplete and inconsistent development of trade secret doctrine and, thus, advocated for a uniform act to make trade secret law more consistent and predictable. As explained in the Prefatory Note to the UTSA, "[n]otwithstanding the commercial importance of state trade secret law to interstate business, this law has not developed satisfactorily." Unif. Trade Secret Act (amended 1985), Prefatory Note, reprinted in Appendix A. Based upon a review of the various drafts of the UTSA, the principal issues of concern were: (1) the definition of a trade secret; (2) the meaning of misappropriation; (3) the availability, scope, and length of injunctive relief; (4) the nature and extent of monetary relief, including punitive damages and attorney's fees; (5) the treatment of trade secrets during litigation; and (6) the effect of the UTSA on other principles of law.

Under the auspices of the American Bar Association (the ABA), an effort was launched in the mid-1960s to draft a uniform law to govern trade secrets, ultimately leading to the adoption of the UTSA by the National Conference of Commissioners of Uniform State Laws (NCCUSL, but now known as the Uniform Law Commission) in August of 1979. Since 1989, after the State of Alaska became the twenty-sixth state to enact its version of the UTSA, the UTSA has been the primary source of trade secret law in the United States. With the recent adoption of the UTSA by Texas (effective September 1, 2013) and New Jersey (effective January 9, 2012), the UTSA has now been adopted (with some variations) by 47 states, the District of Columbia, Puerto Rico, and the U.S. Virgin Islands. The two states that have not yet adopted the UTSA are New York and Massachusetts. North Carolina is often counted among the states that have adopted the UTSA because it enacted a statute that is similar. However, because of certain modifications, the Uniform Law Commission does not consider the North Carolina statute to be an official adoption of the UTSA.

CHAPTER 2
TRADE SECRET SUBJECT MATTER

§ 2.1   DEFINITION OF A TRADE SECRET UNDER THE UNIFORM TRADE SECRETS ACT

One of the motivating factors behind the adoption of the UTSA was concern that some courts were finding trade secret misappropriation without first finding that there was a trade secret. This typically happened in cases where the defendant's wrongful acts were particularly egregious and where the courts emphasized the unfair competition view of trade secret law instead of a more balanced view that included the property perspective. To solve this problem it was felt that a fixed definition of a trade secret was needed that would include both aspects of trade secret theory.

The modern view of trade secret law under the UTSA defines a trade secret very broadly. Almost anything of competitive value to a company can be a trade secret as long as it meets the three requirements of trade secret protection: secrecy, independent economic value, and reasonable efforts to maintain secrecy. These requirements are embedded in the definition of a trade secret under the UTSA, which defines a trade secret as:

[I]nformation, including a formula, pattern, compilation, program, device, method, technique or process, that:

(i) derives independent economic value, actual or potential, from not being generally known to, and not being readily ascertainable by proper means by, other persons who can obtain economic value from its disclosure or use, and

(ii) is the subject of efforts that are reasonable under the circumstances to maintain its secrecy.

Unif. Trade Secrets Act § 1(4) (amended 1985), reprinted in Appendix A.

Based upon the foregoing, a wide range of confidential business information can be protectable trade secrets. This can include inventions of the sort that might be patentable as well as non-patentable information such as customer lists, sales records, pricing information, and customer information. *See Lyn-Flex West, Inc. v. Dieckhaus*, 24 S.W. 3d 693 (Mo. Ct. of App. 1999) (finding a "price book" consisting of a "detailed compilation of technical and non-technical data" to be a trade secret). Some jurisdictions have recognized trade secret protection for secret contract terms, marketing strategies, and industry studies. *See PepsiCo, Inc. v. Redmond*, 54 F.3d 1262, 1265 (7th Cir. 1995) (recognizing strategic financial and marketing information as trade secrets); *Cardinal Freight Carriers, Inc. v. Hunt Transp. Servs., Inc.*, 336 Ark. 143, 149–50 (Ark. 1999) (recognizing trade secret protection for methods, processes, operations, and marketing programs); *ConAgra, Inc. v. Tyson Foods, Inc.*, 342 Ark. 672, 676–78 (Ark. 2000) (holding that certain terms contained in customer contracts may be trade secrets, but were not protected because Plaintiff failed to maintain secrecy). Even "techniques for improving oneself" and spiritual processes have been recognized as trade secrets. *See Religious Tech. Ctr. v. Netcom On-line Commc'ns Servs., Inc.,* 923 F. Supp. 1231 (N.D. Cal. 1995).

As is explained in greater detail *infra*, under the UTSA a trade secret does not need to be "in use" (continuous or otherwise) to be protected. *See* Unif. Trade Secrets Act § 1(4), cmt. Also, negative information—comprised of failed research or an ineffective process—can also be protected. *See infra* § 2.6. Finally, known information that is collected and combined in a novel and unique way and the new information added thereto can be protected if it otherwise meets the requirements of the UTSA. *See infra* § 2.7.

§ 2.2   DEFINITION OF A TRADE SECRET UNDER THE *RESTATEMENT OF TORTS*

As noted previously, the *Restatement of Torts* was the first major effort to synthesize the developing law of trade secrets. The text of the *Restatement of Torts*, however, does not include a definition of a trade secret. Rather, a comment to section 757 provides that:

A trade secret may consist of any formula, pattern, device or compilation of information which is used in one's business, and which gives him an opportunity to obtain an advantage over competitors who do not know or use it . . . it is not simply information as to a single or ephemeral events in the conduct of the business, as for example, the amount or other terms of a secret bid for a contract . . . A trade secret is a process or device for continuous use in the operation of a business . . . .

Restatement (First) of Torts, § 757, cmt. b (1939).

The commentary to the *Restatement of Torts* lists six factors that should be considered in determining whether something is a trade secret. Often referred to as the "*Restatement* factors" or the "six-factor test," these are:

1. The extent to which the information is known outside of the business;

2. The extent to which the information is known by employees and others inside the business;

3. The extent of measures taken to guard the secrecy of the information;

4. The value of the information to the business and competitors;

5. The amount of effort or money expended in developing the information; and

6. The ease or difficulty with which the information could be properly acquired or duplicated by others.

Restatement (First) of Torts, § 757, cmt. b (1939).

In most decisions that apply the *Restatement* factors, it does not appear that all the elements must be satisfied. *See, e.g.*, *In re Bass*, 113 S.W.3d 735, 740 (Tex. 2003) ("We agree with the Restatement and the majority of jurisdictions that the party claiming a trade secret should not be required to satisfy all six factors because trade secrets do not fit neatly into each factor every time.") Rather, courts consider some or all of the factors in an effort to reach a general conclusion on whether the information should be protected as a trade secret. *See, e.g., Learning Curve Toys, Inc. v. PlayWood Toys, Inc.*, 342 F.3d 714, 722–730 (7th Cir. 2003). In practice, where the defendant's actions are particularly egregious or wrong it is likely that the six-factors will be applied in a manner that supports a finding of trade secrecy. This is one reason why the UTSA was adopted, to prevent the loose and inconsistent application of the six-factor test.

Since the adoption of the *Restatement of Torts* provisions on trade secret law in 1939, trade secret doctrine has continued to evolve, so much so in fact that the American Law Institute decided to update its treatment of trade secret law with the publication in 1995 of the *Restatement of Unfair Competition*. However, despite the publication of the *Restatement of Unfair Competition* and the adoption of the UTSA by most states, some courts and commentators continue to cite the *Restatement of Torts* as applicable, if not helpful, authority. *See, e.g., Learning Curve Toys, Inc. v. PlayWood Toys, Inc.*, 342 F.3d 714.

In UTSA jurisdictions, continued reliance on the *Restatement of Torts* appears to be a mistake particularly where the UTSA differs from the common law. *See infra* § 2.4. As noted in the Prefatory Notes of the UTSA, although the UTSA codifies some basic principles of the common law of trade secrecy, it also contributes new material and adopts the "better reasoned cases" in some areas. Moreover, in the remaining non-UTSA jurisdictions, care must be taken to determine whether the common law as expressed in the *Restatement of Torts* or the *Restatement of Unfair Competition* governs and whether the jurisdiction prefers to follow the common law as expressed in its own reported cases rather than the common law as expressed in the *Restatements*.

§ 2.3   DEFINITION OF A TRADE SECRET UNDER THE *RESTATEMENT OF UNFAIR COMPETITION*

The *Restatement of Unfair Competition,* although published after the adoption of the UTSA, includes a definition of a trade secret that is different from that which is contained in the UTSA. Section 39 states:

> A trade secret is any information that can be used in the operation of a business or other enterprise and that is sufficiently valuable and secret to afford an actual or potential economic advantage over others.

Restatement (Third) of Unfair Competition § 39 (1995). However, the associated comment states that: "[t]he concept of a trade secret as defined in this Section is intended to be consistent with the definition of 'trade secret' in § 1(4) of the [UTSA]." *Id*. at cmt. b.

While the intent of the *Restatement of Unfair Competition* may have been to restate the UTSA's definition of a trade secret, and the scope of information that is protectable is conceptually as broad as under the UTSA, the foregoing definition does not include an explicit "reasonable efforts" requirement. Rather, the information need only be "sufficiently secret." As explained in the commentary to Section 39:

> The rule stated in this Section requires only secrecy sufficient to confer an actual or potential economic advantage on one who possesses the information. Thus, the requirement of secrecy is satisfied if it would be difficult or costly for others who could exploit the information to acquire it without resort to the wrongful conduct proscribed under § 40.

Restatement (Third) of Unfair Competition § 39 cmt. f (1995). In comment g it is noted that "[p]recautions taken to maintain the secrecy of information are relevant in determining whether the information qualifies for protection as a trade secret." *Id.* at cmt. g.

The foregoing suggests that information can be a trade secret under the *Restatement of Unfair Competition* even if a trade secret owner does not take affirmative steps to identify and protect such information. This distinction, discussed more fully in § 3.4.2 *infra*, highlights an issue that arises under the UTSA; namely, whether information that was actually secret may be protected as a trade secret if the owner of the information did not undertake reasonable efforts to maintain its secrecy. *Compare Electro-Craft Corp. v. Controlled Motion, Inc.*, 332

N.W.2d 890 (Minn. 1983), *with Rockwell Graphic Sys., Inc. v. DEV Indus., Inc.*, 935 F.2d 174 (7th Cir. 1991). The answer to this question arguably depends upon the purpose of the reasonable efforts requirement. If its purpose is to put others on notice of the existence of trade secrets, then the requirement should not be overlooked. If the requirement only serves an evidentiary purpose on the issue of secrecy, then other evidence may suffice to prove the requisite secrecy.

§ 2.4   COMPARING THE DEFINITIONS OF A TRADE SECRET UNDER THE DIFFERENT SOURCES OF LAW

Because, as detailed above, not all definitions of a trade secret are the same, it is important to understand the practical realities of those differences, particularly where an individual or company wishes to protect trade secrets in multiple jurisdictions. The first thing to realize is that the UTSA, as enacted into law in each UTSA jurisdiction, is primary authority for the definition whereas the *Restatements* are secondary authority. Thus, the three mandatory requirements of trade secrecy under the UTSA should trump the six-factor test of the *Restatement of Torts* in UTSA jurisdictions. Additionally, in non-UTSA jurisdictions, the definition of a trade secret tends to be more flexible because, by definition, the common law that is reflected in the *Restatements* can continue to evolve and adapt.

The foregoing distinction can be illustrated by comparing trade secret cases in non-UTSA and UTSA jurisdictions (and, by extension, by comparing trade secret cases from the United States with trade secret cases from other countries). For instance, *Enterprise Leasing Co. of Phoenix v. Ehmke*, 197 Ariz. 144, is an example of a case where the court carefully applied the three requirements of the UTSA in finding that there were protectable trade secrets. *Gen. Aniline & Film Corp. v. Frantz*, 272 N.Y.S.2d 600 (Sup. Ct. 1966), illustrates the more flexible and less rigorous approach under the *Restatement of Torts*.

Beyond the foregoing, the major differences between the *Restatement of Torts* definition of a trade secret and the more modern UTSA and *Restatement of Unfair Competition* definitions are that: (a) the modern approach does not require that the secret be "in continuous use" by the owner (potential value and single use are enough); and (b) the modern formulations put slightly more emphasis on the trade secret holder's efforts to keep the information a secret. Additionally, it can be argued that factor 5 of the *Restatement of Torts* factors is not part of either the UTSA or *Restatement of Unfair Competition* definitions, except to the extent that the amount of effort or money expended may relate to the readily ascertainable, economic value, and reasonable efforts requirements of the UTSA and the "sufficiently valuable and secret" requirements of the *Restatement of Unfair Competition.*

The continuous use requirement of the *Restatement of Torts,* where it applies, may affect outcomes by narrowing the scope of information that can be protectable as a trade secret. Based upon the use requirement it is generally understood that negative information, unused information, and information that is only used once or for a short period of time cannot be a trade secret. *See, e.g.,* *Lehman v. Dow Jones & Co, Inc.,* 783 F.2d 285, 298 (2d Cir. 1986) (applying N.Y. law) (characterizing information and analysis regarding a particular business deal as the plaintiff's "product," and not "a process or device for continuous use in the operation of the business"). Conversely, in jurisdictions that follow the UTSA and the *Restatement of Unfair Competition,* it is generally understood that negative or unused information can conceivably be protected as a trade secret provided that it meets the other requirements of trade secrecy. However, as a practical matter, it may be difficult to prove that unused information has the requisite independent economic value. *See infra* § 3.3. Moreover, the lack of use is likely to affect the availability of remedies.

Another issue that the use requirement of the *Restatement of Torts* raises is whether trade secrets that once existed can lose their trade secret status once use ceases. *See Victor Chem. Works v. Iliff,* 132 N.E. 806, 813 (Ill. 1921) (noting that plaintiff's discontinued use of a trade secret for two years and resumption of use only after start of the suit may provide grounds for "failure to prove an allegation of irreparable injury" sufficient to entitle it to equitable relief). Under the UTSA and *Restatement of Unfair Competition* definitions of a trade secret, the focus of the inquiry would not be on whether the information is used but on whether it continues to have economic value. In this regard, it is possible for information that once enjoyed trade secrecy to become stale and lose protection as a trade secret. *See Fox Sports Net N., L.L.C. v. Minnesota Twins P'ship,* 319 F.3d 329, 336 (8th Cir. 2003) ("obsolete information cannot form the basis for a trade secret claim because the information has no economic value.").

Finally, although the *Restatement of Unfair Competition* was not intended to modify the law of trade secrecy as expressed in the UTSA, because it addresses some issues that are not addressed by the UTSA, some of its rules may apply to trade secret misappropriation actions that are brought in both UTSA and non-UTSA jurisdictions. However, to the extent the provisions of the UTSA as adopted in a particular state differ from the *Restatement of Unfair Competition*, the applicable UTSA provisions should govern.

§ 2.5   WHAT IS PROTECTABLE "INFORMATION"?

A threshold, but seemingly easy to satisfy, requirement for trade secret protection is that the alleged trade secrets consist of "information"; the idea being that the putative trade secrets provide information that, according to the economic value requirement of trade secret law (discussed *infra* § 3.3), would be of value to someone else. But what is "information"? Neither the UTSA nor the *Restatements* define the term. According to the primary definition in the Merriam-Webster dictionary, information is: "the communication or reception of knowledge or intelligence." Under trade secret law, this knowledge and intelligence can take many tangible and intangible forms.

§ 2.5.1   FORM OF INFORMATION PROTECTED

Although the issue does not come up much in trade secret litigation, sometimes the form of the alleged trade secrets suggests that there is no protectable information. This argument was asserted by the defendant in *Del Monte Fresh Produce Company v. Dole Food Co., Inc.,* 136 F. Supp. 2d 1271 (S.D. Fla. 2001), when Del Monte alleged that the defendant had misappropriated a pineapple. The issue that the court had to consider was whether a pineapple is protectable information. The court refused to grant the defendant's motion to dismiss, in part, based upon a finding that Del Monte sought protection for the genetically engineered material embedded in the pineapple, which could be a trade secret.

In another case, *Religious Tech. Ctr, v. Netcom On-Line Commc'n Servs. Inc.,* 923 F. Supp. 1231 (N.D. Cal. 1995), one issue was whether seemingly non-commercial information (religious texts) could be a trade secret. Scientology doctrine teaches that each of its members must advance through different levels of its teaching to reach spiritual awareness. The highest levels of Scientology are made up of increasingly sophisticated questions and answers. These closely structured questions are located in the "Operating Thetan" documents (OT documents). According to Scientology doctrine, improper disclosure of the OT documents could be detrimental to achieving the desired effect and, therefore, the plaintiff asserted their trade secret status. The court found that the church's status as a religion did not preclude it from having trade secrets in the OT documents, stating that: "there is no category of information that is excluded from protection as a trade secret because of its inherent qualities." *Id.* at 1251.

Although trade secret information usually exists in some tangible form, there is generally no tangibility requirement either for purposes of the type of information that can be protected as a trade secret or the method of misappropriation (memorization can be a form of misappropriation). Thus, cases sometimes arise where the alleged trade secrets only exist in the mind of the trade secret owner or a valued employee. *See, e.g., Bridgestone/Firestone, Inc. v. Lockhart*, 5 F. Supp. 2d 667 (S.D. Ind. 1998) (finding trade secrets in customer and business planning information that did not exist in tangible form). There can be limited exceptions in some jurisdictions. In Georgia, for instance, customer information that is not in tangible form cannot be protected as a trade secret. *See* Allen v. Hub Cap Heaven, Inc., 484 S.E.2d 259, 263 (Ga. Ct. App. 1997). As a practical matter, however, the absence of tangible evidence of putative trade secrets may make it difficult for a plaintiff in a misappropriation case to identify its trade secrets with the required specificity. *See infra* § 4.9.

§ 2.6   NEGATIVE INFORMATION PROTECTED

Even "negative information," or information about what did not work or what not to do, can be protected as a trade secret under modern trade secret law. According to the UTSA, "[t]he definition of [a trade secret] includes information that has commercial value from a negative viewpoint, for example the results of lengthy and expensive research which proves that a certain process will *not* work could be of great value to a competitor." Unif. Trade Secrets Act § 1, cmt., reprinted in Appendix A. The *Restatement of Unfair Competition* also recognizes the availability of such protection. Restatement (Third) of Unfair Competition § 39 cmt. e. This is a modern departure from the *Restatement of Torts*, which required that information be in continuous use to be protected. *See supra* § 2.2.

The protection of negative information under trade secret law may be supported by the realization that, as one court stated, "knowing what not to do often leads automatically to knowing what to do." *Metallurgical Indus. Inc. v. Fourtek, Inc.*, 790 F.2d 1195, 1203 (5th Cir. 1986). Based upon this principle, some courts have been persuaded by the argument that former employees may misappropriate trade secrets by being able to use negative knowledge from their former employer to provide their new employers with a head start or competitive advantage in developing new products. *See, e.g., Novell, Inc. v. Timpanogos Research Grp., Inc.*, 46 U.S.P.Q.2d 1197, 1216–17 (Utah Dist. Ct. 1998). An employee's negative knowledge about an employer's business has even been used to support granting injunctions in inevitable disclosure cases (discussed *infra* in § 7.7) where a company is concerned about a former employee working for a competitor. *See Avery Dennison Corp. v. Finkle*, 2002 WL 241284, at *2 (Conn. Super. Ct. 2002).

§ 2.7   IMPROVEMENTS ON PUBLICLY KNOWN INFORMATION PROTECTED

A basic distinction between information that can be a trade secret and that which cannot relates to the public disclosure or availability of the subject information. *See infra* §§ 2.8 and 3.1. It is recognized, however, that information that seems to be in the public domain because it concerns previously disclosed information may actually involve new and unique kernels of information that are protectable. *See, e.g., Metallurgical Indus. Inc. v. Fourtek, Inc.*, 790 F.2d 1195 (finding trade secrets in improvements on a furnace design even though the general process was well known). Additionally, information that an individual or company adds to publicly available information may qualify for trade secret protection as so-called "combination trade secrets." *See, e.g., Andair Helicopter Supply, Inc. v. Rolls-Royce Corp.*, 663 F.3d 966 (8th Cir. 2011) (helicopter manufacturer's overhaul information letters were protectable trade secrets even though they were compilations of publicly available information and new proprietary information).

Determining whether a collection of information constitutes a protectable combination trade secret requires a careful examination of the pertinent facts. *Rohm and Haas Co. v. ADCO Chemical Co.*, 689 F.2d 424 (3d Cir. 1982), involved the alleged misappropriation of a latex paint making process. The defendant claimed that most of the process was well-known in the trade and the central issue was whether the process qualified as a trade secret in light of its alleged public availability. The court found that, although the various constituent elements of the process were available in the public literature, the particular combination was not expressly revealed and thus could be protected.

In contrast, *Hutchinson v. KFC Corp.*, 51 F.3d 280 (9th Cir. 1995), involved a process for frying skinless chicken. The plaintiff, Hutchinson, alleged that he developed a proprietary process for making skinless fried chicken and that defendant, Kentucky Fried Chicken, misappropriated his process. The lower court characterized Hutchinson's alleged trade secret process as "the general process of cutting, skinning, marinating, dipping and breading, and frying the chicken." *Id.* at 280. While acknowledging that trade secrecy potentially could exist either in the combination of steps for the process as a whole or in the individual steps, the court concluded that such was not the case under the facts. Skinless fried chicken had been publicly available and on sale since 1981 and the basic sequence of steps (skinning, marinating, dipping, breading, freezing if necessary, and frying) were well-known. Because Hutchison had failed to distinguish his process from the general process of making skinless fried chicken, he did not have a protectable trade secret.

Although it is often stated that novelty as it is used in patent law is not a requirement for trade secret protection (*see infra* § 3.2), based upon the foregoing, when combining known information in an attempt to create a trade secret, the novelty of the combination should be taken into consideration. Citing earlier cases, the court in *Strategic Directions Grp., Inc. v. Bristol-Myers Squibb Company*, 293 F.3d 1062, 1065 (8th Cir. 2002), explained: "mere variations on widely used information cannot be trade secrets" and combinations of known information must "achieve the degree of novelty or 'unknownness' needed for a trade secret."

§ 2.8   LIMITATIONS ON TRADE SECRET PROTECTION

All intellectual property rights have limits that are designed to balance the public interest in free competition with the asserted benefits of intellectual property protection. Trade secret rights are no exception. The initial lines of the commentary to the *Restatement of Torts* express this principle when they state: "The privilege to compete with others includes a privilege to adopt their business methods, ideas or processes of manufacture. . . . This privilege has some limitations, however." Restatement (First) of Torts § 757 cmt. a (1939). Similarly, early comments to the *Restatement of Unfair Competition* provide that: "[t]he freedom to engage in business and to compete for the patronage of prospective customers is a fundamental premise of the free enterprise system." Restatement (Third) of Unfair Competition, § 1, cmt. a (1995).

The limitations on the scope, application, and enforcement of trade secret protection are expressed in a variety of ways, including the following:

§ 2.8.1 PUBLIC DOMAIN INFORMATION

While the modern view of trade secret law under the UTSA defines a trade secret very broadly, the range of protectable information is not without limits. It is a general principle of intellectual property and unfair competition law that legal protection will not be provided for information that is already in the "public domain." *See Bonito Boats, Inc. v. Thunder Craft Boats, Inc.*, 489 U.S. 141, 156 (1989) ("[C]oncepts within the public grasp, or those so obvious that they readily could be, are the tools of creation available to all. They provide the baseline of free competition.") Accordingly, information that falls into the public domain cannot be a trade secret even if it started out as a trade secret. In keeping with this principle, the UTSA recognizes that protectable information cannot be "generally known" or "readily ascertainable." Unif. Trade Secrets Act § 1(4) (amended 1985), reprinted in Appendix A.

§ 2.8.2 INFORMATION THAT IS GENERALLY KNOWN

The definition of a trade secret under the UTSA specifically precludes protection for information that is generally known. The phrase "generally known" is not defined by the UTSA, but the commentary to the UTSA and applicable case law recognize that the concept is not limited to information that is known by the public at large. *See* Unif. Trade Secrets Act

§ 1, cmt. (amended 1985). Information can be generally known and ineligible for trade secret protection "[i]f the principal persons who can obtain economic benefit from the information are aware of it." *Id.* This would include information that is generally known within a particular industry or technical or scientific discipline. Thus, the general state of knowledge among the general public and within the field of the alleged trade secrets are relevant in making this determination. *See infra* § 3.1.

If information is not generally known among the general public or within a particular industry it is conceivable that it can be protected by more than one person or entity. In such a case, each person or entity would separately own the same trade secrets. In other words, it is possible for multiple persons and entities to own the same trade secrets as long as that information has not become generally known or readily ascertainable. This may occur, for instance, where each person "independently develops" the same information and thereafter keeps it secret. *See infra* § 2.8.6.

§ 2.8.3   TRADE SECRETS DISCLOSED IN PATENT APPLICATIONS

When an issued patent (or patent application) is published by the United States Patent and Trademark Office (the USPTO) or a foreign patent office, any trade secrets disclosed in the relevant patent documents are lost. *See On–Line Techs., Inc. v. Bodenseewerk Perkin–Elmer GmbH*, 386 F.3d 1133, 1141 (Fed. Cir. 2004). This is because public disclosure destroys secrecy and one of the central purposes of patent law is to enhance the disclosure of inventions. Thus, information disclosed in patents and the associated "file-wrappers" is treated as public information without proof that anyone ever actually accessed it. *See Bondpro Corp. v. Siemens Power Generation, Inc.*, 463 F. 3d 702, 706–707 (7th Cir. 2006) (distinguishing between disclosure in a patent and other "public documents" that may not be generally known).

There are, however, some recognized exceptions to the patent disclosure rule. First, any trade secret information related to a patented invention (or published patent application) that is not specifically identified or disclosed in the patent documents can remain protected as a trade secret, provided the information is beyond what was disclosed in the patent. *See Atlantic Research Marketing Systems, Inc. v. Troy*, 659 F.3d 1345, 1357 (Fed. Cir. 2011). Second, if a trade secret was misappropriated from its owner and the trade secret information later finds its way into an issued patent filed by the misappropriator, the trade secret owner may still initiate a trade secret misappropriation claim. This is an attempt to remedy the unfair competitive advantage that the defendant may have acquired prior to the information becoming publicly available. *See Ultimate Timing v. Simms*, 715 F. Supp. 2d 1195, 1207 (W.D. Wash. 2010). In such circumstances, the defendant may not benefit from the defense that the trade secret information is no longer a trade secret as a result of it appearing in a patent, if he acquired the trade secret prior to its public disclosure. *See Bondpro Corp. v. Siemens Power Generation, Inc.*,

463 F. 3d 702, 707). Similarly, the trade secret owner may have a derivation claim under the Leahy-Smith America Invents Act. *See* Pub. L. No. 112–29, 125 Stat. 284–341, § 135.

§ 2.8.4   INFORMATION THAT IS READILY ASCERTAINABLE

Another limitation on the scope of trade secret protection concerns information that is "readily ascertainable." The readily ascertainable limitation focuses on the ease with which a trade secret could be discovered if anyone attempted to learn it from a source other than the putative trade secret owner. The comments to the UTSA explain: "[i]nformation is readily ascertainable if it is available in trade journals, reference books, or published materials. Often the nature of the product lends itself to being readily copied as soon as it is available on the market." *See infra* Unif. Trade Secrets Act § 1, cmt. (amended 1985). *See also infra* § 3.1.

In *Editions Play Bac, S.A. v. Western Publishing Co., Inc.*, 1993 WL 541219 (S.D. N.Y. 1993), the court examined whether the game concept at issue was readily ascertainable. It looked to Webster's dictionary to determine the common usage of "readily ascertainable," finding that it meant "discoverable with a fair degree of ease, without much difficulty" *Id.* at *4. Based upon this definition, the court found that some aspects of the game were readily ascertainable by examining the publicly available product. However, "know how" from the game concept was not readily ascertainable and could be entitled to trade secret protection. The court defined know how as the "informational and experiential expertise which can be applied to a product." *Id.* at *5.

The cost associated with learning information is a factor to consider in determining whether information is readily ascertainable. According to the court in *Weston v. Buckley*, 677 N.E. 2d 1089, 1092 (Ind. Ct. App. 1997), one way to determine whether information is readily ascertainable is to examine "the degree of time, effort and expense required to duplicate or acquire it by proper means." Where the readily ascertainable requirement is part of the definition of a trade secret, as it is under the UTSA, the putative trade secret owner "must show that duplication of the information or process would require a substantial investment of time, expense and effort." *Id.* Usually this is done by presenting evidence of the time, effort, and expense that the putative trade secret owner incurred to develop its secrets, with the inference being that the defendant would have to expend similar resources. This is one way that factor 5 of the six-factor test of the *Restatement of Torts* arises under the UTSA, not as a factor in its own right, but as a means of proving that the subject information is not readily ascertainable.

§ 2.8.4.1 Patent Law Concepts of "Prior Art" Compared

At the time the UTSA was drafted in the 1970s, the concepts of "public use" and "readily accessible" were well-known to patent lawyers of the time, many of whom worked on the UTSA drafting project. Generally, the concept of "prior art" under pa-

tent law was both broader and narrower than common conceptions of public disclosure. It was narrower because certain forms of information, principally
inventions that were in public use or on sale in a
foreign country but not "printed in a publication,"
did not count as relevant prior art. It was broader
because so-called "secret uses" of inventions within
the U.S. did count as prior art. *See Rosaire v. Nat'l
Lead Co.*, 218 F.2d 72 (5th Cir. 1955) (involving a
process for prospecting for oil that involved under-
ground drilling operations); *Egbert v. Lippmann*,
104 U.S. 333 (1881) (involving a corset-stay invention that was used by the inventor's friend for over
two years before a patent application was filed). As
the Supreme Court in *Kewanee* explained, "[a]n invention may be placed 'in public use or on sale' within the meaning of [patent law] without losing its
secret character." *Kewanee Oil Co. v. Bicron Corp.*,
416 U.S. at 484 (citations omitted). It was also understood that issued patents were publicly available, but confidential or foreign patent applications
were not. *See Julius Hyman & Co. v. Velsicol Corp.*,
123 Colo. 563, 602 (1951).

Whether the definition of "generally known" and
"readily ascertainable" under trade secret law is
now co-extensive with the definition of "prior art"
under patent law, as recently amended by the
Leahy-Smith America Invents Act (the AIA) (Pub. L.
No. 112–29, 125 Stat. 284–341), is an unresolved
question under trade secret law. At a minimum, the
broadening of the definition of prior art under patent law to now include all foreign references will
make it difficult for trade secret claimants to argue

(as some did) that the relevant universe of information on the issues of "generally known" and "readily ascertainable" does not include all foreign information. However, those who want broad trade secret rights (principally plaintiffs), are likely to continue to advocate that secret uses of trade secrets are not "generally known" or "readily ascertainable." *See, e.g., Milgrim on Trade Secrets*, § 1.07.

§ 2.8.4.2 Changing the Burden of Proof on the Readily Ascertainable Issue

Some states, most notably California, do not include the readily ascertainable language in the definition of a trade secret. Rather than requiring the plaintiff in a trade secret misappropriation case to prove a negative—that the information is not readily ascertainable—California's version of the UTSA is structured so that the defendant can assert a defense that the information was readily ascertainable. *See* Cal. Civ. Code § 3426.1(d)(1) (2012); *SkinMedica, Inc. v. Histogen, Inc.*, 869 F. Supp. 2d 1176, 1193 (S.D. Cal. 2012). *See also* 765 Ill. Comp. Stat. 1065/2(d) (2012). The definition of a trade secret under California and Illinois law only includes the "generally known to the public or to other persons who can obtain economic value" language of the UTSA.

§ 2.8.5   GENERAL SKILL AND KNOWLEDGE

Three important social values serve to further limit the scope of trade secret protection: free competition, employee mobility, and the importance of personal growth and improvement. Based upon these values, it is a well-established rule that a person's general skill and knowledge cannot be claimed as a trade secret by his or her employer, in part because he has a right to use the information in his head. *See Dynamics Research Corp. v. Analytic Sciences Corp.*, 9 Mass. App. Ct. 254, 267 (Mass. App. Ct. 1980). One judge captured the policy as follows:

> The courts have recognized that someone who has worked in a particular field cannot be expected to forego the accumulated skills, knowledge, and experience gained before the employee changes jobs. Such qualifications are obviously very valuable to an employee seeking to sell his services in the marketplace. A person leaving one employer and going into the marketplace will seek to compete in the area of his or her greatest aptitude. In light of the highly mobile nature of our society, and as the economy becomes increasingly comprised of highly skilled or high-tech jobs, the individual's economic interests will more and more be buffeted by employers' perceived needs to maintain their competitive advantage. Courts must be cautious not to strike a balance that unduly disadvantages the individual worker.

SI Handling Systems, Inc. v. Heisley, 753 F.2d 1244, 1267 (3d Cir. 1985) (Adams, J., concurring).

The rule is that a former employee may use the general knowledge, skills, and experience acquired during his or her employment even in competition with his or her former employer. Trade secret law only prohibits a former employee from using trade secret information belonging to the former employer, although there is debate whether the scope of information sought to be protected by an employer can be expanded by contract. *See infra* § 7.1. According to the court in *Dynamics Research*, "the employer has a heavy burden of isolating the secret . . . [from] the knowledge and skill [the employee] brought to the job as well as 'what he has learned during the employment.'" 9 Mass. App. Ct. at 268 (citations omitted).

The distinction between that which is an employer's trade secret and an employee's general skill and knowledge is often subject to disagreement and can only be determined by a careful examination of the facts of each case. This is usually done by identifying the skills and knowledge that the employee acquired through formal education and prior experience and by considering the knowledge and skill sets that are common to employees in the same field of endeavor. Additionally, there may be general skills and knowledge that employees acquire while working for a particular company that are not considered trade secrets. In other words, just because an employee acquires skills and knowledge at a particular job, as opposed to acquiring it elsewhere, does not mean that such information qualifies for trade secret protection.

Sometimes the discussion concerning an employee's skills and knowledge involves the concept of "know-how." This term is often used as an umbrella term that refers to intangible information about how to make a product or process work. Sometimes "know-how" qualifies for trade secret protection, sometimes it does not. In *Tempo Instrument, Inc. v. Logitek*, 229 F. Supp. 1 (E.D.N.Y. 1964), for instance, the court noted that the defendant had been employed by numerous electronic firms over the years where he worked with transistor circuits and in those capacities gained skill and knowledge that was attractive to the plaintiff (former employer). Thus, the defendant obviously possessed know-how, but it was not know-how that the plaintiff could claim as its trade secrets.

As a practical matter, general skill and knowledge is arguably a sub-set of information that is "generally known" and, therefore, should be analyzed as part of the definition of a trade secret. However, because it is theoretically possible for an employee to possess general skill and knowledge within a particular field of endeavor that is not known to the public at large (or, perhaps, even within an industry), the rule should also be seen as a special limitation on the scope of trade secret rights that is designed to protect employee mobility and the acquisition of knowledge and experience.

Finally, often the information that is at issue in a trade secret case was developed by the employee in the performance of her work rather than being information that was provided to her by her employer. Such situations implicate questions regarding ownership of the employee developed trade secrets. *See infra* §7.8. The default rule of trade secret law, like that of patent and copyright law, is that the person who develops information owns the intellectual property rights in that information. However, this rule is often modified by an express or implied agreement or by operation of law when the employee was "hired to invent."

§ 2.8.6 INFORMATION THAT IS PROPERLY ACQUIRED

Unlike patent law, which grants a number of exclusive rights to a patent holder, including the exclusive right to use the patented invention (*see* 35 U.S.C. § 271 (2008)), the owner of a trade secret does not enjoy the same level of exclusivity. Not only can identical information be considered a trade secret by more than one owner (provided that each set of information meets the three requirements of trade secrecy), but not all uses of a trade secret constitute an unlawful misappropriation. Only trade secrets that have been acquired, disclosed, or used improperly are protected. *See infra* § 4.5.

There are at least five ways that trade secret information can be properly acquired. *See* Unif. Trade Secrets Act § 1 cmt. (amended 1985) (definition of "proper use"). First, trade secrets can be voluntarily shared between a trade secret owner and another. If there is an adequate duty of confidentiality, either express or implied, between the trade secret owner and the person(s) to whom he discloses his trade secrets, there will be no loss of trade secrecy. The licensing of trade secrets between business enterprises is a form of consensual sharing and a proper means of acquiring trade secrets. *See Metallurgical Industries Inc. v. Fourtek, Inc.*, 790 F. 2d 1195 (5th Cir. 1986) ("We conclude that a holder [of a trade secret] may divulge his information to a limited extent without destroying its status as a trade secret.").

While it is often the case that a trade secret owner will grant another permission to use a trade secret, even without express or implied consent, a party may make lawful use of information if it acquired it through legitimate acts of independent discovery or invention. The typical situation involves an individual or company that is engaged in research and development efforts which leads to the discovery of information that another person or company also discovered and claims as its trade secret. *See, e.g., Bowser, Inc. v. Filters, Inc.*, 398 F.2d 7 (9th Cir. 1968). As is discussed more fully in § 5.3, whether the discovery is truly "independent" is the critical issue.

The third method of proper acquisition of trade secrets is discovery by reverse engineering. Reverse engineering is a process by which a person starts with the known product and works backward to determine either its component parts or the process by which it was developed or manufactured. *See infra* § 5.4. In contrast to the acts of independent discovery, the person or company that engages in reverse engineering will, by definition, have access to the goods or information of another that embodies the other's trade secrets. *See, e.g., Faiveley Transport Malmo AB v. Wabtec Corp.*, 559 F.3d 110 (2d Cir. 2009). The key question in such cases is whether access to such goods or information was properly obtained through, for instance, a legitimate purchase.

As a general rule, as long as the subject goods or information are freely available to the public, anyone is allowed to examine them to discover the trade secrets embedded therein. In the absence of applicable patent, copyright, or trademark protection, they can even make and sell duplicate copies of the goods and information. This is the essential principle of the *Sears/Compco* cases that are discussed in Chapter 1. *See supra* § 1.5.

The concept of reverse engineering in trade secret cases is frequently illustrated by *Chicago Lock Co. v. Fanberg*, 676 F.2d 400 (9th Cir. 1982). The trade secrets at issue were a series of secret codes that locksmiths used to unlock locks, thus uncracking the code that opens the lock. The defendants, the Fanbergs, came up with the very entrepreneurial idea of publishing a manual of all of the codes collected by other locksmiths. The plaintiff, Chicago Lock, conceded that it would have been proper for the Fanbergs to buy and examine the locks on their own and to reverse engineer the key codes. The use of computer programs to generate portions of the key code serial number would have also been permissible reverse engineering. However, Chicago Lock argued that the Fanbergs were not permitted to acquire the (reverse engineered) information from other locksmiths. The court disagreed, finding that the locksmiths did not owe a duty of nondisclosure to Chicago Lock.

Defendants sometimes use reverse engineering and independent discovery arguments simultaneously to explain why their conduct was proper. This can be tricky for a defendant as it usually means that the defendant company may have started down a path of independent discovery but that at some point it obtained the plaintiff's product or information and used it to improve or speed-up its reverse engineering efforts. More problematic is the possible use of information about the plaintiff's trade secrets that were obtained from another who was under a duty of confidentiality, such as a former employee. In such cases, what may have started out as permissible independent discovery or reverse engineering becomes tainted and subject to liability for misappropriation. *See Faiveley Transport Malmo AB v. Wabtec Corp.*, 559 F.3d 110.

The fourth and fifth means of proper acquisition focus on the definition of misappropriation under the UTSA. The comments to the UTSA identify them as discovery by "[o]bservation of the item in public use or on public display" and "[o]btaining the trade secret from published literature." Unif. Trade Secrets Act § 1 cmt. (amended 1985). As is discussed more fully in § 4.4.1 *infra*, where a party learns a trade secret through a disclosure that was not made in breach of a contract or special relationship, or with knowledge of such a breach, she is entitled to use it. In other words, any discovery of a trade secret that does not meet the definition of misappropriation under trade secret law is a proper disclosure. Such discovery could occur, for instance, where a trade secret owner voluntarily discloses information without first establishing a duty of confidentiality. It may also occur where trade secrets are disclosed by accident or mistake. *But see*, Unif. Trade Secrets Act § 1(2)(ii)(C) (providing limited protection in cases where the recipient of the information has knowledge or reason to know that the information was accidentally disclosed); *infra* § 4.4.)

Whether trade secret information is properly or improperly acquired by others, there is always a risk that it will lose its trade secret status. This is because once a trade secret is disclosed and becomes generally known or readily ascertainable, it cannot meet the secrecy requirement of trade secret law. The trade secret owner's only recourse in this situation is to sue the alleged misappropriator for an award of damages or a limited "lead-time" injunction. As the foregoing reveals, however, individuals and companies that properly acquire trade secrets cannot be misappropriators unless they improperly use or disclose those secrets.

§ 2.8.7 PROPRIETARY AND CONFIDENTIAL INFORMATION AND "EXCLUSIVE" DATA

Businesses often claim legal protection for information which they label as their "proprietary and confidential" information or "exclusive data." This body of information, however, must be distinguished from trade secrets. Just because a business labels information as proprietary, confidential, or exclusive does not mean that the information can be protected under trade secret law, or at all. Some of the information may qualify for trade secret protection, but other parts of it may not because it does not meet the requirements for trade secret protection. *See infra* §§ 3.1–3.4. For information that does not qualify for trade secret protection, another theory of liability must apply, such as breach of contract or common law missappropriation.

The *Restatement of Torts*, § 759 (*supra* § 1.2) previously recognized a cause of action where mere business information was improperly acquired with the purpose of "advancing a business rival." However, this cause of action was not carried over into the UTSA or the *Restatement of Unfair Competition*, most likely due to the limits of trade secret protection discussed in *Kewanee v. Bicron Oil Corp.*, 416 U.S. 470. Moreover, state tort claims designed to protect such information are arguably precluded by section 7 of the UTSA. *See infra* § 5.7.

§ 2.9   PRINCIPLES OF FEDERAL PREEMPTION

Preemption issues concern potential conflicts between state and federal laws and can arise anytime a state-law based cause of action appears to conflict with an actual or potential federal claim for relief. To sort out the potential conflicts, courts look first to the language of the federal statute to determine the intent of Congress, particularly where there is an express preemption clause. *See Sprietsma v. Mercury Marine*, 537 U.S. 51, 62–63 (2002). Secondly, courts will examine whether federal preemption should be implied due to either "field preemption" or "conflict preemption." *See Freightliner Corp. v. Myrick,* 514 U.S. 280, 287 (1995). Pursuant to principles of conflict preemption, state law cannot be applied or enforced if it "stands as an obstacle to the accomplishment and execution of the full purposes and objectives of Congress." *Kewanee Oil Co. v.*

Bicron Corp., 416 U.S. 470, 479 (quoting *Hines v. Davidowitz*, 312 U.S. 52, 67 (1941).)

To the extent that inventors and creators pursue or assert different forms of intellectual property protection for different parts of an invention or creation, federal preemption should not be an issue. But where they assert: (1) multiple forms of IP protection for the same parts; or (2) protection for portions of inventions and creations that are not protectable under one or more of the intellectual property laws, a federal preemption defense may arise. *See infra* § 5.8. In this regard, the preemption issue does not just concern the issue of whether multiple forms of intellectual property protection are available for the same bits of information, but whether information that is expressly excluded from protection by one form of intellectual property protection (particularly U.S. patent or copyright law) can be protected under another form of intellectual property law, such as trade secret law.

§ 2.9.1   PATENT PREEMPTION

Principles of federal preemption were first applied by the U.S. Supreme Court to limit the application of state unfair competition law in the famous companion cases of *Sears, Roebuck & Co. v. Stiffel Co,* 376 U.S. 225, and *Compco Corp. v. Day-Brite Lighting, Inc.,* 376 U.S. 234, decided on the same date in March 1964. Noting a conflict between the unfair competition laws of Illinois that prohibited product simulation and federal patent law, the court ruled that the Illinois law was preempted.

Although the *Sears/Compco* cases involved a conflict between the general unfair competition laws of Illinois and federal patent policy, they immediately raised concerns about the continued viability of state trade secret law. In its 1974 decision in *Kewanee Oil Co. v. Bicron*, 416 U.S. 470, the U.S. Supreme Court made it clear that state trade secret law (or at least the U.S. Supreme Court's understanding of Ohio's trade secret law) was not preempted by federal law and could be enforced. The Court's key finding was that trade secret law did not conflict with the objectives of U.S. patent law. Indeed, the Court found the objectives of patent and trade secret law to be consistent.

A critical part of the *Kewanee* Court's opinion described different categories of inventions, both patentable and unpatentable. The Court then examined what it believed was the effect of trade secret law on the behavior of inventors, concluding that patent protection was so superior to trade secret law (which does not protect against independent development), that the owner of a patentable invention would only rarely choose the trade secret alternative. It explained:

> The holder of a trade secret . . . takes a substantial risk that the secret will be passed on to his competitors, by theft or by breach of a confidential relationship, in a manner not easily susceptible of discovery or proof. Where patent law acts as a barrier, trade secret law functions relatively as a sieve. The possibility that an inventor who believes his invention meets the standards of patentability will sit back, rely on trade

secret law, and after one year of use forfeit any
right to patent protection, is remote indeed.

416 U.S. at 490 (citations omitted). Accordingly, the
Court found nothing wrong with overlapping forms
of protection for inventions based upon its assump-
tion that chances were slim that an inventor would
choose trade secret protection over patent protection.

As for unpatentable information covered by trade
secret law, such as customer lists, the Court recognized that there could be no conflict with patent
law. "[T]he holder of [an unpatentable] discovery
would have no reason to apply for a patent whether
trade secret protection existed or not." *Id.* at 483.
Therefore, the court reasoned that abolition of trade
secret protection would not result in increased disclosure to the public of discoveries in the area of
non-patentable subject matter. In so doing, however,
it identified at least one non-patentable item, "business methods," which has since become patentable.

The Court's finding that it was unlikely that inventors would choose trade secret protection over
patent protection was questionable in 1974, but is
particularly questionable today. The general view
that prevails from *Kewanee* is that trade secret law
and federal law can co-exist. To what extent, is the
question, particularly in light of the post-*Kewanee*
enactment of the 1976 Copyright Act (Pub. L. No.
94–553, 90 Stat. 2541 (codified as amended at 17
U.S.C. §§ 101–914 (1976)) and the September 2011
enactment of the Leahy-Smith America Invents Act.
(P.L. Pub. L. No. 112–29, 125 Stat. 284–341). Where

the *Kewanee* Court thought inventors faced a largely binary choice between patent and trade secret law, the current reality is that inventors and creators often pursue and assert multiple forms of intellectual property protection for the same body of information.

§ 2.9.2   COPYRIGHT PREEMPTION

An example of a possible preemption problem concerns the potential overlap of alleged trade secrets and copyrighted materials. While patent and trade secret law protect inventions and information, federal copyright law covers only expression. Nevertheless, copyright preemption questions can arise in trade secret cases where, for instance, the copyrighted material was not published or otherwise made publicly available. If you write a novel and engage in reasonable efforts to keep it secret, it is arguably protected by both copyright and trade secret law until it is published.

Copyright preemption is specifically addressed in the 1976 Copyright Act. *See* 17 U.S.C. § 301 (2012). Assuming a work qualifies as copyrightable subject matter, similar grants of rights under state law are preempted if they are "equivalent" to any of the exclusive rights established by the Act. These include the right of reproduction (copying), the distribution right, and the right to make derivative works. *See* 17 U.S.C. § 106 (2006). The jurisprudence of Section 301 generally establishes that whether a state law is preempted by U.S. copyright law depends on whether there is some "extra element" (e.g., beyond mere copying) that must be proven to establish the state claim.

While some cases have found that the 1976 Copyright Act preempts state trade secret claims, other cases have found no preemption. *Compare Relational Design & Tech., Inc. v. Data Team Corp.*, No. 91–2452–O, 1992 WL 97799, at *1 (D. Kan. Apr. 16, 1992) (holding that because plaintiff's copyright and trade secret claims were based on the same facts, the trade secret claim was preempted by federal copyright law), *and Videotronics, Inc. v. Bend Elecs.*, 564 F. Supp. 1471 (D. Nev. 1983) (holding that trade secret protection under state common law for subject matter which was also covered by the Copyright Act was preempted), *with M. Bryce & Assocs., Inc. v. Gladstone*, 319 N.W.2d 907 (Wis. Ct. App. 1982) (finding no preemption because the "line of demarcation between trade secret and copyright protection is clear"), *and Boeing Co. v. Sierracin Corp.*, 738 P.2d 665 (Wash. 1987) (following the same reasoning to find no preemption).

In trade secret cases, the alleged breach of a duty of confidence often provides the "extra element" that avoids preemption. *See Computer Assocs. Int'l, Inc. v. Altai, Inc.*, 982 F.2d 693 (2d Cir. 1992). The court in *Computer Associates* noted that while unfair competition and misappropriation claims grounded solely in the copying of a plaintiff's protected expression are preempted by section 301, some state claims survive preemption, including those involving breaches of confidential relationships and breaches of fiduciary duties.

> The legislative history of section 301 states that "the evolving common law rights of . . . trade secrets . . . would remain unaffected as long as the causes of action contain elements, such as . . . a breach of trust or confidentiality, that are different in kind from copyright infringement."

982 F.2d at 717. Thus, trade secret claims that are properly pleaded to include allegations of breach of confidentiality or other "improper means" are likely to avoid preemption problems. But it is also important to look beyond the allegations and determine the actual facts of each case.

§ 2.9.3   THE EFFECT OF THE AIA ON THE PREEMPTION ANALYSIS

The adoption in September 2011 of the Leahy-Smith America Invents Act (portions of which went into effect at various times through March of 2013), renewed questions about whether state trade secret law is preempted by federal patent policy. *See supra* § 2.9.1. Although not intended to change trade secret law, the AIA's switch to a first-inventor-to-file system, together with changes to the definition of prior art, arguably create greater conflict between the two means of protection, particularly with respect to patentable inventions. Whether this means that trade secret law will be preempted (at least in part) remains to be seen, but as with the potential overlap between trade secret claims and copyright law, the potential preemption issue should not be ignored.

§ 2.9.4   PREEMPTION AS A LIMIT ON THE SCOPE OF TRADE SECRET RIGHTS

As discussed more fully in § 5.8 *infra*, in the appropriate case federal preemption may be asserted as a defense to a trade secret misappropriation claim. For present purposes, it is important to realize that the availability of patent and copyright protection for a particular body of information may limit the scope of trade secret protection. In this regard, while *Kewanee* recognized that multiple forms of protection for information are conceptually possible, it also recognized that trade secret law cannot be interpreted or applied in a manner that unduly conflicts with federal forms of protection. What saved trade secret protection from preemption in that case was the relatively weak (sieve-like) protection that trade secret law provides compared to patent law. *Kewanee Oil Co. v. Bicron Corp.*, 416 U.S. at 489–90. For this reason, efforts to strengthen trade secret rights either through legislation or a liberal application of trade secret principles are suspect. *See* Sharon K. Sandeen, *Kewanee Revisited: Returning to First Principles of Intellectual Property Law to Determine the Issue of Federal Preemption*, 12 Marq. Intell. Prop. L. Rev. 288 (2008).

§ 2.10   PRACTICAL LIMITATIONS

Several practical considerations affect the universe of protectable information under trade secret law. One such consideration is the requirement that the putative trade secret owner be able to articulate in a very concrete way exactly what it claims to be its trade secret(s). *See Del Monte Fresh Produce Co.*

v. Dole Food Co. Inc., 136 F. Supp. 2d 1271 (S.D. Fl. 2001). While the claimed information need not be identified in great detail, as it would be in a patent application, it cannot be a vague or abstract concept either. *See Nilssen v. Motorola, Inc.*, 963 F. Supp. 664 (N.D. Ill. 1997). Thus, to the extent a trade secret owner cannot describe its trade secrets, the scope of its rights will naturally be limited.

Trade secret owners often have difficulty identifying their trade secrets with specificity. This is usually due to the fact that they do not realize that they own potential trade secrets until a valued employee resigns and goes to work for a competitor. It is only when they consult an attorney that many companies begin to understand what may be a trade secret. It is also because the identification of trade secrets depends upon a number of factors, including the nature and form of the trade secrets (whether they are in tangible or intangible form), who developed or knows the trade secrets, and whether they are a sub-part of a broader set of information.

When individual components of a set of information are generally known, individuals and companies often overlook the fact that trade secrets may exist in the non-disclosed components. *See Del Monte Fresh Produce Co. v. Dole Food Co. Inc.*, 136 F. Supp. 2d 1271. Conversely, there is a tendency for companies who believe they have been "wronged" by former employees or business associates to claim that everything, or nearly everything, is a trade secret. The challenge for trade secret owners is to identify what they claim as their trade secrets without overreaching. This should involve a cost-benefit analysis of what secret information is worth the effort of protection.

Another practical consideration involves the nature of the information sought to be protected and whether it is classified as "technical trade secrets" or "business information." Although there are no explicit exclusions from trade secret protection based on specific categories of subject matter, some cases appear to distinguish between technical and business information. In practice, this distinction can be significant. In some older cases, the term "technical trade secrets" is used to refer to trade secret information for which a patent could be sought. *See, e.g.*, *National Rejectors, Inc. v. Trieman*, 409 S.W.2d 1, 26 (Mo. 1966). Generally, technical information is more likely to be patentable than business information, unless the business information is framed as a patentable "business method." Perhaps because of this difference (or simply due to the lore of inventors), courts in trade secret cases sometimes appear to be more impressed by technical information. Thus, the basic nature of the information sought to be protected can influence the trade secrecy analysis and may determine the outcome of a case.

The final practical consideration concerns the realities and public nature of trade secret litigation. Although the owner of information may be inclined to claim protection for a wide array of business information, there are at least three reasons why trade secret litigants may wish to define their trade secrets more narrowly. First, overreaching in the assertion of trade secrets can backfire and result in a finding that little to no information is protected. *See Litton Sys., Inc. v. Sunstrand Corp.*, 750 F.2d 952, 956 (Fed. Cir. 1984) (denying an injunction where plaintiff claimed "a broad universe of thousands of unidentified trade secrets"). Such overreaching also makes it more difficult to prove the requisite elements of trade secrecy, particularly the reasonable efforts requirement, described *infra* § 3.4.

Second, trade secret litigation is expensive and the more information that is claimed as a trade secret, the greater the costs. According to surveys by the American Intellectual Property Law Association (AIPLA), it can cost anywhere from $400,000 to well over one-million dollars to pursue a trade secret misappropriation case through trial. Because much of the discovery and presentation of evidence in trade secret misappropriation cases involves the identification of trade secrets and proof of trade secrecy, each claimed trade secret adds numerous points of potential dispute.

Third, although protective orders are routinely granted for the purpose of protecting trade secrets during litigation (*see* Unif. Trade Secrets Act § 5 (amended 1985)), there is always a risk that trade secrets will be disclosed during litigation. While protective orders are commonly used to protect trade secrets in the early stages of civil litigation, for important public policy reasons, it is more difficult to protect trade secrets during and after trial. This is due to the presumption that trials and court records are open to the public. *See Citizens First Nat'l Bank of Princeton v. Cincinnati Ins. Co.*, 178 F.3d 943 (7th

Cir. 1999). The fewer trade secrets that are put at issue in a case, the less the risk of loss of trade secrecy.

CHAPTER 3

THE REQUIREMENTS FOR TRADE SECRET PROTECTION

§ 3.1 SECRECY

As numerous cases and commentators note, secrecy is the *sine qua non* of trade secrecy; without it the putative trade secret owner cannot bring a successful trade secret misappropriation claim. *See Computer Print Sys., Inc. v. Lewis*, 422 A.2d 148, 154 (Pa. Super. Ct. 1980); *Hertz v. Luzenac Grp.*, 576 F.3d 1103, 1109 (10th Cir. 2009); *Forest Labs., Inc. v. Formulations, Inc.*, 299 F. Supp. 202 (E.D. Wis. 1969); *Milgrim on Trade Secrets* § 1.03 ("Indispensable to an effective allegation of trade secret is proof that the matter is, more or less, secret.") Because of this, all trade secret cases should begin with the identification of the putative trade secrets and an analysis of whether such information is actually secret. *See Electro-Craft Corp. v. Controlled Motion, Inc.*, 332 N.W.2d 890, 897 ("In defining the existence of a trade secret as the threshold issue, we first focus upon the 'property rights' in the trade secret rather than on the existence of a confidential relationship.") (citations omitted).

The word "secrecy" is not used in the UTSA's definition of a trade secret. Instead, "secrecy" is defined by stating what it is not. According to the UTSA, information is not secret if it is "generally known" or "readily ascertainable." *See supra* §§ 2.8.1–2.8.4. In effect, "secrecy" is the opposite of those two terms, but pursuant to case law there is more to the definition of secrecy than meets the eye. Thus, it is useful to look at the secrecy requirement from a number of different perspectives.

First, although all trade secret owners should attempt to keep their trade secrets as confidential as possible, absolute secrecy is not required to meet the requirements of trade secret protection. Rather, pursuant to the relative secrecy doctrine, the owner of information that would otherwise qualify for trade secret protection does not lose protection if the information is shared with others in a manner that is reasonable under the circumstances to maintain its secrecy. *See Vulcan Detinning Co. v. Am. Can Co.*, 72 N.J. Eq. 387, 396 (N.J. Ct. of Errors and Appeals 1907) ("[T]he secrecy with which a court of equity deals is not necessarily that absolute secrecy that inheres in discovery, but that qualified secrecy that arises from mutual understanding, and that is required alike by good faith and good morals."). *See also infra* § 3.4. Indeed, a stated purpose of trade secret law is to facilitate the efficient sharing of otherwise confidential information. *See Kewanee Oil Company v. Bicron Corp.*, 416 U.S. at 486–87.

Second, the source and development of the subject information should be considered when determining its secrecy. Information that was derived from others is less likely to meet the secrecy requirement than information that is developed by the putative trade secret owner. This is because, as just noted, information that is shared can only meet the secrecy requirement if it is kept "relatively secret." Additionally, information that is derived from others is more likely to be generally known.

Third, even if information is independently developed and zealously guarded, it may lose its secrecy due to no fault of the developer of the information. This is because the same information may be independently developed and subsequently disclosed by another, and this can happen throughout the "secret life" of the putative trade secret owner's information. In other words, information that was once a trade secret can become "generally known" and "readily ascertainable" and thereby lose its secrecy. While this may seem unfair, the fleeting nature of trade secret protection is one of the reasons that the Supreme Court found that trade secret law was not preempted by U.S. patent law. *Kewanee Oil Co. v. Bicron Corp.*, 416 U.S. at 490.

Finally, although "secrecy" is principally defined by what it is not, secrecy is also a requirement separate from the requirement that the information not be generally known. *See Kewanee Oil Co. v. Bicron Corp.*, 416 U.S. at 475 ("The subject of a trade secret must be secret, and must not be of public knowledge or of general knowledge in the trade or business."). As discussed in § 3.4 *infra*, evidence of reasonable efforts to maintain secrecy is not only relevant to satisfy the reasonable efforts requirement of the UTSA, it also helps to establish the factual requirement of secrecy. This makes sense when you consider that information may be freely used and distributed within a company and not become generally known or readily ascertainable.

How evidence of what is "generally known" and "readily ascertainable" is presented at trial is an interesting aspect of trade secret litigation. The plaintiff in a trade secret case has the burden of proving the existence of a trade secret which, by definition, means it must establish that the information it claims as a trade secret is not generally known or readily ascertainable. Usually, it will attempt to do this by describing how the information was developed and by presenting expert testimony of the state of the art before the development of the claimed trade secret. For instance, in *Rohm and Haas Co. v. Adco Chem. Co.*, 689 F.2d 424 (3d Cir. 1982), on the issue of whether the alleged trade secrets were generally known, the plaintiff presented evidence that: (1) it was the only manufacturer to use the allegedly secret process; (2) other competitors had tried and failed to put competing products on the market; and (3) some of the elements of the process were previously unknown. *Id.* at 431–32.

Plaintiffs in trade secret cases often attempt to establish that their alleged trade secrets are not generally known by presenting evidence of the efforts that they have engaged in to protect such secrets. In other words, the same evidence that they present to meet the reasonable efforts requirement, discussed *infra*, is cited as proof of the fact that the plaintiff's putative trade secrets are not generally known. Often, the focus of such evidence is on the security measures that the plaintiff instituted to protect the information rather than on the state of public knowledge. Thus, it does not directly address whether the subject information is generally known and is, at best, circumstantial evidence of a lack of public or industry knowledge. In practice, however, it may be enough to shift the burden of presenting evidence on the issue of secrecy to the defendant.

The "not readily ascertainable" requirement is conceptually more difficult to prove because it requires not only an examination of information that is generally known, but information that could be easily found if one were to look for it. Thus, a plaintiff in a trade secret case might retain a person who is skilled in the art of the subject trade secret to testify that the putative trade secrets are unknown generally and that a search of relevant and available resources failed to reveal such information. *See, e.g., Applied Materials, Inc. v. Advanced Micro-Fabrication Equip. Co.*, No. C 07–05248JW, 2009 WL 3429575, at *1 (N.D. Cal. Oct. 22, 2009); *Milgrim on Trade Secrets* § 15.01. Additionally, or in the alternative, the plaintiff may present evidence of the time, effort, and expense that would be required to duplicate the information, thereby disproving the "readily" aspect of the requirement. *See supra* § 2.8.4.

As a practical matter, once the plaintiff in a trade secret case puts on some evidence that its alleged secrets are *not* generally known or readily ascertainable, it is up to the defendant to find and present evidence of "prior art" to establish that the alleged secrets are either generally known or readily ascertainable. With respect to both issues, and unlike applicable patent law, this evidence can consist of information that existed both before and after the development of plaintiff's alleged trade secrets.

Thus, an important defense strategy is for a defendant in a trade secret case to first determine what the alleged trade secrets are, and then to search publicly available information to see if the information exists elsewhere. As discussed previously, this information could conceivably include all publicly known or readily ascertainable information from throughout the world. *See supra* §§ 2.8.1–2.8.4.

§ 3.2   THE NOMINAL NOVELTY REQUIREMENT OF TRADE SECRET LAW

Those who are familiar with the details of patent law know that a patent will not be granted unless the claimed invention is both novel and non-obvious. *See* 35 U.S.C. §§ 101–103 (2008) (§ 102 as amended by Pub. L. 112–29, § 3(b)(1), Sept. 16, 2011, 125 Stat. 285). These are very stringent requirements which require the patent examiner to carefully compare the claims of an invention with the relevant prior art. Because of the stringency of the requirements, it is often said that trade secret protection does not require novelty in the patent law sense. *See* Restatement (Third) of Unfair Competition, § 39, cmt. f (1995). However, this does not mean that there is no novelty requirement under trade secret law. Conceptually, it is part of the generally known and readily ascertainable inquiries which examine what is known and knowable.

Novelty is sometimes raised as an issue in trade secret cases separate and apart from the generally known and readily ascertainable analyses. *See, e.g., Arco Indus. Corp. v. Chemcast Corp.*, 633 F.2d 435, 441–42 (6th Cir. 1980) (applying Michigan law);

Jostens, Inc. v. Nat'l Computer Sys., Inc., 318 N.W.2d 691, 699 (Minn. 1982). This is because the alleged trade secrets sometime constitute basic, common-sense information that the defendant asserts is not worth protecting, but where the low value of the information makes it difficult to prove that it is not generally known or readily ascertainable. This frequently occurs in idea submission cases (discussed *infra* in § 4.6.6) where an "idea man" (or woman) alleges that he shared his valuable trade secret with the defendant pursuant to a promise of confidentiality or compensation. *See Wal-Mart Stores v. P.O. Mkt.*, 66 S.W.3d 620 (Ark. 2002).

Theoretically, where there is insufficient evidence that putative trade secrets are generally known or readily ascertainable, the "independent economic value" requirement of trade secrecy (discussed next) should preclude a finding of trade secrecy for alleged secrets of little value. For a number of reasons, however, including underdeveloped state laws and frequent misapplication of the economic value requirement, courts will sometimes find a lack of novelty instead. In *Jostens,* for instance, the court found that: "Clearly, the [putative trade secrets], as the combination of three generally known subsystems, does not achieve the degree of novelty or "unknownness" needed for a trade secret." *Jostens, Inc. v. Nat'l Computer Sys., Inc.*, 318 N.W.2d at 699.

§ 3.3   INDEPENDENT ECONOMIC VALUE

The independent economic value requirement of trade secrecy is an often overlooked and misapplied part of the trade secrecy analysis. Technically, the "value" that is required is not any value viewed in the abstract, but a particular kind of value. The plaintiff in a trade secret misappropriation case has the burden of pleading and proving that its putative trade secret: (1) derives; (2) independent; (3) economic value, actual or potential; (4) from not being generally known or readily ascertainable; (5) to others who can obtain economic value from its disclosure or use. Unif. Trade Secrets Act § 1(4) (amended 1985), reprinted in Appendix A.

The specifics of the economic value requirement are often given short attention by courts and litigants. Frequently, courts assume that the alleged trade secrets must have the requisite economic value otherwise the plaintiff would not have initiated litigation. *See, e.g., Editions Play Bac, S.A. v. Western Pub. Co., Inc.*, No. 92 Civ. 3652 (JSM), 1993 WL 541219 (S.D.N.Y. Dec. 28, 1993) (holding that the plaintiff's alleged trade secret had economic value because the defendant and another company considered licensing the rights to the secret); *MAI Sys. Corp. v. Peak Computer, Inc.*, 991 F.2d 511, 521 (9th Cir. 1993) (holding that plaintiff's customer database had potential economic value because it would allow competitors to direct efforts to potential customers already using the plaintiff's services). Plaintiff's tend to discount or obscure the requirement in an effort to make it easier for them to prove their *prima facie* case.

The drafting history of the UTSA reveals that the economic value requirement was not simply a rhetorical flourish but was intended to limit the scope of information that can be protected to information that has actual or potential commercial value. Like the reasonable efforts requirement that is discussed *infra* at § 3.4, the requirement serves important identification and notice functions. Because the plaintiff in a trade secret misappropriation case has the burden on the issue, it must first be able to identify the information which it considered to be valuable at the time of the alleged misappropriation. Then it must show that such information has the requisite value. Fundamentally, as noted in *Taylor v. Babbitt*, 760 F. Supp. 2d 80 (D.D.C. 2011), the information in question must be of value to the putative trade secret owner. However, it is not just the value to the plaintiff that will suffice. It must also have "independent" value derived from its secrecy and be of "value to others."

Although the distinction is a fine one, information can have economic value for a number of reasons other than because of its secrecy. For instance, a recipe may be valuable because it results in the production of tasty food. However, unless it also has "independent" (or additional) value because it is secret, it can be argued that it does not meet the economic value requirement of the UTSA. Similarly, simply because a body of information has value to its owner does not mean that the same body of information is of value to others. Thus, in the right case, the "value to others" requirement can be a significant limitation on the scope of trade secret protection. As an example, it may be of value to a company to keep records of its polluting activities secret, but such information would not have economic value to competitors. Thus, information regarding polluting activities should not be treated as a trade secret by government regulators or the courts.

One of the first cases to explicitly discuss the independent economic value requirement is *Electro-Craft Corp. v. Controlled Motion, Inc.*, 332 N.W.2d 890, which involved the common scenario of a former employee deciding to start a competing business and allegations that the product produced by the new company (servo motors) included trade secrets that were misappropriated. The evidence revealed a number of troublesome facts, including the former employee's decision to start a competing business while still in the employ of plaintiff and his solicitation of co-workers to join his new company. Evidence was also presented to show that the former employee had access to and knowledge of the inner workings of plaintiff's product and that his company's new product was nearly identical to the plaintiff's product.

Based upon the evidence that was produced at trial, the trial judge found for the plaintiff and enjoined the defendant from competing in the subject market for twelve months. *Electro-Craft Corp. v. Controlled Motion, Inc.*, 332 N.W.2d at 896. The judge also awarded punitive damages of $50 for each offending servo motor that defendant sold. On appeal, the appellate court reversed, noting "[w]ithout a proven trade secret there can be no action for misappropriation, even if defendants' actions were wrongful." *Id.* at 897. Based upon a careful consideration of the statutory definition of a trade secret as spelled-out in Minnesota's version of the UTSA, the court concluded that the plaintiff had not met the reasonable efforts requirement of the UTSA.

On the issue of economic value, the appellate court found that plaintiff's alleged trade secrets (the ECC 1125 motor) did provide the plaintiff with economic value from its secrecy. This finding was based upon consideration of both the language and purpose of the economic value requirement and the evidence presented. The court first noted that the economic value requirement "carries forward the common law requirement of competitive advantage." *Id.,* at 900–01. It refused, however, to accept the defendant's contention that plaintiff must prove that it is the only company in the market. Instead, the applicable test was expressed as follows: "If an outsider would obtain a valuable share of the market by gaining certain information, then that information may be a trade secret if it is not known or readily ascertainable." *Id.* Ultimately, because the plaintiff presented evidence of the time and money that would be required for a prospective competitor to produce a comparable motor, the appellate court found that there was sufficient evidence to support the lower court's finding on the issue of economic value.

From the foregoing, evidence of independent economic value may be presented in two ways. The first method provides direct evidence of economic value by focusing on the actual competitive advantage that the putative trade secret holder gains from its information. As stated in *Yield Dynamics, Inc. v. TEA Sys. Corp.*, 154 Cal. App. 4th 547, 564 (Cal. Ct. App. 2007), "The advantage 'need not be great,' but must be 'more than trivial'" (citations omitted). The second method is based upon circumstantial evidence, including the resources invested in producing the information, the reasonable efforts that were engaged in to protect the information, and the willingness of others to pay for access to the information. *See also, Religious Tech. Ctr. v. Netcom on-Line Commc'n Servs., Inc.,* 907 F. Supp. 1361 (N.D. Cal. 1995); Restatement (Third) of Unfair Competition, § 39 cmt. e (1995).

In *Buffets, Inc. v. Klinke,* 73 F.3d 965 (9th Cir. 1996), the court addressed both the "economic value" and "value to others" prongs of the economic value requirement. The court noted that the mere fact that the plaintiff's food tasted better than its competitors was not sufficient proof of economic value. The plaintiff also had to show that its competitors were at a competitive disadvantage because of their inferior food. In other words, plaintiff failed to show that the alleged lack of success of its competitors was caused by the fact that they did not have access to plaintiff's small-batch cooking recipes.

§ 3.4   REASONABLE EFFORTS TO MAINTAIN SECRECY

Whether a state follows the *Restatement of Torts,* the UTSA, or the *Restatement of Unfair Competition,* the reasonable efforts requirement is an important part of the analysis in every trade secret case. In almost every state, the reasonable efforts requirement is embedded in the threshold legal question of the misappropriation analysis: whether the plaintiff owns a legally protectable trade secret. In fact, based upon the emphasis that is placed upon it by courts and litigants, the reasonable efforts requirement of trade secrecy is arguably the most important requirement, although for reasons that are explained below there are cases that seem to ignore it altogether.

Often the cases focus on the various steps and techniques that a plaintiff undertook to protect its information and whether such efforts appear reasonable under the circumstances. However, it is equally important to understand the purposes of the requirement and the various practical functions it serves.

§ 3.4.1   THE PURPOSES AND FUNCTIONS OF THE REASONABLE EFFORTS REQUIREMENT

To understand the purposes and functions of the reasonable efforts requirement (and to a lesser extent the economic value requirement) it is useful to engage in a thought experiment. Imagine that you are an employee of a company and you want to do the right thing and respect and protect company trade secrets. Also assume that as an employee you are routinely given access to a variety of information ranging from the mundane to highly technical data. How are you to know whether, and to what extent, the information constitutes trade secrets? Should you assume that all of the information is a trade secret even though it is likely that such is not the case?

The foregoing illustrates the principal purpose and function of the reasonable efforts requirement; namely, to require trade secret owners to identify their putative trade secrets and put others on notice of the existence of their property rights before an act of trade secret misappropriation occurs. Because trade secrets need not exist in tangible form (like copyrights), be evidenced by a government certificate (like patent rights), or be registered or publicly used (like trademarks), the reasonable efforts requirement provides some evidence of both the existence and identification of trade secrets. The notice function of the reasonable efforts requirement also plays a fairness and due process role, particularly given the potential civil and criminal liability for trade secret misappropriation.

Evidence of reasonable efforts can also serve as circumstantial evidence of: (1) secrecy (*supra* § 3.1); (2) the economic value of the putative trade secrets (*supra* § 3.3); (3) misappropriation (*infra* § 4.3); and (4) the actual harm suffered by the plaintiff (*infra* § 6.4). However, in UTSA jurisdictions it is important to keep the evidentiary functions of reasonable efforts separate from the reasonable efforts requirement itself. Just because there is some evidence of efforts to maintain the secrecy of information that may suffice to help prove secrecy or economic value does not mean that those efforts meet the reasonable efforts requirement. What is "reasonable" requires a highly factual and contextual analysis. *See infra* § 3.4.2. Conversely, just because a putative trade secret owner engaged in significant efforts to protect its information does not mean that trade secrets exist. No amount of effort can turn generally known and readily ascertainable information into trade secrets.

§ 3.4.2 SOURCES AND STANDARDS OF THE REASONABLE EFFORTS REQUIREMENT

The UTSA includes reasonable efforts as part of the definition of a trade secret. *See* Unif. Trade Secrets Act § 1(4)(ii) (amended 1985), reprinted in Appendix A. The reasonable efforts requirement specifies that in order to qualify for trade secret protection, the information must be "the subject of efforts that are reasonable under the circumstances to maintain its secrecy." *Id.* Thus, what is reasonable depends upon the circumstances, including the nature of the information and the risks that are posed to the secrecy of the information.

Like the economic value requirement before it, the inclusion of a reasonable efforts requirement in the UTSA's definition of a trade secret was by design. The drafters of the UTSA wanted to limit the information that could qualify for trade secret protection and avoid situations where trade secrets were found to exist even though the putative trade secret owner did nothing to identify or secure them prior to the alleged misappropriation. In this regard, early drafts of the UTSA included a requirement that trade secrets be fixed in tangible form. When this requirement was rejected, the reasonable efforts requirement became an alternative means to ensure the veracity of claims of trade secrecy. Accordingly, courts applying the UTSA have found that the failure of a plaintiff to put on any evidence of reasonable efforts is fatal to the plaintiff's claim, even if the alleged trade secrets were actually secret. *See Electro-Craft Corp. v. Controlled Motion, Inc.* 332 N.W. 2d 890.

The states that have not adopted the UTSA often rely on the older version of trade secret law as expressed in the *Restatement of Torts*. However, in contrast to the UTSA which codified the reasonable efforts requirement, the *Restatement of Torts* includes "the extent of measures taken by [the trade secret owner] to guard the secrecy of the information" as one of six factors to be considered in determining whether information qualifies as a trade secret. Restatement (First) of Torts § 757 cmt. b (1939). Because of this, reasonable efforts is not viewed as an independent requirement of trade secrecy and can therefore be overlooked or downplayed in non-UTSA jurisdictions, particularly in cases where there is evidence of egregious wrongdoing. *See, e.g., In re Cooper Tire & Rubber Co.*, 313 S.W.3d. 910–915 (Tex. App. Ct. 2010) (noting that in Texas "the party claiming a trade secret is not required to satisfy all six factors. . .") (citations omitted). Nonetheless, a defendant in a trade secret case, whether in a non-UTSA jurisdiction or not, should always try to hold the plaintiff to the burden of proving reasonable efforts.

Unlike the UTSA, the *Restatement of Unfair Competition* does not include the words "reasonable efforts" in its definition of a trade secret (*see* Restatement (Third) of Unfair Competition § 39 (1995)) and, accordingly, does not view reasonable efforts as an independent requirement. Rather, in keeping with the evidentiary functions of reasonable efforts and the *Restatement of Torts* factors, evidence of precautions taken by an information owner to protect information may be relevant on a number of different trade secret issues. Restatement (Third) of Unfair Competition, § 39, cmt. g (1995).

As explained in comment g to section 39 of the *Restatement of Unfair Competition*:

> Whether viewed as an independent requirement or as an element to be considered with other factors relevant to the existence of a trade secret, the owner's precautions should be evaluated in light of the other available evidence relating to the value and secrecy of the information. Thus, if the value and secrecy of the information are clear, evidence of specific precautions taken by the trade secret owner may be unnecessary.

In effect, the *Restatement of Unfair Competition* approves of the case decisions that the drafters of the UTSA appear to have rejected, those which found trade secrets even in the absence of evidence of reasonable efforts.

Under the *Restatement of Unfair Competition*'s formulation of trade secrecy, reasonable efforts is also an important part of the second question in the misappropriation analysis; namely, whether the defendant misappropriated the trade secret. Restatement (Third) of Unfair Competition § 43 cmt. c (1995). In determining whether a defendant's acquisition of a trade secret was improper, the *Restatement of Unfair Competition* calls for an evaluation of "the extent to which the acquisition was facilitated by the trade secret owner's failure to take reasonable precautions against discovery of the secret by the means in question." *Id.* The *Restatement of Unfair Competition* further suggests that the "foreseeability of the conduct through which the secret was acquired" should be relevant to determining reasonableness. *Id.*

Similar to the UTSA, the Economic Espionage Act ("EEA"), the federal criminal trade secret statute, includes a reasonable efforts requirement in its definition of a trade secret. *See infra* § 10.2 for further discussion of the EEA. The EEA requires that "the owner [of the alleged trade secrets] has taken reasonable measures to keep such information secret." 18 U.S.C. § 1839(3)(A) (2006). This provision withstood a void for vagueness challenge, with the court finding that the term "reasonable measures" is not unconstitutionally vague. *See United States v. Kai-Lo Hsu*, 40 F. Supp. 2d 623, 628 (E.D. Pa. 1999).

In summary, the modern view of trade secret law under the UTSA (and the EEA) makes the reasonable efforts requirement a separate requirement for secrecy, whereas the alternative common law view in the *Restatements* treats it as evidence of secrecy and other trade secret issues. As a practical matter (at least for the defendant in a trade secret case), it makes sense to treat the reasonable efforts requirement as a separate requirement because it encourages courts and litigants to filter out those putative trade secrets whose value is only recognized by the plaintiff after the alleged misappropriation occurs. In addition, the requirement helps clarify that each of the requirements of trade secrecy are important.

§ 3.4.3   INTERPRETATION BY THE COURTS

The above sources of law do not provide precise standards to the courts on how to determine whether the reasonable efforts requirement has been met. The commentary to the UTSA § 1 simply lists some precautions to be considered, including "advising employees of the existence of a trade secret, limiting access to a trade secret on a 'need to know basis,' and controlling plant access." However, the interpretation of the reasonable efforts requirement in both UTSA and non-UTSA states appears to be similar.

Whether a trade secret owner has utilized appropriate safeguards sufficient to meet the reasonable efforts requirement is a question of fact, based on the particular circumstances. *See Rockwell Graphic Sys., Inc. v. DEV Indus., Inc.*, 925 F.2d 174, 176–77 (7th Cir. 1991). Generally, a review of the circumstances necessitates balancing the value and nature of the putative trade secrets and the cost of precautions with the realities of the putative trade secret owner's business. The inquiry necessarily varies in each case based on the costs of the protective measures relative to the risks of misappropriation and the attendant benefits of protecting the information. The costs to the trade secret owner not only include direct financial costs, but also indirect costs, such as the ability to make appropriate use of the information in the business by sharing it with employees and others who need to use it.

Although the level of efforts that are required will vary, it is clear that the necessary level of reasonable efforts does not require absolute secrecy. *See Computer Assocs. Int'l v. Quest Software, Inc.*, 333 F. Supp. 2d 688, 696 (N.D. Ill. 2004). Rather, the standard is one of relative secrecy; a trade secret owner needs to take steps that are reasonably necessary under the circumstances to maintain secrecy. *See Sheets v. Yamaha Motors Corp.*, 849 F.2d 179, 183–84 (5th Cir. 1988). At a minimum, the plaintiff must take affirmative steps and show concrete efforts to preserve the confidentiality of the alleged secret information. *See Niemi v. Am. Axle Mfr. & Holding, Inc.*, 2007 WL 29383, at *4 (Mich. Ct. App. Jan. 4, 2007).

As noted previously, efforts to protect secrecy are also tied to the requirement that trade secrets have value and, indeed, whether or not a company took adequate steps to protect a secret is evidence of the subjective belief that the information was a trade secret and thus worthy of protection. *See Metallurgical Indus. Inc. v. Fourtek, Inc.*, 790 F.2d 1195, 1199–1200 (5th Cir. 1986). Some courts may reason that there is a direct relationship between the value of the information and the extent to which the company made efforts to protect it such that the more valuable the information to the company, the more costly or extensive the measures ought to be to protect it.

Because relationships are often at the heart of trade secret claims (*see infra* § 4.6), the nature of the relationship between a putative trade secret owner and the alleged misappropriator will often influence the reasonable efforts analysis. Generally, the closer the relationship between the parties, and the more it is imbued with trust or fiduciary duties (as opposed to simple duties of confidentiality), the less efforts should be required. For instance, it should not be necessary for an inventor to require a written confidentiality agreement from his attorney since the attorney is under a professional and ethical obligation to maintain the confidentiality of attorney/client communications. *See* Model Rules of Prof'l Conduct R. 1.6 (1983). Whether this should be the case with respect to lesser relationships, such as the employer/employee relationship or arms-length business transactions, is another question.

Where a plaintiff makes a strong showing of reasonable efforts to protect trade secret information, a court is more likely to infer that the defendant used improper means to obtain the information. As one court aptly noted:

> If [plaintiff] expended only paltry resources on preventing its drawings from falling into the hands of competitors, why should the law, whose machinery is far from costless, bother to provide [plaintiff] with a remedy? The information contained in the drawings cannot have been worth much if [plaintiff] did not think it worthwhile to make serious efforts to keep the information secret.

Rockwell Graphic Sys., Inc. v. DEV Indus., Inc., 925 F.2d 174, 179 (7th Cir. 1991). Indeed, even when a plaintiff creates a trade secret protection plan which provides for how the secrets will be safeguarded, but fails to adequately follow it, a court could find such conduct to be unreasonable vis-a-vis the hypothetical reasonable person. *See Gemisys Corp. v. Phoenix Am., Inc.*, 186 F.R.D. 551, 558, 567 (N.D. Cal. 1999).

There are a variety of steps that a putative trade secret owner can take to protect its information, all of which are based more upon common sense than the dictates of law. As a practical matter, because trade secret litigation can be expensive, there is no guaranty of success, and trade secrets can be lost in the process, a trade secret owner should institute measures that are necessary to achieve strong security. This is particularly true with respect to the "crown jewels" of a company. In order to meet the reasonable efforts requirement of trade secret law, however, something less than strong security is often enough.

§ 3.4.4   EVIDENCE OF REASONABLE EFFORTS

The plaintiff in a trade secret case has the burden of producing sufficient evidence to prove that the alleged trade secret was the subject of reasonable efforts to protect its secrecy. *See Gillis Associated Indus., Inc. v. Cari-All, Inc.*, 564 N.E.2d 881, 886 (Ill. App. Ct. 1990). In order to meet its burden, the plaintiff is likely to present evidence of both the general security procedures of its place of business and specific measures related to the information in question.

Examples of available security measures abound. The language the courts use is not always consistent, but courts often look for the use of the fol-

lowing kinds of security measures in assessing reasonableness: (1) confidentiality agreements; (2) exit
interviews reminding departing employees of their
confidentiality obligations; (3) security badges to
enter the premises or secured areas; (4) security
guards and closed-circuit television cameras; and (5)
computer passwords or access codes restricting access to certain personnel.

It is usually recommended that all employees and
outside entities that are given access to trade secret
information be required to sign written confidentiality agreements. *See infra* § 7.4. Some courts note
that in addition to requiring employees to sign confidentiality agreements, "reasonable efforts" can
include "advising employees of the existence of a
trade secret, limiting access to the information on a
'need to know basis,' and keeping secret documents
under lock." *See Religious Tech. Ctr. v. Netcom On-
Line Commc'n Servs.*, 923 F. Supp. 1231, 1253. The
use of security guards, closed-circuit television mon-
itors, access codes for information stored on a computer, and varying security access levels for different areas of the facilities have also proven reasonable. *See Schalk v. State*, 767 S.W.2d 441, 447–48
(Tex. Ct. App. 1988).

In testing the adequacy of the plaintiff's efforts,
the trier of fact will usually focus on the plaintiff's
security measures and whether any sharing of the
trade secrets were subject to express or implied duties of confidentiality. If the trade secrets exist in
written or digital form, evidence should be presented to show where and how the information is stored
and who has access to it. If the trade secrets are

part of a manufacturing process, then general efforts to maintain secrecy usually involve efforts to restrict the visibility of the process.

Even where a trade secret owner implements security measures internally with employees it must be mindful of external protections, such as with customers and vendors, as failure to do so could lead to a court denying trade secret protection. *See Flotec, Inc. v. S. Research, Inc.*, 16 F. Supp. 2d 992, 1004–05 (S.D. Ind. 1998). Thus, although there is a tendency among plaintiffs to put forth any and all evidence of security precautions, arguably the relevant precautions relate to the specific trade secrets and acts of misappropriation that are alleged. For instance, it makes little sense for a plaintiff to argue that it engaged in reasonable efforts to keep its formula under lock and key when it had a practice of sharing the formula with customers. The relevant inquiry is whether the customers were under an adequate duty of confidentiality.

As a practical matter, what suffices as reasonable efforts often depends upon the perceived egregiousness of the defendant's acts of misappropriation. The more "wrongful" the acts of the defendant, the more likely the plaintiff's efforts are to be found reasonable. This is because there is a natural tendency among courts and juries not to want to reward perceived wrongdoers. Arguably, however, what constitutes reasonable efforts should be based, at least in part, on an objective standard that considers the availability of security measures.

CHAPTER 4

TRADE SECRET LITIGATION

§ 4.1 INTRODUCTION

There are many aspects to trade secret litigation, including substantive, procedural, and strategic considerations. This chapter gives an overview of trade secret litigation primarily from the perspective of the plaintiff who bears the burden of pleading and proving a claim for relief. It begins with a consideration of the essential elements of a cause of action for trade secret misappropriation, focusing on the critical element of misappropriation. It then discusses a variety of issues that are likely to arise during the pleading and discovery phases of trade secret cases, including: (1) the requirement that trade secrets be identified with specificity; and (2) the need to protect trade secrets during litigation. While issues related to defending against a trade secret misappropriation claim are mentioned throughout this chapter, Chapter 5 provides a detailed description of applicable defenses.

§ 4.2 THE ESSENTIAL ELEMENTS OF A CAUSE OF ACTION FOR TRADE SECRET MISAPPROPRIATION

In order to establish a claim for trade secret misappropriation under the UTSA, a plaintiff has the burden of pleading and proving that: (1) it owns a trade secret; (2) that one or more of its trade secrets have been or are threatened to be misappropriated by the defendant; and (3) that it is entitled to a remedy. *See Clorox Co. v. S.C. Johnson & Son, Inc.,* 627 F. Supp. 2d, 9554, 968 (E.D. Wisc. 2009) (listing the elements of a *prima facie* case for trade secret misappropriation under California's version of the UTSA). Because the available remedies (discussed in Chapter 6) are broad, the focus of trade secret misappropriation cases is usually on the first and second requirements. Generally, the determination whether specific information is a trade secret is a mixed question of law and fact. *See, e.g., APAC Tele-services, Inc. v. McRae,* 985 F. Supp. 852, 864 (N.D. Iowa 1997).

Chapters 2 and 3 examined the meaning of a trade secret. This chapter explores the meaning of misappropriation, first by detailing the statutory definition and then by breaking that definition into its constituent parts.

§ 4.3   "MISAPPROPRIATION" AS DEFINED BY THE UTSA

To understand the meaning of misappropriation it is necessary to carefully consider the statutory definition and then break it down into its constituent parts. In this regard, although the UTSA's definition of misappropriation does not apply in non-UTSA jurisdictions, it generally codifies common law principles. *See* Unif. Trade Secrets Act, Prefatory Note, (amended 1985), reprinted in Appendix A.

Section 1(2) of the UTSA defines "misappropriation," as:

(i) acquisition of a trade secret of another by a person who knows or has reason to know that the trade secret was acquired by improper means; or

(ii) disclosure or use of a trade secret of another without express or implied consent by a person who:

(A) used improper means to acquire knowledge of the trade secret; or

(B) at the time of disclosure or use, knew, or had reason to know, that his knowledge of the trade secret was:

(I) derived from, or through, a person who had utilized improper means to acquire it;

(II) acquired under circumstances giving rise to a duty to maintain its secrecy or limit its use; or,

(III) derived from, or through, a person who owed a duty to the person seeking relief to maintain its secrecy or limit its use; or

(C) before a material change of his position knew or had reason to know that it was a trade secret and that knowledge of it had been acquired by accident or mistake.

In keeping with tort law generally, the definition of misappropriation defines both the requisite wrongful acts and the requisite state of mind of the defendant.

Focusing on the verbs used in section 1(2) of the UTSA, there are three acts that may subject an individual or company to liability for trade secret misappropriation: wrongful acquisition, disclosure, or use. With respect to such acts, there are three potential "wrongs": acquisition by improper means; disclosure or use in violation of a duty of confidentiality; and acquisition by accident or mistake.

It is not necessary in UTSA jurisdictions for plaintiffs in trade secret cases to prove actual harm. The UTSA specifically provides that trade secret owners may file a lawsuit to protect against both threatened and actual misappropriation. This might happen, for instance, where trade secrets were acquired improperly but have not been used or disclosed. In such situations, the plaintiff may obtain injunctive relief but not an award of damages because no actual harm to the trade secrets has occurred. *See infra* § 6.4.

§ 4.4   THE KNOWLEDGE REQUIREMENT

An aspect of trade secret law that is different from patent, copyright, and trademark law is its knowledge requirement. The definition of misappropriation under all formulations of trade secret law requires that the defendant "know or have reason to know" of the alleged trade secrets and the wrongful acts of misappropriation. *See* Unif. Trade Secrets Act § 1(4) (amended 1985); Restatement (Third) of Unfair Competition, § 40 (1995). In contrast, patent, copyright, and trademark laws are similar to strict liability torts in that a defendant may be held liable for patent, copyright, and trademark infringement even if he did not know or have reason to know of the existence of plaintiff's intellectual property rights. How a plaintiff attempts to prove the requisite knowledge in trade secret cases depends upon the facts of each case, but direct evidence of actual knowledge is not required. Knowledge or reason to know can be inferred from circumstantial evidence.

Where a defendant directly engages in the wrongful acts that constitute misappropriation, the requisite knowledge of such wrongful acts is relatively easy to prove. *See, e.g., Beard Research, Inc. v. Kates*, 8 A.3d 573, 599 (Del. Ch. 2010). The key in such cases is to prove that the defendant knew or had reason to know that the information he acquired, disclosed, or used was trade secret information. This is where the reasonable efforts requirement intersects with the misappropriation analysis. As noted *supra* in § 3.4.1, one of the purposes of the reasonable efforts requirement is to put individuals and companies on notice of the trade secret status of information. Thus, the same evidence that might be cited to meet the reasonable efforts requirement and prove the existence of trade secrets can be used to establish part of the knowledge that is needed to prove misappropriation.

In practice, the two parts of the knowledge analysis (knowledge of wrongdoing and knowledge of trade secrets) often work in tandem, with evidence with respect to one part being used to infer the other. For instance, where a defendant acquired knowledge of the plaintiff's trade secrets under circumstances giving rise to a duty to maintain secrecy, as is typical in the employment context, a court may infer knowledge of the trade secret status of the subject information. *See Data General Corp. v. Grumman Systems Support Corp.*, 825 F. Supp. 340,

360 (D. Mass. 1993). A defendant's knowledge that the information was a trade secret is also evidence of misappropriation under the *Restatement of Torts*. *See* Restatement (First) of Torts, § 757 (1939).

Circumstantial evidence can be weighed to determine the likelihood that the defendant knew of the misappropriation, and a defendant cannot shield himself by "studious ignorance of pertinent 'warning' facts." *See Curtiss-Wright Corp. v. Edel-Brown Tool & Die Co.*, 407 N.E.2d 319, 324 (Mass. 1980). A defendant's constructive notice that the information was a trade secret is sufficient.

The *Restatement of Tort*'s definition of notice provides further guidance:

> One has notice of facts . . . when he knows of them or when he should know of them. He should know of them if, from the information which he has, a reasonable man would infer the facts in question, or if, under the circumstances, a reasonable man would be put on inquiry and an inquiry pursued with reasonable intelligence and diligence would disclose the facts.

Restatement (First) of Torts § 757, cmt. 1 (1939). Accordingly, if the evidence suggests that a reasonable person would have been on notice that the information received was the wrongfully disclosed trade secret of another, then the defendant should be liable for misappropriation.

§ 4.4.1   KNOWLEDGE BY THIRD-PARTIES

The knowledge requirement of trade secret law poses problems when third-parties come to possess trade secrets that were earlier misappropriated by someone else. *See, e.g., Cabot Corp. v. Thai Tantalum Inc.*, Civ. A. No. 12580, 1992 WL 172678, at *2 (Ct. of Chancery, Del. 1992). As detailed *infra* in § 4.8, generally, it must be established that the defendant either owed a duty of confidentiality to the plaintiff or acquired the trade secrets by improper means. However, a third-party usually has no direct relationship with the trade secret owner that gives rise to a duty of confidentiality and, by definition, there is no evidence that the third-party acquired the information by improper means. Thus, unless there is another basis upon which to hold the third-party liable for trade secret misappropriation, he is free to use information that he receives from another. (*See infra* § 4.7)

When read with potential third-party liability in mind, the UTSA sets forth five factual circumstances where a third-party may be held liable for trade secret misappropriation. Generally, a third-party may be held liable for trade secret misappropriation if he knew or has reason to know of the wrongdoing by the direct misappropriator. This would arise where it is proven that the third-party knew or had reason to know that the trade secrets were: (1) acquired [by another] by improper means; (2) derived from or through a person who used improper means to acquire them; (3) acquired [by another] under circumstances giving rise to a duty to maintain or limit their use; and (4) derived from or through a person who owed a duty to maintain their secrecy or limit their use. Unif. Trade Secrets Act § 1(2)(ii)(A) and (B) (amended 1985). A third-party may also be held liable in the case of accident or mistake where he knew or had reason to know that the information disclosed to him "was a trade secret and that knowledge of it had been acquired by accident or mistake." *Id.* § 1(2)(ii)(C).

As noted previously, actual evidence of knowledge is not needed; circumstantial evidence is enough. However, if the trade secret owner provided notice to the defendant in a timely fashion that the information was a trade secret, then third-party liability is more likely. *See* Unif. Trade Secrets Act §1(b) (amended 1985); *Colony Corp. of America v. Crown Glass Corp.*, 102 Ill. App. 3d 647, 650 (Ill. App. Ct. 1981).

§ 4.5   MISAPPROPRIATION BY IMPROPER MEANS

The simplest form of trade secret misappropriation occurs when a trade secret is acquired directly by improper means by a person who knows or has reason to know that the information is a trade secret. Such activity can also constitute corporate espionage and may subject the perpetrator to criminal responsibility in addition to a civil lawsuit. *See* Chapter 10. Liability for trade secret misappropriation may also be imposed where a person acquires a trade secret indirectly from another person when he knows (or has reason to know) that the trade secret was obtained through improper means. *See IMED*

Corp. v. Sys. Eng'g Assocs. Corp., 602 So.2d 344, 346 (Ala. 1992).

§ 4.5.1   SOURCES AND MEANING OF "IMPROPER MEANS"

The term "improper means" first appears in section 1(2)(i) of the UTSA and includes the mere unauthorized acquisition of trade secrets by a person "who knows or has reason to know that the trade secret was acquired by improper means." Next, section 1(2)(ii)(A) uses the term with respect to the alleged disclosure or use of trade secrets by a person who (directly) acquired the trade secrets by improper means. Finally, the term is used in section 1(2)(ii)(B)(I) to cover a situation where the alleged discloser or user derived (indirectly acquired) the trade secrets from another with knowledge or reason to know that the other had acquired them by improper means.

"Improper means" is defined in section 1(1) of the UTSA to include, but not be limited to, "theft, breach or inducement of a breach of a duty to maintain secrecy, or espionage through electronic or other means." Clearly, criminal activity that is engaged in for the purpose of acquiring trade secret information is considered improper means. However, the methods that are used to acquire trade secrets need not be criminal to be considered improper. Activity that is merely tortious can suffice, including actions that would be considered acts of "unfair competition" under common law. *See Precision Automation, Inc. v. Technical Serv., Inc.*, No. 07–CV–707–AS, 2007 WL 4480736, at *1–3 (D. Or. Dec. 14, 2007);

Penrose Computer Marketgroup, Inc. v. Camin, 682 F. Supp. 2d 202, 214–16 (N.D.N.Y. 2010).

The *Restatement of Torts* does not include a definition of "improper means." This may be explained by the fact that the *Restatement of Torts* does not define the wrongful acquisition of trade secrets as an actionable wrong (although some common law cases found a trade secret misappropriation in such circumstances). Rather, only the wrongful use or disclosure of trade secrets (or, in some cases, the threatened use or disclosure of trade secrets) after being acquired either rightfully or wrongfully, is actionable under the *Restatement of Torts*. Under both the UTSA and the *Restatement of Unfair Competition*, the wrongful acquisition of trade secrets is explicitly actionable, provided a basis for remedies is established.

Section 43 of the *Restatement of Unfair Competition*, defines what it means to "improperly acquire trade secrets." Similar to the language of the UTSA, improper acts of acquisition include: "theft, fraud, unauthorized interception of communications, inducement of or knowing participation in a breach of confidence, and other means wrongful in themselves or wrongful under the circumstances of the case." As further explained in the commentary to section 43, improper means can include all manner of tortious and criminal conduct and other unspecified wrongful acts not rising to the level of a crime or a tort. Restatement (Third) of Unfair Competition § 43, cmt. c (1995). This language is undoubtedly based upon the holding of *E.I. DuPont v. Christopher*, 431

F.2d 1012 (5th Cir. 1970), a case that was decided before the adoption of the UTSA.

In *Christopher,* the court addressed the question whether actions that are not criminal or otherwise tortious can nonetheless constitute improper means for purposes of a trade secret misappropriation claim. *Id.* at 1015–17. DuPont had developed a secret process for producing methanol and was in the process of constructing a plant for that purpose. The defendants, who were hired by an unidentified third-party, allegedly acquired secrets about DuPont's process by taking aerial photographs of the methanol plant. Because the plant was still under construction, parts of the process were exposed to view from directly above the construction area. DuPont alleged that the photos would enable a skilled person to deduce its secret process for making methanol.

The defendants argued that "improper means" required a trespass, other illegal conduct, or breach of a confidential relationship. Because the photographers broke no laws and did not otherwise commit a tort in taking the pictures, they contended they could not be liable for trade secret misappropriation. The court in *Christopher* did not agree. Focusing on the perceived unfairness of acquiring information through aerial photography, the court stated: "To obtain knowledge of a process without spending the time and money to discover it independently is improper unless the holder voluntarily discloses it or fails to take reasonable precautions to ensure its secrecy." *E.I. DuPont v. Christopher*, 431 F.2d at 1015–16.

There are two ways to look at the *Christopher* case. First, it can be viewed as simply defining an act of unfair competition which, consistent with the common origins of trade secret law, should not be allowed among civilized businesses. On the other hand, it may be criticized as extending the definition of improper means too far. Either way, unless *Christopher* is explicitly overruled it is likely to be cited by trade secret plaintiffs who would benefit from a broad conception of the meaning of improper. How broad that definition of improper should extend is a question that is open for debate in trade secret cases.

§ 4.5.2   EVIDENCE OF IMPROPER MEANS

As the foregoing suggests, the best way for a plaintiff in a trade secret misappropriation case to prove that the defendant acquired trade secrets by improper means is to establish that the defendant engaged in a crime or tort that resulted in the acquisition of trade secrets. However, given the nefarious purposes and methods of individuals who commit crimes or torts in order to acquire trade secrets, there is often no direct evidence in the form of eyewitness testimony that can be presented. Frequently, all that the plaintiff can show is that its trade secrets are missing and that the defendant appeared to behave oddly or improperly. Common scenarios of odd behavior include after-hours copying of documents, the unexpected packing and moving of boxes, and secretive behavior. *See, e.g., United States v. Martin*, 228 F.3d 1, 6 (1st Cir. 2000).

In the absence of direct evidence of improper activity, a plaintiff must rely on circumstantial evidence of a defendant's use of improper means to obtain its trade secrets. *See Milgrim on Trade Secrets* § 15.01[1]. In *Pioneer Hi-Bred Int'l v. Holden Foundation Seeds, Inc.*, 35 F.3d 1226 (8th Cir. 1994), the plaintiff did just that. The alleged misappropriation consisted of the improper acquisition and subsequent use of genetic messages from corn seed. Plaintiff claimed that the defendant improperly acquired one of plaintiff's "inbred parent seed lines" (Pioneer H3H or H43SZ7) and used it to develop its own seed line (LH38–39–40, developed from an internal line L120). The defendant argued that there was no evidence that it used improper means to acquire the genetic messages.

The court upheld the lower court's finding of acquisition by improper means, reasoning that although there was no direct evidence of industrial espionage, sufficient circumstantial evidence was presented. Among the evidence presented was: (1) defendant's long history of attempts to find Pioneer's genetic material; (2) defendant's searches of "friendly farms;" (3) inadequate explanation of faulty record-keeping (that might have shown the independent development that Holden claimed); (4) expert testimony that the independent development of Holden's seed line was highly unlikely; and (5) proof that Holden's seed was derived from Pioneer's.

§ 4.5.3   PROPER MEANS: REVERSE ENGINEERING AND INDEPENDENT DEVELOPMENT

Another way to understand the meaning of "improper means" is to consider how trade secrets can be acquired properly. According to the commentary to section 1 of the UTSA, proper means include: (1) discovery by independent invention; (2) discovery by reverse engineering; (3) discovery under a license from the owner; (4) observation of the item in public use or on public display; and (5) obtaining the trade secret from published literature. Proper acquisition also includes the outright purchase of trade secrets from a trade secret owner and a trade secret owner's act of "sharing" trade secrets with others pursuant to an implied duty of confidentiality.

§ 4.5.4   COMPETITIVE INTELLIGENCE

As a matter of public policy, competition is good; it helps to lower prices and can improve the quality of goods and services. *See F.T.C. v. Superior Court Trial Lawyers Ass'n*, 493 U.S. 411, 423 (1990). Often, in order to compete effectively, companies need to acquire information about their competitors and to do so they frequently seek competitive intelligence. Competitive intelligence about another company can be acquired from a number of different sources, including required government filings, industry and company websites and blogs, trade journals and newspaper reports, patent filings, trade shows, and Freedom of Information Act (FOIA) requests. As long as these efforts focus on publicly available or readily ascertainable information, they are not deemed improper even if the end result is the loss of business profits due to increased competition. Sometimes, however, actions that are believed to be lawful acts of competitive intelligence go too far and constitute actionable trade secret misappropriation. *See, e.g., Microstrategy, Inc. v. Business Objects, S.A.*, 513 F. Supp. 2d 396 (E.D. Va. 2004).

§ 4.6   MISAPPROPRIATION BY BREACH OF A DUTY OF CONFIDENTIALITY

Although cases involving the misappropriation of trade secrets by improper means often present intriguing facts of corporate espionage by electronic or other technological methods, the majority of trade secret cases involve alleged breaches of a duty of confidentiality. In this regard, it is important to note that the definition of improper means includes "breach of a duty to maintain secrecy," generally referring to acts leading to the acquisition of trade secrets. In contrast, the provisions of the UTSA that do not use the term "improper means" start with the premise that the subject information was acquired properly, but involve a situation where disclosure or use has occurred (or is threatened to occur) in violation of a duty of confidentiality. This situation often arises in the employment context when a former employee of a company discloses trade secrets he rightfully learned from a former employer to his new employer.

§ 4.6.1 SOURCES AND MEANING OF "DUTY OF CONFIDENTIALITY"

The UTSA does not use the phrase "duty of confidentiality" and, accordingly, does not define the scope and meaning of a duty of confidentiality in either the text of the UTSA or its commentary. However, it does define "misappropriation" to include disclosing or using a trade secret of another with knowledge or reason to know that it was acquired "under circumstances giving rise to a duty to maintain its secrecy." Unif. Trade Secrets Act § 1(2)(ii)(B)(II) (amended 1985), reprinted in Appendix A.

Because a duty of confidentiality is not defined by the UTSA, its meaning is generally to be determined by the common law of each individual state and in practice can prove to be a very malleable requirement. Two critical questions are: (1) whether the duty of confidentiality for purposes of trade secret law is different from, and perhaps more loose than, concepts of a duty of confidentiality, generally; and (2) how the applicable definition of a duty of confidentiality relates to similar concepts such as fiduciary and trust duties and an employee's duty of loyalty. *See, e.g., BlueEarth Biofuels, LLC v. Hawaiian Elec. Co., Inc.*, 123 Hawai'i 314, 321–22 (2010).

The *Restatement of Torts* does not include a definition of the duty of confidentiality in either its text or commentaries, but a definition is included in the *Restatement of Unfair Competition*. Pursuant to sections 41 of the *Restatement of Unfair Competition*, there are two ways that a duty of confidentiality may arise. It may be based upon an actual agreement between the parties (either written, oral, or implied-in-fact) or it may arise as a matter of law from the circumstances (implied-at-law). However, "no duty of confidence will be inferred unless the recipient has notice of the confidential nature of the disclosure." Restatement of Unfair Competition, § 40, cmt. b (1995).

§ 4.6.2   CONTRACTUAL DUTIES OF CONFIDENTIALITY, EXPRESS AND IMPLIED

The most obvious example of an express duty of confidentiality is a binding written contract. *See B.F. Goodrich v. Wohlgemuth*, 192 N. E. 2d 99, 105 (1963) ("The written contract expressly binds the employee. . . not to misuse special confidential knowledge of trade secrets secured by him while the contractual relationship of employment existed.") Thus, if a trade secret owner wants to create a duty in another to maintain the confidentiality of his information, the best way to do so is to get the promise in writing before any disclosure occurs. This can take the form of a confidentiality clause in an agreement which deals primarily with other matters (for instance a clause in an employment agreement or a license agreement) or a separate "Confidentiality Agreement" or "Non-Disclosure Agreement" (also referred to as an "NDA") *See infra* § 7.4.

When no express oral or written agreement exists to impose a duty of confidentiality on the defendant, the plaintiff in a trade secret misappropriation case must plead and prove the existence of an implied duty. Generally, under principles of contract law, such a duty may either be implied-in-fact or implied-at-law. *See* 17A Am. Jur. 2d Contracts § 12 (2013) (explaining the difference between express, implied, and constructive contracts).

An implied-in-fact contract (like an express written or oral agreement) is based on the intentions of the parties. "'It arises where the court finds from the surrounding facts and circumstances that the parties intended to make a contract but failed to articulate their promises and the court merely implies what it feels the parties really intended.'" *See Reeves v. Alyeska Pipeline Service Company*, 926 P. 2d 1130 (Sup. Ct. of AK 1996) (quoting *Martens v. Metzgar,* 524 P.2d 666, 672 (Alaska 1974)). Such contracts often arise in the context of so-called idea submission cases where a person with an idea conditions the disclosure of the idea on a promise of compensation.

§ 4.6.3   DUTIES OF CONFIDENTIALITY IMPLIED-AT-LAW

An implied-in-fact contract differs from an implied-at-law (or quasi) contract because with an implied-at-law contract there is no finding of intent to enter into a contract. *See* 17A Am. Jur. 2d Contracts § 12. Instead, a contract is implied from the circumstances based upon equitable considerations. *See Demodulation, Inc. v. U.S.*, 103 Fed. Cl. 794, 807 (Fed. Cl. 2012). Under applicable principles of contract law, a number of factors are considered in determining whether an implied-in-fact contract exists, including mutuality of intent to contract, consideration, and lack of ambiguity in offer and acceptance. *See City of El Centro v. U.S*, 922 F.2d 816, 820 (Fed. Cir. 1990).

Generally, to establish an implied-at-law duty of confidentiality in a trade secret case, the plaintiff should present evidence of the nature and character of the relationship between the parties and the circumstances that led to the disclosure of the putative trade secrets; the goal being to show that the equities demand a finding of an implicit promise of confidentiality. Evidence disclosed in written and oral communications may be highly relevant to determining whether a duty of confidentiality should be implied. Where, however, an express contractual arrangement on confidentiality existed between the parties, it may not be controverted by an implied agreement, and its terms will serve to define the duty of confidentiality, if any. *See Nilssen v. Motorola, Inc.*, 963 F. Supp. 664, 679–82 (N.D. Ill. 1997).

Arguably, "the circumstances" that give rise to an implied duty of confidentiality in trade secret cases should be the same as those that give rise to an implied-at-law contract under contract law. However, some authorities suggest a broader conception of an implied duty of confidentiality when trade secrets are involved, arguing that the mere sharing of information with another who knows the information is considered to be a trade secret can create a duty of confidentiality. *See* Restatement (First) of Torts § 757 cmt. b (1939); *Milgrim on Trade Secrets*, § 3.03. Defendants should insist on a higher degree of proof of the existence of an implied duty of confidentiality.

§ 4.6.4   DUTIES OF CONFIDENTIALITY IN THE EMPLOYMENT RELATIONSHIP

While plaintiffs in trade secret cases are inclined to argue for a broad application of equitable principles to establish a duty of confidentiality, the focus of the analysis in most cases is on the nature of the relationship between the trade secret owner and the alleged misappropriator. Generally, the closer the relationship between a trade secret owner and another, the more likely it is that an implied-at-law duty of confidentiality will be found. However, even seemingly close relationships—like the employer/employee relationship—do not create a duty of confidentiality in all cases and under all circumstances. *See, e.g., Shatterproof Glass Corporation v. Guardian Class Company, Inc.*, 322 F. Supp. 854 (E.D. Mich. 1970). This is particularly true with respect to low-level employees and employees who have no knowledge of either the existence of trade secrets or the expectation of confidentiality.

Despite the foregoing, and based upon principles of agency and employment law (and the statutes of some states), it is often found that the employment relationship imposes a duty of confidentiality on employees. *See also* Chapter 7, *infra*. While the precise scope and nature of the duty should differ depending upon the particular facts of a case and the law of a given jurisdiction, it often includes a duty to maintain the confidentiality of known trade secrets. *See Town & Country House & Homes Service, Inc. v. Evans*, 150 Conn. 314 (Conn. Sup. Ct 1963). In some jurisdictions, it may also require employees to maintain the confidentiality of proprietary business information that does not meet the definition of a trade secret. *See, e.g., Willis of New York, Inc. v. DeFelice,* 299 A.D.2d 240, 242–43 (N.Y. App. Div. 2002).

Town & Country House & Homes Service, Inc. v. Evans, involved a dispute between a house cleaning business and its former employee in which the plaintiff former employer argued that the defendant owed an implied-at-law duty of confidentiality. The trial court highlighted a critical factor to consider when determining if an implied-at-law duty of confidentiality arose; namely, whether the employee was given access to confidential or trade secret information. 150 Conn. at 319–20. The trial judge determined that the relationship between the plaintiff and defendant was "an ordinary one of employer and employee" that did not include a duty of confidentiality.

The appellate court had a different viewpoint. The essence of the appellate court's holding is that if an employer gives an employee trade secret information, the law will impose a duty on the employee not to use the trade secrets "for his own benefit, to the detriment of the employer." *Town & Country House & Homes Service, Inc. v. Evans,* 150 Conn. at 319. The appellate court overturned the lower court's decision, not on the basis of a finding that the defendant had been given access to trade secret information, but because there was no indication in the record that the lower court had determined whether the customer information was in fact a trade secret.

Often in trade secret cases involving employees, the plaintiffs will invoke other principles of law in an attempt to bolster the argument that there is an implied duty of confidentiality. In particular, they may rely upon the "duty of loyalty" that is said to exist between an employer and an employee. *See Scanwell Freight Express STL, Inc. v. Chan,* 162 S.W.3d 477, 481 (Mo. 2005). Or they might cite to statutes, like California's, which provide that employers own everything that is provided to an employee in the course and scope of the employment relationship. *See Mattel, Inc. v. MGA Entm't,* 782 F. Supp. 2d 911, 998 (C.D. Cal. 2011). Care should be taken to ensure that the existence of these "other" duties does not subsume the trade secret analysis. Arguably, the trade secret analysis requires a finding that the defendant was under the specific duty to protect particular trade secrets.

§ 4.6.5   DUTIES OF CONFIDENTIALITY IN NON-EMPLOYMENT RELATIONSHIPS

Not all trade secret cases involve the employment relationship. In such cases, it can be difficult to establish an implied duty of confidentiality, particularly if the relationship involves an arm's- length transaction or parties who possess equal bargaining strength and sophistication. The most obvious example of a relationship outside of the employment relationship that can give rise to a duty of confidentiality is a trust or fiduciary relationship, such as the attorney/client relationship. When the relationship involves trust or fiduciary duties, it is generally easy for the trier of fact to find an implied duty of confidentiality. *See Fischer v. Viacom Intern., Inc.*, 111 F. Supp. 2d 535, 543 (D. Md. 2000); *Djowharzadeh v. City Nat. Bank and Trust Co. of Norman*, 646 P.2d 616, 619 (Okla. Civ. App. 1982). At the other end of the spectrum are arm's-length transactions that generally do not include a duty of confidentiality. *See Smith v. Snap-on Tools*, 833 F.2d 578 (5th Cir. 1987). In between these two extremes are relationships that may give rise to a duty of confidentiality in some cases.

Whether a particular business relationship gives rise to an implied duty of confidentiality requires a fact-intensive inquiry and a weighing of the totality of the circumstances. Two important circumstances being: (1) whether trade secrets existed and were shared with another; and (2) whether the other was made aware of the expectation of confidentiality. Another important factor, albeit not identified as such, is the perceived wrongfulness of the former employee's behavior.

The types of relationships where (based upon the specific facts of each case) an implied duty of confidentiality was found include: a manufacturer and its suppliers (*see Flotec, Inc. v. Southern Research, Inc.*, 16 F. Supp. 992, 998 (S.D. Ind. 1998)); a manufacturer and an independent contractor (*see Hicklin Engineering, L.C. v. Bartell*, 439 F.3d 346 (7th Cir. 2006)); the seller of a business and a potential buyer (*see Smith v. Dravo Corp*, 203 F.2d 369 (7th Cir. 1953)); *Phillips v. Frey*, 20 F. 3d 623 (5th Cir. 1994)); a licensor and licensee (*see Hyde Corp. v. Huffines*, 314 S.W. 2d 763 (Tex. 1958)); an independent inventor and a potential manufacturer of his invention (*see Kamin v. Kuhnau*, 232 Or. 139 (Sup. Ct. Or. 1962)); and where a trade secret owner provides a product for testing and evaluation (*see Mineral Deposits Ltd. v. Zigan*, 773 P.2d 606, 608 (Colo. App. 1988)). In *Morton v. Rank America, Inc.*, 812 F. Supp. 1062, 1074 (C.D. Cal. 1993), the court ruled that a duty of confidentiality may even exist between joint owners of a trade secret.

In practice, the line between an interaction that gives rise to an implied duty of confidentiality and those that do not can be a very fine one. Where the line is drawn often depends upon whether the disclosure of information was unsolicited. Although it may seem "unfair" for a business to use information that it received from others without paying for it, such businesses do not want to be subjected to trade secret misappropriation claims merely because they listened to someone's "pitch." Thus, courts have held that the mere act of disclosing information to a third-party does not create a duty of confidentiality. *See Smith v. Snap-on Tools Corp.*, 833 F.2d 578, 579–580 (1988) ("[W]hen parties are dealing at arm's length, one party's disclosure of an alleged trade secret to another does not automatically create a confidential relationship.") If one hands over an idea without an understanding or agreement, it is considered a gift. *See Liautaud v. Liautaud*, 221 F.3d 981, 985 (7th Cir. 2000); *Interox America v. PPG Industries*, Inc., 736 F.2d 194, 202 (5th Cir. 1984). Among other reasons, disclosing what one believes to be a trade secret without alerting the recipient that it is a trade secret that must be protected fails to put the other on notice of the existence of trade secrets.

Despite the foregoing, there is commentary in the *Restatement of Torts (*and cases applying it) to the effect that the act of sharing information, when coupled with "notice" that it is a trade secret, can be enough to create a duty of confidentiality. *See Phillips v. Frey*, 20 F.3d 623, 632 (5th Cir. 1994) (*citing* the Restatement of Torts § 757 cmt. j (1939)) ("[N]o particular form of notice is needed; the question raised is whether the recipient of the information knew or should have known that the information was a trade secret and the disclosure was made in confidence."). The cases that apply this broad conception of an implied duty of confidentiality often involve information that was expressly solicited (or enthusiastically welcomed) by the alleged misappropriator. *See, e.g., Moore v. Marty Gilman, Inc.*, 965 F. Supp. 203, 215 (D. Mass. 1997). The circumstances surrounding the disclosures and the positions of power between the parties are additional factors that often lead to a finding of an implied duty of confidentiality. *See Learning Curve Toys, Inc. v. PlayWood Toys, Inc.*, 342 F.3d 714, 725–26 (7th Cir. 2003).

Note, however, that even where an implied duty of confidentiality is found, the existence of such a duty may not be enough to meet the reasonable efforts requirement of trade secrecy. Thus, a plaintiff in a trade secret case may "win the battle" of showing a duty but "lose the war" due to an inability to establish the existence of a trade secret. *See Incase*

Incorporated v. Timex Corporation, 488 F.3d 46 (1st Cir. 2007).

§ 4.6.6 RELATIONSHIPS WITH IDEA MEN AND WOMEN

Idea-submission cases (discussed in greater detail *infra* in § 4.13) often involve power differentials between the plaintiff "idea man" and the alleged misappropriator that can prove difficult for a defendant in a trade secret case to overcome. *See Rogers v. Desa Intern., Inc.*, 183 F. Supp.2d 955, 957–58 (E.D. Mich. 2002). However, unlike the employment relationship or an ongoing business relationship, the short-term nature of the relationship is a factor that weighs against finding an implied duty of confidentiality. *See Smith v. Snap-On Tools Corp.*, 833 F.2d at 580–81. Moreover, a distinction should be made in such cases between an implied contractual obligation that may serve as the basis of a breach of contract claim and an implied duty of confidentiality that is needed to support a trade secret misappropriation claim. *See generally, Reeves v. Alyeska Pipeline Serv. Co.*, 926 P.2d 1130 (explaining the requirements for claims based upon implied contracts). Also, if the plaintiff is relying on a trade secret theory, the existence or non-existence of a confidential relationship is relevant on the issue of reasonable efforts. *See Daktronics, Inc. McAfee*, 599 N.W. 2d 358 (S.D. Sup. Ct. 1999).

Companies will sometimes require those who submit ideas to them to sign an explicit acknowledgment that no implied duty of confidentiality exists between them. *See infra* § 4.13. Such waivers must be carefully worded in order to be enforced, but are generally recommended to avoid imposition of an implied-at-law or implied-in-fact duty. *See Burten v. Milton Bradley Co.*, 763 F.2d 461 (1st Cir. 1985). Where a receiving party clearly indicates in advance that he will not enter into a confidential relationship and is only dealing at arm's length, the party disclosing the information cannot unilaterally create a confidential relationship. *See Hisel v. Chrysler Corp.*, 94 F. Supp. 996 (W.D. Mo. 1951).

§ 4.6.7   DETERMINING THE NATURE AND SCOPE OF THE DUTY OF CONFIDENTIALITY

Once a relationship that includes a duty of confidentiality is shown to exist, the next step in the misappropriation analysis requires an examination of the nature and scope of the duty and whether the defendant breached the duty of confidentiality as so defined. This is largely a factual analysis.

Sometimes the person who is under a duty of confidentiality has the right to possess and use the subject trade secrets but not a right to share them with others. *See, e.g., Abernathy-Thomas Engineering Co. v. Pall Corp.*, 103 F. Supp.2d 582, 604–06 (E.D.N.Y. 2000). Other times the person who is under a duty of confidentiality is shown to be in breach of the duty because they exceeded the terms of a license agreement. *See Dun & Bradstreet Software Serv., Inc. v. Grace Consulting, Inc.*, 307 F.3d 197, 219 (3d Cir. 2002); *Lizalde v. Advanced Planning Serv., Inc.*, 875 F. Supp 2d 1150, 1162 (S.D. Cal. 2012). Still other times the breach of a duty of confidentiality will be found based upon the failure of an employee to return trade secrets at the end of his employment with the trade secret owner. *See Zahodnick v. Int'l Bus. Machines Corp.,* 135 F.3d 911, 912, 915 (4th Cir. 1997); *Haught v. Louis Berkman LLC,* 417 F. Supp. 2d 777, 780–81 (N.D. W. Va. 2006). Thus, the act of an employee in secreting away trade secrets before changing jobs (for instance by downloading them onto a flash drive) may constitute both a breach of a duty of confidentiality and acquisition of the trade secrets by improper means. *See Uncle B's Bakery, Inc. v. O'Rourke,* 920 F. Supp. 1405, 1429–30 (N.D. Iowa 1996).

When discussing the existence of an implied duty of confidentiality, many cases do not carefully dif-ferentiate between information that would meet the definition of a trade secret and other proprietary and business information. *See, e.g., North Atlantic Instruments, Inc. v. Haber,* 188 F.3d 38, 47–48 (2d Cir. 1999). Technically, however, the nature of the information is important because it dictates which causes of action and remedies are available. Thus, it is theoretically possible that someone could breach a duty of confidentiality but not be subjected to a suc-cessful claim for relief for trade secret misappropri-ation. This could happen, for instance, where: (1) the information is not a trade secret, and therefore no trade secret claim could be brought successfully; (2) the duty of confidentiality is not a contractual duty, so no breach of contract claim could be assert-ed successfully; and (3) where the particular juris-diction interprets section 7 of the UTSA to preclude tort claims not based upon the misappropriation of a trade secret. *See infra* § 5.7 for a fuller discussion of section 7 of the UTSA.

§ 4.7   ACQUISITION BY ACCIDENT OR MISTAKE

Although by comparison it does not come up much in trade secret litigation, there is a third way that a defendant in a trade secret misappropriation case may be found liable: if he acquired trade secret information by accident or mistake. This may include, for instance, the inadvertent disclosure of trade secrets during the discovery phase of a trade secret case or the accidental release of trade secret information by a governmental agency. *See*, e.g. *Myers v. Williams*, 819 F. Supp. 919 (D. Or. 1993).

In *Myers*, pursuant to regulatory oversight by the Food and Drug Administration (FDA), the chemical composition of the drug Halcion was submitted by Upjohn to the FDA. This information was then provided by the FDA (through a Freedom of Information Act (FOIA) request) to a prison inmate (Myers) who claimed that his felony had been committed while under the influence of the drug. Upjohn contacted Myers and demanded that he return the information and sought a preliminary injunction to enjoin Myers' use or sale of the information he obtained about Halcion. Myers argued that he received the information legally and was entitled to do with it as he saw fit. The court, applying the Oregon UTSA, ordered an injunction and found that Myers knew or had reason to know the information was a trade secret and that is was acquired by mistake. 819 F. Supp. at 921.

The UTSA's definition of misappropriation provides that a person who acquired trade secrets by accident or mistake will be liable if, before a material change in position he knew or had reason to know: (1) that the information was a trade secret; and (2) knowledge of it was acquired by accident or mistake. Unif. Trade Secrets Act § 1(2)(ii)(C) (amended 1985), reprinted in Appendix A. The comments to this section note that providing timely notice to a previously innocent acquirer "suffices to make the third party a misappropriator thereafter." *Id.* This departs from the common law as stated in the *Restatement of Torts* which excused a good faith user (and *bona fide* purchaser) from any liability. *See* Restatement (First) of Torts § 758 (1939). It also departs from the *Restatement of Unfair Competition* which treats the issue as one relating to remedies and not misappropriation. Restatement (Third) of Unfair Competition § 45, cmt. e (1995).

What constitutes an accident or mistake is not defined by the UTSA or the *Restatements*, so the common definition of those terms generally applies. In the comments to the *Restatement of Unfair Competition*, it is explained that the accident or mistake may be by the owner of the trade secret, the alleged misappropriator, or a third-party. Restatement (Third) of Unfair Competition, § 40, cmt. e (1995). However, in some situations the accidental or mistaken disclosures will constitute a failure of reasonable efforts to maintain the secrecy of the information, thereby destroying the trade secrecy of the information.

In *Defiance Button Machine Co. v. C & C Metal Products Corp.*, 759 F.2d 1053 (2d Cir. 1985), the plaintiff treated its customer list as a trade secret, keeping it in a locked room. However, the lists were inadvertently left on a computer sold to the defendant, and the source books with the file name and password to the lists were accessible to the defendant. Accordingly, the court held that the plaintiff's failure to erase the files from the computer and segregate the source books indicated a lack of adequate measures to protect the alleged trade secrets. 759 F.2d at 1063–64. Thus, even if the defendant had used improper means to access the information, there is no liability because trade secret protection was lost due to a failure to exercise reasonable efforts.

§ 4.8   THIRD-PARTY LIABILITY

The prototypical trade secret case involves the actual or threatened disclosure of trade secrets by a person (often a former employee) who knew or should have known of the existence of the trade secrets and subsequently acted in a manner that constitutes misappropriation of those trade secrets. As long as the subject trade secrets remain in the possession of the direct misappropriator, a lawsuit against that person should suffice to protect the interests of the trade secret owner. Sometimes, however, the direct misappropriator will disclose the trade secrets to another and the issue of third-party (or indirect or secondary) liability arises.

As discussed *supra* in § 4.4.1, the key to imposing liability on third-parties who did not participate in the original misappropriation of trade secrets is to prove that they knew or had reason to know that the information they acquired, disclosed, or used is trade secret information that was misappropriated by someone else. In practice, trade secret owners can enhance the possibility of imposing third-party liability by putting competitors and other potential defendants on notice of the existence of trade secrets and the potential that such trade secrets were (or are about to be) misappropriated. Typically, this is done in a "Notice Letter" in which counsel for a trade secret owner advises a third-party of his client's trade secret rights and ongoing obligations of confidentiality. Such letters should be drafted carefully so as not to disclose the trade secrets and in a manner that does not constitute defamation or an act of unfair competition.

§ 4.8.1   SECONDARY LIABILITY UNAVAILABLE

If liability under the third-party provisions of the UTSA cannot be proven, then the only recourse against a third-party who possesses and threatens to use or disclose trade secrets is to come up with another theory of liability. Consistent with general tort theory, a theory of direct liability may be pursued whereby the third-party is shown to have engaged in a wrongful act that provides an independent basis for tort liability. *See* Sharon K. Sandeen, *The Third Party Problem: Assessing the Protection of Information through Tort Law*, in Intellectual Property Protection of Fact-based Works, Copyrights and Its Alternatives (Robert Brauneis, ed. 2009). Or a theory of indirect or secondary liability may be asserted if applicable.

Unlike patent and copyright law, trade secret law does not have an established doctrinal mechanism for secondary liability such as a contributory infringement pathway. *See* Robert G. Bone, *Secondary Liability for Trade Secret Misappropriation: A Comment*, 22 Santa Clara Computer & High Tech L. J. 539 (2006). In particular, it is currently unclear whether the doctrine of *respondeat superior* can be used to impose liability upon a principal for the trade secret misappropriation of its agents. *See Newport News Industrial v. Dynamic Testing, Inc.*, 130 F. Supp. 2d 745, 750–52 (E.D. Va. 2001). Arguably, such a theory would be inconsistent with the knowledge requirement of both the common law of trade secrecy and the UTSA. However, some courts have allowed it. *See, e.g., Thola v. Henschell*, 140 Wash. App. 70, 80–81 (Ct. App. Wash. 2007).

§ 4.8.2   DISCLOSURES ON THE INTERNET

Trade secret disclosures over the Internet can raise very interesting third-party issues, especially where a third-party, having no connection to or involvement with the original misappropriator who posted the trade secret on the Internet, thereafter discovers the trade secret and uses or discloses it. *DVD Copy Control Association, Inc. v. Bunner*, 116 Cal. App. 4th 241 (Cal. Ct. of App., 6th Dist., 2004), provides a useful illustration.

In *Bunner*, DVD CCA was the plaintiff and putative trade secret owner. The alleged wrongdoers were a number of individuals (including Jon Johansen and other unidentifiable individuals) who were accused of acquiring the alleged trade secrets either through contractually restricted reverse engineering or improper means. According to defendant Bunner's testimony, however, he acquired the alleged trade secrets from the Internet after they were posted by others and did not know that they constituted trade secrets.

As noted by the court, the Internet posting of the trade secrets posed a number of challenges for DVD CCA. *DVD Copy Control Association, Inc. v. Bunner*, 116 Cal. App. 4th at 251–52. First, the posting may have destroyed the trade secret status of the information by making it "generally known" or "readily ascertainable." Second, even if the information was a trade secret at the time that Bunner acquired it, the subsequent dissemination of the information before the issuance of the injunction by the trial court would have eliminated the need for interim relief. Finally, on the question of whether Bunner "knew or had reason to know" that the information was misappropriated by someone else, the court did not accept the assertion that the widespread publicity about the case imposed the requisite knowledge on Bunner.

The current state of trade secret law suggests that a third-party is entitled to use information she obtained from the public domain, assuming that she did not employ improper means to obtain the trade secret, has no knowledge that it was obtained by improper means, and is not bound by any contractual or special relationship with the trade secret

en by the parties and the willingness of courts to compel early disclosure. Some plaintiffs will resist identification as long as possible, while some defendants will demand disclosure too early. Ideally, the parties and the court will agree on the proper sequencing of the litigation to include a date for the identification of trade secrets.

If more specificity is deemed to be required at the pleading stage, ordinarily the issue will be raised in a motion to dismiss (or demurrer) for failure to state a cause of action. *See, e.g.,* *All Business Solutions, Inc. v. NationsLine, Inc.,* 629 F. Supp. 2d 553 (W.D. Va. 2009). Even if the motion to dismiss is not granted, it can focus the court's attention on the issue and is likely to result in plaintiff making arguments that will shed more light on its claims. Moreover, in jurisdictions without a tradition of requiring the early identification of trade secrets, such a motion may be advisable to avoid discovery delays.

California law circumvents many of the pleading issues that arise in other jurisdictions by recognizing that a plaintiff in a trade secret misappropriation case need not identify its trade secrets with detailed specificity in the complaint. Rather, California Code of Civil Procedure § 2019.210 provides that: "before commencing discovery relating to the trade secret, the party alleging the misappropriation shall identify the trade secret with reasonable particularity." Consistent with the language of the statute, defendants have been known to resist all discovery efforts until the plaintiff meets its statutory obligation. Thus, it is generally in the best interest of a trade secret plaintiff in California (and elsewhere) to begin the process of identification as soon as possible after the complaint is filed so that discovery will not be delayed, provided that an adequate Protective Order is in place before any disclosure of trade secrets occur.

In trade secret cases that are brought in federal court based upon diversity jurisdiction and that apply California law, there is a question whether California Code of Civil Procedure § 2019.210 applies at all. The answer depends upon whether the California statute is considered to be procedural or substantive. *See Funcat Leisure Craft, Inc. v. Johnson Outdoors, Inc.*, No. S–06–0533 GEB GGH, 2007 WL 273949, at *1–3 (E.D. Cal. Jan. 29, 2007).

If identification of the relevant trade secrets is to occur during the discovery process, then careful consideration should be given to the sequencing of discovery efforts. Logically, the defendant should be allowed to conduct the first round of discovery to ascertain the specific trade secrets at issue. For strategic or tactical reasons, however, plaintiffs will not always agree to such sequencing because they wish to learn which information the defendant possesses before identifying their alleged trade secrets. The fear is that if the plaintiff identifies its trade secrets too early, relevant evidence of such secrets in the hands of the defendant will disappear. Conversely, the fear of the defendant is that if the trade secrets are identified too late, the plaintiff will use the information it learns during the course of discovery to help define its trade secrets.

Although plaintiffs (or their counsel) will often try, they should not be allowed to avoid the timely identification of the alleged trade secrets for fear of their disclosure and loss of trade secrecy. Such is an inherent risk of trade secrecy and a recognized risk of trade secret litigation. Moreover, to ameliorate these risks, the UTSA specifically authorizes courts to issue appropriate protective orders. *See* Unif. Trade Secrets Act § 5 (amended 1985); *infra* § 4.10.

§ 4.9.2   WHAT LEVEL OF SPECIFICITY IS REQUIRED?

An issue that arises both in California (before discovery) and other states (during or after discovery) is whether the plaintiff's disclosure of its trade secrets has been adequate. The court in *Advanced Modular Sputtering, Inc. v. Superior Court*, 132 Cal. App. 4th 826, 835 (Cal. Ct. App. 2005), explained that the level of specificity does not mean that "every minute detail" of the alleged trade secret must be disclosed prior to discovery but only an amount that is reasonable under the circumstances: (1) to allow the trial court to control the scope of discovery; (2) to protect the parties' confidential information; and (3) to allow the defendants to prepare a defense.

In practice, what constitutes an adequate identification of trade secrets depends upon the nature of the trade secrets, the facts of a case, and the jurisdiction where the case is venued. *See,* e.g., *Perlan Therapeutics v. Superior Court of San Diego County*, 178 Cal. App. 4th 1333 (Cal. Ct. App. 2009). Instead of accepting broad categories of information in response to interrogatories, one court required a plaintiff to supplement with "specific characteristics of each trade secret, such as a particular drawing, process, procedure, or cost/pricing data." *Knights Armament Co. v. Optical Systems Technology, Inc.*, 254 F.R.D. 463, 467 (M.D. Fla. 2008). Other courts have held that the production of the very information alleged to be a trade secret (subject, of course, to a protective order) can constitute the required identification. *See, e.g., Static Control Comp., Inc. v. Darkprint Imaging, Inc.*, 200 F. Supp. 541, 544–45 (M.D.N.C. 2002).

§ 4.9.3   CONSEQUENCES OF FAILING TO IDENTIFY TRADE SECRETS WITH SPECIFICITY

There are a number of possible substantive and procedural consequences for failing to identify trade secrets with specificity, often depending upon when the issue is raised during a case. If the plaintiff fails to timely identify its trade secrets with sufficient particularity, the defendant can file a motion either before or during trial and assert that such failure is fatal to plaintiff's claim. *See, e.g., Nilssen v. Motorola, Inc.*, 963 F. Supp. 664 (N.D. Ill. 1997). *See also Bondpro Corp. v. Siemens Power Generation, Inc.*, 463 F.3d 702, 710 (7th Cir. 2006) (judgment in favor of the defendant where plaintiff's disclosures were not sufficiently precise).

If, as is discussed in § 2.7, the claimed trade secrets are improvements on known processes, the failure to detail the improvements may result in a finding that the claimed secrets are generally known and therefore not protectable. *See CVD, Inc. v. Raytheon Co.*, 769 F.2d 842, 853 (1st Cir. 1985).

In other words, although a plaintiff in a trade secret case may wish to speak about its trade secrets in broad generalities, being specific may be the only way to prove that trade secrets actually exist.

Finally, where a plaintiff in a trade secret case cannot identify trade secrets with specificity or where the information that it specifies does not qualify for trade secret protection, the defendant may assert a bad faith claim and obtain an award of attorney's fees. These findings are generally made when a plaintiff has failed to produce sufficient evidence of the existence of a trade secret and it was apparent that the plaintiff had this knowledge prior to initiating the action. *See,* e.g., *Gemini Aluminum Corp. v. California Custom Shapes, Inc.*, 95 Cal. App. 4th 1249 (Cal. Ct. of App. 2002).

§ 4.10   PROTECTING TRADE SECRETS DURING LITIGATION

Because of the right of defendants in trade secret cases to learn the identification and details of the plaintiff's putative trade secrets, there is an obvious risk that whatever trade secrets exist will be revealed during the course of the litigation. As a practical matter, when presenting its case at trial (either to a judge or jury) the plaintiff will have to explain what its trade secrets are as part of its *prima facie* case. This explains why many plaintiffs are reluctant to identify their trade secrets with particularity and why they will often fight hard to delay the disclosure of any information concerning their alleged secrets (although it may also be the case that they cannot identify their trade secrets because none exist).

§ 4.10.1 PROTECTING TRADE SECRETS DURING DISCOVERY

The discovery phase of litigation can be lengthy and costly. In trade secret cases these costs are frequently incurred early and in a compressed timeframe due to the regular use of expedited discovery. In fact, expedited discovery is one thing that sets trade secret litigation apart from other kinds of business litigation. It occurs because these cases often present as preliminary injunction cases (*see infra* § 6.2) where the early discovery of relevant facts is critical to both sides. For this reason the parties will generally agree to, or the judge will order, expedited discovery.

In order to facilitate the discovery process in trade secret cases, most courts will issue protective orders that are designed to protect plaintiff's information during the pendency of litigation. Indeed, section 5 of the UTSA requires courts to do so. It states: "[A] court shall preserve the secrecy of an alleged trade secret by reasonable means, which may include granting protective orders in connection with discovery proceedings, holding in-camera hearings, sealing the records of the action, and ordering any person involved in the litigation not to disclose an alleged trade secret without prior court approval." Unif. Trade Secrets Act § 5 (amended 1985), reprinted in Appendix A.

Despite the ability of courts to enter protective orders to facilitate the discovery process, the early stages of trade secret litigation can be consumed by costly and time-consuming disagreements regarding the appropriate language of protective orders and the appropriate scope of discovery. A typical topic of dispute is how and to whom the information will be revealed.

Protective orders can be structured in many different ways and can be quite lengthy, detailed, and draconian. Typically, there are one or more levels of access that are defined in a protective order with respect to different classes of information. The plaintiff in a trade secret case will often argue for a very restrictive protective order that precludes any individual defendant, the employees of a corporate defendant, and even trial experts and consultants from seeing the information (often referred to as an "attorney's-eyes only" protective order). The plaintiff may even insist that the disclosure of its secrets only occur at certain places and under specified conditions. For instance, at a secure facility (such as plaintiff's offices) and that the information be kept under lock and key at all other times. The defendant, on the other hand, will argue that it needs to be able to show the information to potential witnesses, including expert witnesses and consultants, and that it can be trusted to hold the information in confidence.

The challenge for courts is to figure out how to accommodate the demands of due process (the need of defendant to know the details of the claims being made against it) while crafting an order that is sufficient to protect plaintiff's putative trade secrets. Because severely restrictive protective orders prevent the parties (particularly a defendant in a trade secret case) from accessing materials and engaging in full and complete discussions with counsel, it is important that courts ensure that they are not granted without careful consideration and adequate justification. The parties can assist the courts by working together to craft a stipulated protective order. In some cases, the court will appoint a special master or disinterested expert to hear secret information and report conclusions to the court.

§ 4.10.2 PROTECTING TRADE SECRETS AT TRIAL

Generally, it is easier to protect trade secrets during the pleading and discovery phases of litigation than it is during trial. This is because of the strong public policy favoring open and publicly accessible judicial proceeding. *See Citizens First Nat. Bank of Princeton v. Cincinnati Ins. Co.*, 178 F. 3d 943 (7th Cir. 1999). As explained by the court in *Citizens First:*

> The public at large pays for the courts and therefore has an interest in what goes on at all stages of a judicial proceeding. . . . That interest does not always trump the property and privacy interests of litigants, but it can be overridden only if the latter interest predominates in the particular case.

Id. at 945 (citations omitted). In light of this policy, it is not surprising that most trade secret cases settle before trial. Nevertheless, courts will sometimes restrict public access to court proceedings in order to protect trade secrets, once the appropriate showings have been made regarding trade secrecy status and the lack of other reasonable alternatives to protect the information. *See Publicker Indus., Inc. v. Cohen*, 733 F.2d 1059 (3d. Cir. 1984).

§ 4.11   COMPELLING THE PRODUCTION OF TRADE SECRETS

As noted above, the need for defendants to learn the specifics about the alleged trade secrets is a necessary part of every trade secret misappropriation case. However, it is not uncommon for a party to other types of litigation to request the production of information that is deemed to be a trade secret. In this "private-party litigation," as opposed to FOIA-litigation (discussed *infra* in §§ 8.5 and 8.6), the requested information either concerns the trade secrets that were allegedly misappropriated or which are relevant to an issue in non-trade secret litigation (for instance, product-liability of environmental cases).

The courts' approaches to solving discovery disputes concerning alleged trade secrets and determining whether to compel disclosure are guided by general discovery and evidentiary rules. *See* Elizabeth A. Rowe, *Striking a Balance: When Should Trade-Secret Law Shield Disclosures to the Government?*, 96 Iowa L. Rev. 791, 819–21 (2011). Typically, in such instances, the party from whom the information is sought will first object to production, perhaps coupling its objection with a request for a

protective order. Within the scheme of evidentiary
and discovery privileges, there is no absolute privilege to refuse to disclose trade secrets. However,
unless the trade secret owner seeks to "conceal
fraud or otherwise work injustice," it is generally
recognized that the trade secret owner has a qualified privilege to resist discovery if such disclosure
will cause harm. *See Upjohn Co. v. Hygieia Biological Labs.*, 151 F.R.D. 355, 358 (E.D. Cal. 1993).

Following an evidentiary-law framework, after a
party to litigation asserts objections to a discovery
request based upon an argument that the requested
information constitutes trade secrets, the other party will usually file a motion to compel production, at
which point the burden is on the moving party to
demonstrate that the information that is sought is
relevant and necessary to the litigation. *See Hartley
Pen Co. v. U.S. Dist. Court for the S. Dist. of Cal.*,
287 F.2d 324 (9th Cir. 1961). In support of the objection to the discovery request, the party asserting the
qualified trade secret privilege must ordinarily present some evidence to show: (1) that the information
is indeed a trade secret; and (2) that disclosure of
the trade secret might be harmful. *See Upjohn Co. v.
Hygieia Biological Labs.*, 151 F.R.D. 355, 358). Although a party may have a legitimate interest in protecting its trade secrets, "that interest must yield to
the right of the plaintiff to discover the full truth of
the facts involved in the issues of the case" where
"the issues cannot be fairly adjudicated unless this
information is available." *Melori Shoe Corp. v.
Pierce & Stevens, Inc.*, 14 F.R.D. 346, 347 (D. Mass.
1953).

Courts consider a wide range of factors that are neither definitive nor exhaustive in deciding whether to grant a motion to compel the production of trade secrets and issue protective orders. One important consideration is whether the information qualifies as a trade secret. Other issues of concern include the purpose for which the information is sought and the relevance and necessity of the information. Courts will often balance the requesting party's need for the information against the injury that might result if disclosure is permitted. Note that when these disputes involve obtaining discovery from third-parties (who are not named in the litigation), courts are generally more protective of the third-parties and far less likely to compel disclosure of their trade secrets. *See, e.g., Snowden ex rel. Victor v. Connaught Labs., Inc.*, 136 F.R.D. 694, 699 (D. Kan. 1991).

Generally, once relevance and need are established, and unless the risk of harm to the trade secret owner outweighs the need for discovery (an unlikely event given the liberal discovery rules), the court will compel disclosure of the requested trade secrets. *See Pochat v. State Farm Mut. Auto. Ins. Co.*, No. Civ. 08–5015–KES, 2008 WL 5192427, at *3–4 (D.S.D. Dec. 11, 2008). Exceptions to the general rule include cases where compliance with the discovery request would be "unreasonable, oppressive, annoying, or embarrassing." *See Centurion Indus., Inc. v. Warren Steurer & Assocs.*, 665 F.2d 323, 326 (10th Cir. 1981).

It is entirely within the sound discretion of the trial court to decide whether trade secrets are relevant and whether the need outweighs the harm of disclosure. Likewise, the appropriate safeguards that should attend the disclosure of trade secrets (usually by means of a protective order) are also a matter within the trial court's discretion. The "trade secret privilege" in the context of the law of evidence recognizes the fact that disclosure of trade secret information destroys the value of the property. Thus, when balancing the need for the evidence against the trade secret owner's property right, it is treated as a qualified privilege insofar as disclosure is compelled only under the control of a protective order. *See Wearly v. FTC*, 462 F. Supp. 589, 594 (D.N.J. 1978). *See also* Fed. Rule Civ. Proc. Rule 26(c)(7) (2008).

§ 4.12   PRACTICAL PRE-LITIGATION CONSIDERATIONS

Trade secret holders contemplating the filing of trade secret litigation should undertake a cost-benefit analysis that includes assessment of the direct and indirect costs associated with the initiation of an action. This risk assessment, if based on the practical reality of the potential consequences of litigation as well as the procedural and substantive requirements, could lead to more sound decisions about whether to file a lawsuit.

Trade secret actions tend to be characterized by emotional undertones, especially where the parties had a prior relationship such as in the employment context. It is not unusual for trade secret plaintiffs to be motivated, at least in part, by the need to "send a message" to defendants and others that they will not tolerate what they perceive as betrayal or disloyalty. Where, for instance, a former employee has left to start a new competing company, a plaintiff may view one "benefit" of the litigation as the potential to "cause excruciating pain to the start-up enterprise." *See* Tait Graves, *Bad Faith and the Public Domain: Requiring a Pre-Lawsuit Investigation of Potential Trade Secret Claims*, 8 VA. J.L. & TECH. 12, ¶ 3, 6 (2003). It is therefore especially important that counsel for both sides identify these emotional incentives and serve as the voice of reason, exercising sound judgment that ethically and professionally avoids inappropriate litigation tactics. Three key considerations are summarized below.

§ 4.12.1   ENCOURAGING DISCLOSURE BY THREATENING TO SUE

When a company threatens to sue a defendant for trade secret misappropriation, it takes the risk that the defendant may respond to the threat by disclosing the trade secret. Litigation may also draw attention to the trade secret. Depending on the nature of the trade secret, news reports about the litigation or the threat of litigation may raise awareness about, and generate greater interest in, discovering the secret. In one case, for example, the defendant published trade secret materials about the plaintiff company on his web site after the trade secret owner threatened the defendant with litigation. *See Ford Motor Co. v. Lane*, 67 F. Supp. 2d 745, 747–48 (E.D. Mich. 1999).

Further, if the trade secret is disclosed on the Internet, it could mean that the trade secret status of the information will be destroyed and the owner will be powerless to save it. *See supra* § 4.6.2. To make matters worse, there may be very little satisfactory recourse against the defendant. Even if, at the conclusion of the litigation, the court finds that the defendant committed misappropriation, such a holding may be of little comfort to the plaintiff. This is especially so in the majority of cases where defendants cannot afford to pay damages.

§ 4.12.2 THE RISK OF EXPOSING TRADE SECRETS

Another major concern for plaintiffs considering trade secret litigation is the protection of their confidential information during the litigation process. *See supra* § 4.10. Without reasonable safeguards to protect confidentiality, the trade secret status of the information may be lost. The public nature of the court system can be dangerous when information needs to be kept secret. To that end, the parties may agree to protect the information or the court may issue a protective order. *See infra* § 4.10. Despite these various precautions, however, the risk of loss does not disappear.

§ 4.12.3 COSTS OF LITIGATION

In addition to the possible risks to trade secrets described above, the actual cost of filing and maintaining a trade secret misappropriation action is very high. On average it costs several hundred thousand dollars to litigate a trade secret case through trial, and that average can easily climb higher in larger stakes cases. The fact-intensive nature of these cases requires thorough investigation during both pre-litigation and discovery. Moreover, because of the injunction process, the initial cost to a trade secret misappropriation plaintiff is greater than the mere cost of filing a complaint. Plaintiffs in trade secret cases typically must bear the costs associated with temporary restraining order hearings and briefs, expedited discovery, and preliminary injunction hearings and briefs. Accordingly, the decision to proceed with this kind of action is not one to be made lightly, especially if the value of the information does not warrant it.

There are also a variety of indirect litigation costs that may detract from the plaintiff's business activities. Key employees with relevant knowledge and information will likely need to devote a substantial amount of time to the investigation and discovery process as the litigation continues. Other employees may also be distracted by litigation, whether through casual discussions in the hallways or by conflicts over possible support for the former-coworker-turned-defendant. This kind of sideline participation by employees can negatively affect employee morale and productivity. In addition, companies who sue for trade secret misappropriation may have difficulty recruiting employees. An even greater concern for plaintiffs may be jeopardizing their relationships with third-parties who are important to their business. Customers, vendors, or even investors may need to become involved in the litigation as reluctant witnesses, and the mere mention of the trade secret misappropriation may cause the company to suffer a loss in stock value.

§ 4.13   IDEA SUBMISSION CLAIMS

While trade secret law was developing through a series of cases brought between competing businesses or employers and employees, another body of related cases also became part of the legal landscape. Often referred to as "idea submission cases," these cases typically involve an individual who develops an idea that he thinks would be of value to a business, the submission of that idea to a business (usually unsolicited), and the alleged use of the idea by the business without compensation. Frequently, they involve ideas of potential interest to the entertainment industry, such as a concept for a movie or a new television show (see e.g., *Desny v. Wilder,* 46 Cal 2d 715 (1956)), but they can include any idea that may be of interest to a business, such as ideas for new products, ways to improve business processes, or the idea for Facebook.

To the extent an idea was secret before it was disclosed to a prospective user or purchaser, there is a possible overlap between idea submission claims and trade secret claims. If the idea qualifies for trade secret protection, then the idea generator is likely to assert a trade secret misappropriation claim if his idea is disclosed or used by another without consent. When idea submission claims are brought as trade secret misappropriation claims they are usually of the breach of confidentiality variety. *See infra* § 4.6. In such cases, it is not enough for the plaintiff to prove the existence of a duty of confidentiality; the plaintiff must also prove that the subject information was a trade secret.

Daktronics, Inc. McAfee, 599 N.W.2d 358 (S.D. Sup. Ct. 1999) is an example of an idea submission case that is based upon trade secret principles. The key question addressed by the court was whether or not the information at issue was a trade secret at the time of its disclosure. Because the court found that the information was generally known, and therefore not a trade secret, the plaintiff was denied relief.

Idea submission cases are not necessarily dependent on the existence of a trade secret or even a novel idea. If the plaintiff in an idea submission case can prove the existence of an express or an implied-in-fact contract, some courts are willing to provide recovery for ideas that would not qualify for trade secret protection. *See Reeves v. Alyeska Pipeline Service Company*, 926 P. 2d 1130, 1136 (noting that the protectability of information and whether it needs to be novel depends upon the theory of recovery pursued). Contractual claims of this sort are not precluded by the enactment of the UTSA. *See infra* § 5.7. However, there is ongoing debate about the types of information that can be protected by contract. On one side of the debate are those who advocate for freedom of contract and urge a broad definition of protectable information. On the other side of the debate are those who tout the benefits of a rich public domain and counsel against private efforts to restrict access to public information. *See* Raymond Nimmer, *Information Law*, § 1.02[2].

In many idea submission cases, the courts resort to language of concreteness or novelty in an attempt to distinguish between information that can be the subject of a successful idea submission claim and that which cannot. *See Murray v. National Broad Co., Inc.*, 844 F.2d 988 (2d Cir. 1988). As noted in *Reeves*, there has historically been a split of authority between New York and California on whether novelty is required in express contract cases, with New York requiring novelty and California not requiring novelty. *Reeves v. Alyeska Pipeline Srv. Co.*, 926 P.2d at 1137 (citations omitted). The novelty question may, however, be an issue in implied contract and trade secret cases. *See supra* § 3.2.

Pursuant to the UTSA's definition of a trade secret, ideas that are generally known and readily ascertainable cannot be trade secrets. Similarly, ideas that are generally known cannot serve as the basis of a pre-disclosure contract claim because the public availability of the ideas means they are of no actual value to the buyer and the contract fails for want of consideration. Similarly, information that has no economic value or that has become obsolete cannot be protected. *See Fox Sports Net N., L.L.C. v. Minnesota Twins P'ship*, 319 F.3d 3329 (8th Cir. 2003).

Unlike the employment relationship or an ongoing business relationship, proving reasonable efforts to protect an idea can be a challenge for the plaintiff idea generator. Generally, if one hands over an idea without an understanding or agreement, it is considered a gift. *See Liautaud v. Liautaud*, 221 F.3d 981, 985 (7th Cir. 2000); *Burten v. Milton Bradley Co.*, 763 F.2d 461, 463 (1st Cir. 1985). Thus, without a pre-disclosure agreement, the plaintiff in an idea submission case will have difficulty proving that the "idea" which it communicated to the defendant qualifies as a trade secret and that it took the requisite steps to protect it. In cases where a pre-disclosure agreement can be proven, the principal question under the reasonable efforts analysis is whether such an agreement, alone, is enough.

In placing the foregoing requirements on idea submission claims, courts recognize that even outside the context of trade secret litigation there should be limits on the type of information that can be protected under the law. What these limits are and how to articulate and apply them is an unsettled aspect of what has fairly recently been labeled "information law." *See* Nimmer, *Information Law*, § 1.02[2]. For purposes of trade secret law, if an idea man is relying on a trade secret theory, he has the burden of proving all of the essential elements of a claim for trade secret misappropriation.

In order to avoid claims by idea generators, it is important for companies to adopt idea submission policies and procedures to preclude the creation of an express, implied-in-fact, or implied-at-law duty of confidentiality. This is because creative and inventive people who come up with new ideas will always pitch their ideas and inventions to large enterprises. One way to avoid potential lawsuits by idea generators is to adopt an iron-clad policy that unsolicited ideas will not be accepted.

To implement an anti-solicitation policy, companies should screen all incoming phone calls, e-mails, and other correspondence to be certain that no ideas are being received by employees other than the limited few who are charged with screening the correspondence. They should also engage in an extensive campaign to educate their workforce on how to handle unsolicited ideas.

While some companies may choose an iron-clad policy against unsolicited ideas, the reality is that many companies (particularly those that are engaged in research and development or the creative arts) want new ideas and are willing to pay a reasonable price for them. They just do not want to be surprised by a claim for compensation after the fact or be forced to pay someone for an idea that they, coincidentally, developed in-house. Thus, the consequences and meaning of the sharing of ideas should be carefully detailed in a written agreement before any disclosure occurs.

§ 4.14   THE COMPUTER FRAUD AND ABUSE ACT

The Computer Fraud and Abuse Act ("CFAA") is a federal criminal statute enacted in 1984 that was later amended to provide a civil cause of action. *See* 18 U.S.C. §1030(g) (2006); *infra* § 10.3. Given the large scale involvement of computers in trade secret misappropriation cases, both a claim of trade secret misappropriation and a claim under the CFAA may be applicable under a set of facts where a computer was used to access trade secret information. However, a plaintiff in a CFAA case does not need to establish that the information accessed was a "trade secret" in order to state a claim.

To make out a claim under the CFAA, a plaintiff essentially needs to show: (1) that its information was on a protected computer; (2) that the defendant obtained the information through unauthorized access or access exceeding authorization; and (3) that it has lost at least $5,000 as a result. *See* 18 U.S.C. §§ 1030(a)(2)(C)(g) (2006). The statute provides for federal subject-matter jurisdiction over a CFAA claim, which also means that a trade secret claim which is part of the same case or controversy may also be heard in federal court pursuant to the supplemental jurisdiction statute. *See* 28 U.S.C. § 1367 (2006).

Whether the defendant's access to the plaintiff's computer was unauthorized or exceeded existing authorization is at the heart of a CFAA claim. In some ways, this focus on the defendant's conduct seems analogous to the improper means requirement for misappropriation under the UTSA. However, it is unclear whether they mean the same thing or whether the CFAA requirement is broader or narrower than the UTSA.

There is currently a split in authority among jurisdictions about how to define "unauthorized access," in employment relationships. Specifically, can employees who have permission to access their employer's computers ever be deemed to have accessed these computers "without authorization"? The answer depends on whether the interpretation of the statute is broad or narrow. Some courts reason that a breach of loyalty or other break in the agency relationship resulting from a purpose that is contrary to the interests of the employer is an unauthorized

access. *See Int'l Airport Ctrs., LLC v. Citrin*, 440
F.3d 418, 420–21 (7th Cir. 2006) (finding that former employee who destroyed data on former employer's computer prior to resigning to join competitor exceeded authorization to access). According to
Judge Posner in *Citrin*, "when an employee accesses
a computer or information on a computer to further
interests that are adverse to his employer, he violates his duty of loyalty, thereby terminating his
agency relationship and losing any authority he has
to access the computer or any information on it." *Id.*
at 203.

Other courts look to the employers' specific employment policies delineating the kinds of computer
access that are permissible for employees and which
are prohibited. *See,* e.g., *EF Cultural Travel B.V. v.
Zefer Corp*, 318 F.3d 58, 63 (1st Cir. 2003); *United
States v. John*, 597 F.3d 263, 269, 272 (5th Cir.
2010). Still other courts find unauthorized access
without regard to company policies, where the employee used the computer for an improper or non-
business related purpose. *See United States v. Tolliver*, 2011 WL 4090472 *5 (former bank teller provided confidential customer account information to
others for criminal purpose); *United States v.
Teague*, 646 F.3d 1119 (8th Cir. 2011) (employee of a
government contractor of the U.S. Department of
Education viewed President Obama's student loan
records without a business purpose).

The narrowest view of the meaning of "without
authorization" looks to whether the defendant has
circumvented any technological barriers to access
the information. Under this view, violations of com-

pany policies or unauthorized use of information obtained from a computer are not enough to trigger the statute. Rather, the focus is more on computer hacking-type behavior. The manner of access, not the use of the information after it has been accessed, is critical. *See United States v. Nosal*, 676 F.3d 854 (9th Cir. 2012) ("the phrase 'exceeds authorized access' does not extend to violations of use restrictions"). The court in *Nosal* reasoned that the CFAA only applies to outsiders who have no authorized access to the computer at all or those insiders or employees whose initial access to a computer is authorized but who access unauthorized information.

Similarly, in *WEC Carolina Energy Solutions LLC v. Miller*, 687 F.3d 199, 207 (4th Cir. 2012) the court held that the CFAA applies only to "individuals who access computers without authorization or who obtain or alter information beyond the bounds of their authorized access." The defendants in *WEC* were former employees who allegedly downloaded proprietary company information and used it to solicit a new customer in competition with WEC. In pleading its CFAA claim, the company alleged that the defendant's conduct was in violation of its policies "prohibiting the use of any confidential information and trade secrets unless authorized" and prohibiting the "download[ing] [of] confidential and proprietary information to a personal computer." *Id.* at 207. Because the defendants in *WEC* had legitimate access to the subject information as employees, the court found that while they may have misappropriated information, they did not access a computer without authorization or exceed their authorized access in violation of the CFAA.

Generally, courts that adopt a narrow approach to interpreting the CFAA are concerned about the policy ramifications of the broader view. One fear is that, "any employee who checked the latest Facebook posting or sporting event scores in contravention of his employer' use policy . . . would be left without any authorization to access his employer's computer systems." *Id.* at 206. A related concern is the lack of notice of potentially wrongful behavior, particularly considering that under a broad view of the CFAA, Internet users might commit a federal crime simply by "clicking to agree" a Terms of Use Agreement which restricts the use of a website or its content. *See, e.g.,* H.R. [Discussion Draft], 113th Cong. (1st Sess. 2013), *available at* http://lofgren.house.gov/images/stories/pdf/aarons%20law%20revised%20draft%20013013.pdf (last visited Mar. 27, 2013).

§ 4.15 OTHER (ANCILLARY) CLAIMS FOR RELIEF

Often in trade secret cases, the plaintiff will allege a number of causes of action in addition to a claim for trade secret misappropriation. Many of these causes of action are based upon common law and can broadly be described as tort claims for unfair competition. Depending upon the facts, claims for breach of contract may also be asserted, as is often the case with idea submission claims, discussed *supra* at § 4.13.

The tort claims that are alleged in conjunction with trade secret misappropriation claims are frequently labeled as actions for breach of confidentiality, breach of trust, breach of the duty of loyalty, or breach of fiduciary duty. A general claim of "unfair competition" may also be alleged. *See,* e.g., Cal. Bus. & Prof. Code §§ 17200–17210. If the trade secret information exists in tangible form, a property claim, such as for conversion, may be asseted. *See, e.g., Hauck Mfg. Co. v. Astec Indus., Inc.*, 375 F. Supp. 2d 649, 661 (E.D. Tenn. 2004); *Glynn v. EDO Corp.*, 641 F. Supp. 2d 476, 483–84 (D. Md. 2009). Where it is alleged that the defendant or a third-party owed a duty of confidentiality, a claim for intentional interference with contract or prospective economic advantage may be brought. *See, e.g., Harris Grp., Inc. v. Robinson*, 209 P.3d 1188, 1206–07 (Colo. App. 2009).

The breach of contract claims that are often alleged in trade secret cases can take two basic forms. First, the plaintiff may allege that the defendant was a party to an express oral or written non-disclosure agreement or other obligation of confidentiality. Second, it may allege that the defendant owed an implied duty of confidentiality. These are the same sort of allegations that can establish the breach of confidentiality form of trade secret misappropriation, but may be asserted separately as a breach of contract claim.

As discussed in section 5.7 *infra*, many of the ancillary tort claims may be precluded by Section 7 of the UTSA. The principal problem with any breach of contract claim is that available remedies are generally more limited than those that are available for trade secret misappropriation.

CHAPTER 5

DEFENSES TO TRADE SECRET MISAPPROPRIATION

§ 5.1 ATTACKING PLAINTIFF'S PRIMA FACIE CASE

The first line of defense for any defendant in a trade secret misappropriation case is to attack plaintiff's *prima facie case*. To do so requires both an understanding of the essential elements of a claim for trade secret misappropriation and who has the burdens of production and persuasion on those issues. In practice, this can only be determined by researching the law of a given jurisdiction, but as noted previously, generally, the plaintiff has the burden of pleading and proving: (1) that it owns (or is the exclusive licensee of) a trade secret; (2) that the trade secret was misappropriated by the defendant; and (3) that it is entitled to one or more remedies. *See supra* § 4.2. *See* also, *Worldwide Prosthetic Supply, Inc. v. Mikulsky*, 246 Wis. 2d. 461, 467–68 (Wis. Ct. App. 2001).

During the presentation of plaintiff's case-in-chief, a defendant—by cross-examining plaintiff's witnesses and questioning the sufficiency of plaintiff's evidence—will attempt to disprove one or more of the essential elements of plaintiff's case. Typically, in most trade secret cases, this will include the assertion that the claimed trade secrets do not qualify for trade secret protection and that there was no act of misappropriation. It may also include an ar-

gument—particularly where the putative trade secrets have not been disclosed or used—that the
plaintiff cannot prove any actual or threatened
harm.

§ 5.2   ADDRESSING THE BURDEN OF PERSUASION AND ASSERTING AFFIRMATIVE DEFENSES

If the plaintiff does not produce sufficient evidence to shift the burden of production to the defendant on the essential elements of a trade secret
misappropriation claim, then the defendant is entitled to move for a judgment as a matter of law (also
known as a "directed verdict") at the close of the
plaintiff's case. *See, e.g.*, Fed. Rule Civ. Proc. Rule
50 (2008). If this motion is denied, the defendant
can choose to either "rest" and let the case go to the
jury (or the judge if it is a bench trial) as presented
or can produce his own evidence in an attempt to
meet the burden of persuasion on the essential elements of the trade secret claim. Additionally, the
defendant may attempt to prove any affirmative
defenses that he timely raised in answer to the
plaintiff's complaint. *See, e.g.*, Fed. Rule Civ. Proc.
Rule 8 (2008) (describing the general rules of pleading in federal courts).

Technically, what constitutes an affirmative defense depends upon which party has the burden of
production and persuasion (collectively the burden
of proof) on a given issue. *See, e.g., Sargent Fletcher,
Inc. v. Able Corp.*, 110 Cal. App 4th 1658, 1667–68
(Cal. Ct. App. 2003) (explaining the difference between the burden of persuasion (or proof) and the

burden of producing evidence, particularly as the concepts apply in a trade secret case and stating that reverse engineering and independent development are not affirmative defenses).

If an issue is part of plaintiff's *prima facie case*, by definition the negative assertion of that issue is not an affirmative defense. According to *Black's Law Dictionary*, an affirmative defense is "[a] defendant's assertion of facts and arguments that, if true, will defeat the plaintiff's. . . claims, even if all the allegations in the complaint are true." Thus, except where special pleading rules apply, a defendant in a trade secret case does not have to plead and subsequently prove that the information is not a trade secret because proving the existence of a trade secret is part of plaintiff's burden of proof. Rather, the defendant should be able to put both the trade secret status of the subject information and the alleged misappropriation at issue by filing an answer which (generally or specifically, depending upon applicable rules of pleading) denies plaintiff's allegations.

In practice, defendants in trade secret cases often allege as affirmative defenses arguments that technically go to an essential element of plaintiff's case. This is done for fear of not being able to raise the issue at trial or because they wish to allege the factual basis for their defense arguments. For instance, the defense arguments of reverse engineering and independent development, which arguably relate to the essential element of misappropriation, are often pleaded as affirmative defenses. By doing so, as opposed to simply denying plaintiff's allegations of misappropriation, the defendant in a trade secret case can tell his side of the story early, sometimes leading to an early settlement of the case.

At times, the assertion of defense arguments as affirmative defenses is not only done out of an abundance of caution or to reveal facts about the case, but because the substantive law of the jurisdiction (including case law and statutes) place the burden of proof on the issue on the defendant. For instance, as noted previously, under California's version of the UTSA, defendants have the burden of pleading and proving that information is "readily ascertainable" and, accordingly, should raise the issue as an affirmative defense. *See Abba Rubber Co. v. Seaquist*, 235 Cal. App. 3d 1, fn 9 (Cal. Ct. App. 1991) ("While ease of ascertainability is irrelevant to the definition of a trade secret, 'the assertion that a matter is readily ascertainable by proper means remains available as a defense to a claim of misappropriation.'") (*citing* Legis. committee cmt. to Cal. Civ. Code § 3426.1). Similarly, the laws of some jurisdictions specify the defense arguments that must be alleged as affirmative defenses. *See, e.g.*, Fed. Rule Civ. Proc. Rule 8 (2008).

With the foregoing in mind, the affirmative defenses that are typically raised in trade secret cases are: (1) independent development; (2) reverse engineering; (3) readily ascertainable (in California and other states where it is a defense); (4) statute of limitations; (5) loss of trade secrecy; and (6) section 7 preclusion. Defendants may also allege that they were authorized to acquire, disclose, or use plaintiff's trade secrets pursuant to an express or implied license. The affirmative defenses of federal preemption (*see supra* § 2.9) and violation of the First Amendment right of free speech (*see infra* § 5.9) may also be raised in appropriate cases. Defendants should also consider standard equitable defenses such as laches and estoppel (*see, e.g., Anaconda Co. v. Metric Tool & Die Co.,* 485 F. Supp. 410 (E.D. Pa. 1980)) and possible procedural defenses like lack of subject matter or personal jurisdiction.

§ 5.3   INDEPENDENT DEVELOPMENT

Although the plaintiff in a trade secret misappropriation case has the burden of pleading and proving that its trade secrets were misappropriated (and independent development is not a method of misappropriation), defendants in trade secret cases often plead independent development as an affirmative defense. As a practical matter, pleading independent development as an affirmative defense allows the defendant to allege facts that may demonstrate to the plaintiff that its case is weak or, at the very least, that it is more complicated than first thought.

Neither the defense of independent development nor the defense of reverse engineering (discussed *infra*) are set forth in the substantive portions of the UTSA or the *Restatement of Torts*. However, it is undisputed that they are long-standing and well-established defenses to a claim for trade secret misappropriation. *See Kewanee Oil Co. v. Bicron Corp.,* 416 U.S. 470, 476. *See also,* Cal. Civ. Code § 3426.1(1) (specifically stating that reverse engineering and independent derivation are not improper means of acquiring trade secrets). This is consistent with the view that the "wrong" of trade se-

cret misappropriation is not merely the use of the
trade secrets (as is the case with patent rights), but
the means by which the trade secrets were acquired.
See supra § 4.5. Without acquisition by improper
means, the only way for a defendant to be liable for
trade secret misappropriation is if he breached an
express or implied duty of confidentiality. *See supra*
§ 4.6.

The key to proving the defense of independent development is the word "independent." It must be
shown that the subject information was developed
by the defendant (or his associates) and not derived
from or tainted by the plaintiff's trade secrets. This
may be proven by showing that the information was
developed in a clean-room environment where no
bits of the plaintiff's trade secrets were present. *See
Modular Devices, Inc. v. Brookhaven Science Associates, LLC.*, No. CV 08–3267(ARL), 2011 WL
1885719 (E.D.N.Y. May 18, 2011). If no clean-room
was established then the defendant must otherwise
show that he did not have access to or use plaintiff's
trade secrets. *See, e.g., RTE Corp. v. Coatings, Inc.*,
84 Wis. 2d 105 (Wis. 1978). Circumstantial evidence
in the form of significant time and money expended
by the defendant to develop his information is often
helpful in proving independent development.

Sometimes the information that the defendant is
using or disclosing (and for which independent discovery is claimed) is not identical to plaintiff's information. In such cases, the defendant is apt to argue that the differences prove independent development. It is not necessary, however, for a plaintiff
in a trade secret case to prove that the defendant is

using identical information; use of a substantial amount of plaintiff's trade secrets is enough. Restatement (Third) of Unfair Comp. § 40, cmt. c (1995). The court in *Mangren Research and Development Corp. v. National Chemical Co, Inc.,* 87 F. 3d. 937 (7th Cir. 1996) (quoting *In re Innovative Constr. Sys., Inc.,* 793 F.2d 875, 887 (7th Cir.1986)) explained: "the user of another's trade secret is liable even if he uses it with modifications or improvements upon it effected by his own efforts, so long as the substance of the process used by the actor is derived from the other's secret."

A frequent scenario in trade secret cases occurs when an individual or company starts to independently develop a new product but runs into difficulties and seeks "assistance" from others. On the surface, these others may appear to be independent consultants or companies, but in fact they may have acquired information improperly from someone else. Once outsiders are brought in and information starts to be shared, it may be difficult for a company to prove the independence of its own discoveries. This is particularly true where information was shared pursuant to a written confidentiality agreement.

A 2011 lawsuit involving Best Buy that resulted in a $27 million judgment provides a case in point. The plaintiff, TechForward, alleged that Best Buy misappropriated its trade secrets. *See TechForward v. Best Buy Co., Inc.,* No. CV–11–01313 ODW, 2011 WL9522240 (C.D. Cal April 22, 2011) (Amended Complaint for Misappropriation of Trade Secrets and Breach of Contract). The essential allegations

were that Best Buy first sought out plaintiff's assistance in developing a "Guaranteed Buy Back Program" but then canceled the resulting business relationship once access to plaintiff's alleged trade secrets were obtained. After canceling the agreement,
Best Buy allegedly proceeded to use the information
provided by plaintiff without permission or compensation. Under these circumstances, even if BestBuy
acted as it did because it concluded that plaintiff's
information was not protected by trade secrecy, the
fact that it obtained the information from the plaintiff and then used it, apparently looked really bad to
the jury.

To avoid the unwanted "taint" of outsider information, companies receiving information from outside sources should first determine the trade secret
status of the information before allowing it to be
used or disclosed within their business operations.

§ 5.4   REVERSE ENGINEERING

Reverse engineering is defined as "starting with
the known product and working backward to divine
the process which aided in its development or manufacture." *Kewanee Oil Co. v. Bicron Corp.*, 416 U.S.
470, 476. The issue of reverse engineering comes up
in two ways in trade secret litigation. As noted
above in § 2.8.4, the ease with which something can
be reversed engineered relates to the readily ascertainable prong of the definition of secrecy. If putative trade secret information can be easily ascer-
tained from publicly available information, including products and services that are on the market,
then the information is not "secret" in the first in-

stance. How easily information can be derived from publicly available information is the critical inquiry with respect to this aspect of reverse engineering. *See CheckPoint Fluid Systems Intern., Ltd. v. Guccione*, 888 F. Supp. 2d 780, 797 (E.D. La 2012) (explaining that the fact that plaintiff's products could be reverse engineered did not bar a trade secret claim where it appears that the defendant did not engage in reverse engineering, "as long as the pumps cannot be reverse engineered so quickly as to be 'readily ascertainable'").

The second way that the issue of reverse engineering comes up in trade secret cases concerns the defendant's assertion (either as part of plaintiff's *prima facie* case or as an affirmative defense) that the information in his possession was acquired through reverse engineering. The fact that the issue arises as a defense usually means that sufficient evidence of the existence of a trade secret was already presented. Thus, the question is not whether the information could, theoretically, be easily reversed engineered. Rather, it examines how the defendant actually came to possess the information that the plaintiff claims as its trade secret. In other words, it relates to the issue of misappropriation.

It is the public policy of the U.S., and most free-market economies, that copying and imitation is not only allowed, but highly desirable. *See Bonito Boats v. Thunder Craft Boats, Inc.,* 489 U.S. 146 (calling imitation and refinement though imitation the "lifeblood of a competitive economy"). This is because copying and imitation help to increase competition and reduce prices to consumers and often lead to improvements. Thus, except where a product or device is protected by patent law, there is nothing legally or morally wrong with acquiring a product or device in the free market and then breaking it down to discover how it works. If, in the process, trade secret information is discovered, such discovery is not an act of misappropriation.

The defense of reverse engineering is not without its limits. Similar to the required "independence" of the independent development defense (*see supra* § 5.3), reverse engineering is only permissible with respect to information that has been properly acquired, usually from public domain sources. *See Kadant, Inc. v. Seeley Machine, Inc.*, 244 F. Supp. 2d 19, 38 (N.D.N.Y. 2003). As the court in *Kadant* explained: "The relevant inquiry is whether the means to obtain the alleged trade secret were proper or 'honest,' as opposed to being obtained by virtue of a confidential relationship with an employer." Thus, the act of reverse engineering a product that is not publicly available may be improper.

§ 5.4.1   CONTRACTUAL RESTRICTIONS ON REVERSE ENGINEERING

An issue that has arisen in trade secret cases, particularly with respect to the licensing of computer software, is whether the ability to reverse engineer a publicly available product can be restricted by an express or implied contract. *See Vault Corp. v. Quaid Software Limited*, 655 F. Supp. 750 (E.D. La 1987) (express license agreement restricting reverse engineering cited by plaintiff to bolster its trade secret misappropriation claims); *Chicago Lock Co. v.*

Fanberg, 676 F.2d 400, 405 (9th Cir. 1982) (finding no implied duty to refrain from reverse engineering). Those who favor the freedom to contract argue that employers and other owners of trade secrets should be allowed to restrict their employees, vendors, and customers from engaging in acts of reverse engineering. *See* Raymond Nimmer, *Information Law*, ¶¶ 2.12[1], 5.05[3], and 5.11[4][b] (1996). Thus, as a practical matter, efforts should always be undertaken to determine if the defendant in a trade secret case is subject to a contract which precludes reverse engineering. If so, the contractual restriction may be cited in response to a reverse engineering defense.

In considering the validity of contractual restrictions on reverse engineering, the information to which the restriction applies should first be identified. If the information is generally known or readily ascertainable, then arguably the restriction is against public policy because it seeks to deny access to otherwise publicly available information. If the information contains trade secrets, however, a restriction on reverse engineering may be a precondition of disclosure; the agreement not to reverse engineer the licensed information is simply part of the price that the licensee must pay to gain access to the information in the first place. This is arguably consistent with the limits on the defense of reverse engineering noted above. *See supra* § 5.4.

§ 5.5   STATUTE OF LIMITATIONS

Pursuant to section 6 of the UTSA, the statute of limitations for a trade secret misappropriation claim is three years. In keeping with the fact that they are only restatements of existing law, neither the *Restatement of Torts* nor the *Restatement of Unfair Competition* discuss the applicable statute of limitations. In non-UTSA jurisdictions (and in some UTSA jurisdictions that have not adopted the UTSA's statute of limitations), the statutes of limitation for tort claims should be consulted to determine the temporal limits of a trade secret misappropriation claim. *See, e.g., Epstein v. C.R. Bard, Inc.,* 460 F. 3d 186 (1st Cir. 2006) (applying Massachusetts law). Also, some UTSA jurisdictions have modified the UTSA's statute of limitations. *See, e.g.,* 765 Ill. Com. Stat. 1065/7 (2012) (5 years); Me. Rev. Stat. Ann., title 10, § 1547 (2012) (4 years).

As with all statutes of limitations, two issues arise in trade secret cases: (1) when does a cause of action for trade secret misappropriation accrue; and (2) is trade secret misappropriation a continuing wrong? The answer to both questions is clear under the UTSA, but may not be so clear in states that have not adopted the UTSA's statute of limitations. A cause of action for trade secret misappropriation accrues under the UTSA when the act of misappropriation "is discovered or by the exercise of reasonable diligence should have been discovered." Unif. Trade Secrets Act § 6 (amended 1985), reprinted in Appendix A. Furthermore, the UTSA explicitly rejects the continuing wrong approach to the statute of limitations, stating that "a continuing misappropriation constitutes a single claim." *Id.* As noted in the associated comments to the UTSA, this rule is

ameliorated somewhat by the discovery rule for accrual.

Cadence Design Systems, Inc. v. Avant! Corp., 29
Cal. 4th 215 (Cal. Sp. Ct. 2002) provides an example
of how the concept of a continuing wrong is applied
under the UTSA. The case concerned the alleged
misappropriation of trade secrets following a confidential settlement agreement between the parties.
Defendant Avant! argued that the settlement
agreement covered all claims concerning the continuing or future use of the trade secrets that were the
subject of the settlement agreement. The court
agreed, holding that "for statute of limitations purposes, continuing misappropriation is viewed as a
single claim." *Id.* at 222. The court noted a distinction between a claim for misappropriation and multiple acts of misappropriation, finding that a claim
for misappropriation arises only once with multiple
instances of misappropriation merely enhancing the
potential remedies.

Although trade secret misappropriation is not a
continuing wrong under the UTSA, there can be
multiple acts of misappropriation that are engaged
in by different defendants, each having different
dates of accrual. *See Cadence Design Systems, Inc. v.
Avant! Corp.*, 29 Cal. 4th at 224. This could occur,
for instance, in third-party situations where the
original misappropriator later discloses a trade secret to a third-party who has knowledge or reason to
know of the misappropriation. *See Cypress Semi-
conductor Corp. v. Superior Ct.*, 163 Cal. App. 4th
575, 583–84 (Cal. Ct. App. 2008). Thus, when a
statute of limitations defense is raised in a trade

secret misappropriation case, care should be taken to identify with respect to each of the alleged acts of misappropriation: (1) the alleged misappropriator(s); (2) the alleged act(s) of misappropriation; and (3) when each alleged act of misappropriation occurred.

For each initial act of misappropriation by a defendant that occurred less than three years before the filing of the complaint in the action, a statute of limitations defense should not prevail. If the alleged acts of misappropriation occurred more than three years before the filing of the complaint then the plaintiff should argue: (1) that each occurrence was not discovered (or could not have been discovered) before a date that is less than three years before the filing of the complaint; or (2) that there are reasons to toll the running of the statute of limitations.

In jurisdictions that have not adopted the statute of limitations provision of the UTSA, including non-UTSA jurisdictions and foreign countries, care must be exercised to determine: which statute of limitations applies; when a cause of action for trade secret misappropriation accrues; and whether trade secret misappropriation is considered to be a continuing wrong. Additionally, if a trade secret owner wishes to initiate a trade secret misappropriation claim against a governmental entity, applicable government tort liability rules should be consulted.

§ 5.6   LOSS OF TRADE SECRECY

Proof of the existence of a trade secret is part of plaintiff's *prima facie case* but sometimes the defendant in a trade secret misappropriation case can prevail by pleading and proving that information that was once a trade secret has lost its status as a trade secret. The loss of trade secrecy can happen in two basic ways. First, the information may have been acquired (properly or improperly) by a third-party and subsequently disclosed in such a way that it has become generally known or readily ascertainable. *See Religious Technology Center v. Lerma*, 897 F. Supp. 260 (E.D. Va. 1995) (finding a public disclosure of the alleged trade secrets despite the plaintiff's extraordinary efforts to keep them secret). Second, information that was once a trade secret may be inadvertently or voluntarily disclosed by the plaintiff. *See Flotech, Inc. v. Southern Research, Inc.*, 16 F. Supp. 2d 992, 1004–05 (finding the voluntary and unrestricted disclosure of information to defendant to be fatal to plaintiff's trade secret claims despite other efforts to maintain secrecy).

§ 5.6.1   PRIOR ART SEARCH

When an individual or company is sued for trade secret misappropriation they should initiate a process to learn the past and present state of the art in the field of the alleged trade secrets. This is much like a "prior art search" in patent litigation where publicly known or accessible information is reviewed to determine if the subject patent is invalid for want of novelty or non-obviousness. *See* 35 U.S.C. §§ 102 and 103 (2006). In trade secret cases, if it can be established that the alleged trade secrets were generally known or readily ascertainable at the time of the alleged misappropriation, then the plaintiff cannot prevail even if the information was once a valuable trade secret. *See supra* §§ 2.8.2–2.8.4.

In contrast to the prior art search that is conducted in patent cases, which according to recent changes to U.S. patent law is limited to the "art" that was publicly known and accessible before the date on which the subject patent application was filed, the search for prior art in trade secret cases should continue throughout the pendency of the litigation and beyond. *See* 35 U.S.C. § 102 (2006) (as amended Pub. L. 112–29, § 3(b)(1), Sept. 16, 2011, 125 Stat. 285). This is because if the alleged trade secrets lose their trade secrecy during the pendency of litigation or thereafter, available remedies will be affected. *See infra* §§ 6.1–6.5.

§ 5.6.2 SCRUTINIZING THE ACTIVITIES OF THE TRADE SECRET OWNER

In addition to looking for publicly available information to determine whether information that may have once been a trade secret has lost its trade secrecy, a defendant in a trade secret misappropriation case should consider how the putative trade secrets are being used and distributed by the plaintiff. This inquiry will necessarily overlap with the reasonable efforts requirement that plaintiff has the burden of proving, but it comes at the issue of trade secrecy from a slightly different and broader direction.

Many trade secret owners may have the intent to protect their trade secrets and may institute efforts that are reasonable under the circumstances to protect them. However, if those efforts fail and their secrets are disclosed to third-parties, a defendant can argue that trade secrecy has been lost. The loss of trade secrecy could occur, for instance, where one unit of a company (often the marketing or public relations department) discloses trade secret information even while the research and development department is zealously guarding it. It might also occur in connection with the trade secret owner's dealings with its customers because companies are generally unwilling to impose duties of confidentiality on their customers. Moreover, the potential loss of trade secrets for information that is stored "in the Cloud" should not be ignored, particularly since many cloud storage contracts explicitly disclaim a duty of confidentiality.

§ 5.7   UTSA § 7: PRECLUSION OF ANCILLARY STATE CLAIMS

As noted *supra* in Chapters 1 and 4, before the adoption of the UTSA, plaintiffs who brought trade secret misappropriation claims would do so pursuant to a number of common law causes of action, including a variety of tort, unfair competition, property, and breach of contract claims. This was undoubtedly due to the underdeveloped state of trade secret doctrine, but was also because of the tendency of careful attorneys to plead "everything but the kitchen sink." *See, e.g., MKS Instruments, Inc. v. Emphysys, Inc.*, 30 Mass. L. Rptr. 346 (Mass. 2012).

During the drafting process leading to the adoption of the UTSA, careful consideration was given to whether the common law panoply of possible trade secret related causes of actions should continue to exist or whether the UTSA should displace some or all of them. *See* Sharon K. Sandeen, *The Evolution of Trade Secret Law and Why Courts Commit Error When They Do Not Follow the Uniform Trade Secrets Act,* 33 Hamline. L. Rev. 493 (2010). With the adoption of section 7 of the UTSA it was decided that a claim for trade secret misappropriation under the UTSA would be the only tort claim, but that contract claims could continue unabated.

Based upon section 7 of the UTSA, where a plaintiff alleges tort claims in addition to a cause of action for trade secret misappropriation under the UTSA, the defendant may assert the defense of section 7 preclusion. In essence, the defendant would argue that all ancillary tort claims that relate to the alleged wrongful acquisition, disclosure, or use of information should be dismissed. Because ancillary breach of contract claims are not precluded, causes of action (often idea-submission claims) that are based upon the existence of an express or implied-in-fact contract would not be precluded.

Whether a defense based upon section 7 of the UTSA will work depends upon a number of different factors, including the facts of the case. Although, in theory, a trade secret plaintiff should not be able to bring a trade secret misappropriation case under the guise of a different tort claim, it is possible that the actions of a defendant constitute separate and distinct wrongs with separate and distinct essential elements and harms. For instance, a defendant who is accused of improperly acquiring trade secrets may, given the right set of facts, also be liable for

conversion or interference with prospective economic advantage. Thus, in applying the section 7 defense, care must be taken to identify the alleged
"wrong" of each alleged tort. Ancillary causes of action which involve the wrongful acquisition, disclosure, or use of plaintiff's information are arguably
precluded despite what they are labeled.

Another difficulty with the section 7 defense relates to disagreements among the courts of some
states regarding the meaning, intent, and scope of
the provision. *Compare Burbank Grease Services,
LLC v. Sokolowski*, 294 Wis. 2d 274 (2006) *with
Blueearth Biofuels, LLC v. Hawaiian Elec. Co., Inc.*,
123 Hawaii 314 (2010). *See also Mortgage Special-
ists, Inc. v. Davy*, 904 A.2d 652, 664–666 (N.H.
2006). The essence of the disagreement concerns: (1)
whether the defense only applies where there is a
finding that plaintiff's information constitutes trade
secrets, in which case ancillary causes of actions to
protect such secrets are precluded; or (2) whether
the defense was intended to preclude any tort claim
that is designed to protect plaintiff's information,
even if the information does not qualify as a trade
secret. The unfortunate use of the word "trade secrets" in section 7 seems to suggest the first scenario, while the public policy underlying the provision
and its drafting history suggest the second scenario.

While reasonable minds can differ, the authors of
this book (and an emerging majority of courts) believe that the position of the Hawaii Supreme Court
in *Blueearth Biofuels* is the better reasoned view.
See also, John Cross, *UTSA Displacement of Other
State Law Claims*, 33 Hamline L. Rev. 445 (2010).

This belief is informed by the drafting history of the UTSA and the ghosts of *Sears/Compco* and *Kewanee* that animated the drafting debates. Recall from Chapter 1 that at the time of the initial drafting of the UTSA there was great concern among practicing attorneys that the reasoning of the *Sears/Compco* decisions would preclude all state regulation of acts of unfair competition or, at least, severely limit the application of such laws. *See supra* § 1.5. For this reason, the UTSA was carefully drafted to be consistent with the limited scope of trade secret protection described in *Kewanee*.

Viewed in the context of the foregoing history, section 7 can be seen as an additional effort to ensure that state trade secret law is not preempted by federal law. Moreover, as noted by the court in *Blueearth Biofuels*, a narrow interpretation of the preclusive effect of section 7 "would undermine the purpose of the UTSA, which was to resolve the 'uncertainty concerning the parameters of trade secret protection' and create a uniform law to remedy trade secret misappropriation." *See Blueearth Biofuels, LLC v. Hawaiian Elec. Co., Inc.*, 123 Haw. at 320. This interpretation is also consistent with the failure of the UTSA and the *Restatement of Unfair Competition* to carry forward the tort described in Section 759 of the *Restatement of Torts. See supra* § 2.8.7.

Of course, section 7 preclusion does not apply in non-UTSA jurisdictions unless a similar limitation has been (or will be) developed by case law. Additionally, some states that have adopted the UTSA have not adopted section 7 of the UTSA at all (*see, e.g.*, Iowa) or in the identical language of the UTSA. *See, e.g.,* Cal. Civ. Code § 3426.7 (2013); Ga. Code Ann. § 10–1–767 (2012); 765 Ill. Comp. Stat. 1065/3 (2012). Although section 7 of California's version of the UTSA is worded differently from the language of the UTSA, the court in *KC Multimedia, Inc. v. Bank of America Technology & Operation, Inc.*, 171 Cal. App. 4th 939, 962 (Cal. Ct. App. 2009), held that it precludes common law causes of action that are based "on the same nucleus of facts as trade secret misappropriation."

§ 5.8   FEDERAL PREEMPTION

If not precluded by section 7 of the UTSA, then ancillary state law claims may be preempted by federal law for the same reasons that state trade secret law was challenged in *Kewanee* and state unfair competition claims were challenged in the *Sears/Compco* cases. *See supra* § 2.9. In addition, and in spite of the holding of *Kewanee*, a defendant can defend against a trade secret misappropriation claim by alleging that the application of state law with respect to the particular factual allegations would unduly conflict with federal law.

Because the general rule is that a state trade secret claim, as with any state claim, will be preempted by federal copyright law where the rights granted under the state law are equivalent to those granted under the federal copyright law (*see supra* § 2.9.2), care must be taken to consider the nature and scope of trade secret claims and to determine if, in fact, they are copyright cases in disguise. In practice this means that if the trade secret claim is based merely on the alleged copying of information (a wrongful "use" offense under trade secret law), the trade secret claim is likely to be preempted.

The essence of a preemption argument is that the plaintiff is trying to assert a trade secret misappropriation claim for what amounts to a patent or copyright infringement claim. *See C.G.H., Inc. v. Nash Finch, Inc.*, 2012 WL 1070116 (Minn. App. 2012) (finding plaintiff's claims preempted because they alleged patent infringement). For an illustration of a successful federal preemption argument to preclude a trade secret claim beyond the date when the alleged trade secrets were disclosed in plaintiff's patent, see *Evans v. General Motors Corp.*, 51 Conn. Supp. 44, 62 (2007).

§ 5.9   FIRST AMENDMENT VIOLATION

Trade secret misappropriation claims do not always raise First Amendment issues, but where the plaintiff seeks to enjoin the defendant from disclosing (and thereby speaking about) trade secrets, the First Amendment is implicated. *See Ford Motor Company v. Lane*, 67 F. Supp. 745 (E.D. Mich. 1999). This is because the grant of an injunction to prevent the disclosure of trade secrets would constitute the requisite government action under the First Amendment and the scope of the injunction may abridge free speech.

§ 5.9.1   COMMERCIAL VS. OTHER SPEECH

The principal difficulty with a First Amendment defense is that principles of free speech do not preclude all limitations of speech. Sometimes the speech at issue in many trade secret misappropriation cases is not speech that is fully protected by the First Amendment because trade secret cases often involve commercial speech. The U.S. Supreme Court has defined commercial speech as "speech which does no more than propose a commercial transaction." *Bolger v. Youngs Drug Prods. Corp.*, 463 U.S. 60, 66 (1983). Speech may be treated as commercial speech even if it both proposes a commercial transaction and addresses social or political issues. *Id.* at 66–68. Merely because speech concerns a commercial subject, however, does not necessarily make it commercial speech for First Amendment purposes. *See City of Cincinnati v. Discovery Network, Inc.*, 507 U.S. 410, 421 (1993). The speech must be evaluated as a whole, including consideration of the purpose of the speech.

Although commercial speech is afforded some First Amendment protection, it is lesser protection than that given to other kinds of speech, such as political speech. *See Central Hudson Gas & Elec. Corp. v. Pub. Serv. Comm'n of New York*, 447 U.S. 557, 562–63 (1980). Therefore, any assessment of First Amendment conflicts that arise under trade secret law must consider the type of speech that is involved and account for the weaker level of protection that is currently applicable to commercial speech. *See* Elizabeth A. Rowe, *Introducing A Take-Down for Trade Secrets on the Internet*, 2007 Wisconsin L. Rev. 1041, 1071–73 (2007).

§ 5.9.2   ANTI-SLAPP STATUTES

Defendants sometimes seek to dismiss trade secret actions alleging that such complaints violate state anti-SLAPP (strategic lawsuits against public participation) statutes. These statutes (where they exist) usually prohibit the filing of suits against those who exercise their right to free speech in connection with a public issue. *See, e.g.*, Cal. Code Civ. Proc. § 425.16 (2013). In trade secret disputes between competitors or in disputes involving former employees, however, this argument is unlikely to be successful because the threshold requirement of speech on a matter of "public" concern cannot be met. *See, e.g.*, *World Fin. Group, Inc. v. HBW Ins. & Fin. Servs.*, 92 Cal. Rptr. 3d 227, 233–38 (Cal. Ct. App. 2009).

Ultimately, in practical terms the goal of trade secret law is to strike the proper balance between restricting disclosures to protect legitimate trade secrets while permitting disclosures that are more readily recognized as being in the public interest. For instance, one may be privileged to disclose trade secret information "that is relevant to public health or safety, or to the commission of a crime or tort, or to other matters of substantial public concern." Restatement (Third) of Unfair Competition § 40 cmt. c (1995). Some whistleblowing statutes also privilege disclosures of information that potentially include trade secrets. *See, e.g.*, 5 U.S.C. § 2302(b)(8) (2006). However, free speech concerns do not automatically outweigh the other significant interests recognized by trade secret law. *See* Elizabeth A. Rowe, *Trade Secret Litigation and Free Speech: Is it Time to Re-*

strain the Plaintiffs?, 50 Boston College Law Rev. 1425, 1435–38 (2009).

§ 5.10   FIFTH AMENDMENT PRIVILEGE AGAINST SELF-INCRIMINATION

The Fifth Amendment to the U.S. Constitution states that: "No person . . . shall be compelled in any criminal case to be a witness against himself." It has been held to apply anytime an individual is compelled to give potentially incriminating testimonial evidence in "any proceeding, civil or criminal, administrative or judicial, investigatory or adjudicatory." *See Kastiger v. United States*, 406 U.S. 441, 444 (1972). The critical issue under the Fifth Amendment is not whether an individual is likely to be prosecuted for a crime, but whether such prosecution is "more than fanciful." *See Warford v. Medeiros*, 160 Cal App. 3d 1035, 1043–44 (Cal. Ct. App. 1984).

As with the First Amendment defense, a defense based upon the Fifth Amendment privilege against self-incrimination only arises in trade secret cases in very particular situations involving compelled testimony. The requisite government action can be an order of the court in the form of an injunction or a discovery demand that requires an individual to essentially admit that he possesses trade secrets. Since the misappropriation of trade secrets can be a state and federal crime (*see infra* Chapter 10), such an admission amounts to compelled and potentially incriminating testimony.

When determining the potential applicability of
the Fifth Amendment privilege against self-
incrimination, three critical facts must be considered. First, it only applies to individuals, not business entities. *See Bellis v. United States*, 417 U.S. 85
(1974). Second, as noted above, the ability of an individual to invoke the Fifth Amendment privilege is
not limited to criminal cases. The privilege may also
be invoked in civil and regulatory proceedings, the
key being whether there is a risk of subsequent
criminal prosecution. Third, the privilege can arise
when an individual is compelled to provide any testimonial evidence, including by means of oral testimony, the production of testimonial documents, or
the mere act of producing documents. *See Fisher v.
U.S.*, 425 U.S. 391, 407–412 (1976).

Based upon the foregoing, there are a number of
points in time during the course of a trade secret
misappropriation case when an individual defendant may wish to invoke the Fifth Amendment privilege against self-incrimination. The most obvious
scenario is when an individual defendant is called to
testify at trial. The privilege may also be asserted
when an individual is asked questions at a deposition or in written interrogatories related to whether
he misappropriated trade secrets. Similarly, a mandatory injunction or discovery request which requires an individual to produce trade secrets or other incriminating testimonial documents can be opposed on the basis of the privilege.

The invocation of the Fifth Amendment privilege
in a trade secret misappropriation case is not without potential negative consequences. As a practical

matter, it will indicate to the plaintiff that its claims of misappropriation are not farfetched. Additionally, unlike the invocation of the privilege in criminal cases, the invocation of the privilege against self-incrimination can be used in a civil case to infer wrongdoing. *See Baxter v. Palmigiano*, 425 U.S. 308, 318–319 (1976). This adverse inference may even be extended to a party who is associated with a witness who invokes the Fifth Amendment privilege. *See LiButti v. United States*, 107 F.3d 100, 120–21 (2d Cir. 1997).

When the Fifth Amendment privilege against self-incrimination is invoked in a case where one attorney is representing more than one defendant (for instance an employee and his current employer), conflicts of interest may arise that will have to be addressed. However, since the privilege is a Constitutional right, the ultimate decision of whether to invoke the privilege should be made by the holder of the privilege and not his counsel or employer.

In the appropriate case, the invocation of the privilege against self-incrimination may be coupled with a request to stay the civil proceeding pending the outcome of any criminal investigation or prosecution. *See Afro-Lecon, Inc. v. United States*, 820 F.2d 1198 (Fed. Cir. 1987). This is one of the unintended consequences of criminalizing business torts such as trade secret misappropriation, but a consequence that can often be used to a defendant's advantage. If the motion to stay the civil proceeding is granted, all pleadings, discovery, and trial preparations in the civil case must cease. However, settlement of the civil action is still possible. A defendant's motion to

stay a pending civil trade secret case is likely to be
granted if there is an ongoing investigation criminal
investigation.

CHAPTER 6

REMEDIES FOR TRADE SECRET MISAPPROPRIATION

§ 6.1   INTRODUCTION TO REMEDIES

One of the reasons that statutes are often drafted in cases where there are similar common law claims for relief is due to the limited scope of common law remedies. This is certainly true with respect to common law intellectual property torts, such as trade secret misappropriation. At common law it was often difficult for trade secret plaintiffs to prove actual damages or the basis for injunctive relief. The remedies provisions of the UTSA help solve this problem by specifying the types of available remedies and the conditions under which they will be granted. *See* Unif. Trade Secrets Act §§ 2–5 (amended 1985), reprinted in Appendix A. In non-UTSA jurisdictions, the available remedies as developed in each jurisdiction apply.

The following discussion is based upon the UTSA unless otherwise noted. In states that have not yet adopted the UTSA, the common law or state statutes must be examined to determine the scope of available remedies.

§ 6.2   PRELIMINARY INJUNCTIVE RELIEF

The filing of a claim for trade secret misappropriation is ordinarily accompanied by a request for a temporary restraining order (TRO), a preliminary injunction (PI), or both. This is because trade secret protection can be lost forever if trade secrets are disclosed in a manner that makes them generally known or readily ascertainable. Requests for preliminary (or provisional) relief are therefore usually designed to prevent such disclosure. More broadly, "the purpose of a preliminary injunction is merely to preserve the relative positions of the parties until a trial on the merits can be held." *University of Texas v.* Camenisch, 451 U.S. 390 (1981).

Both the UTSA and the *Restatement of Unfair Competition* contain provisions that allow courts to grant appropriate injunctive relief. *See* Unif. Trade Secrets Act § 2 (amended 1985); Restatement (Third) of Unfair Competition § 44 (1995). Although these provisions do not specifically mention preliminary injunctions, they state that both the actual and threatened misappropriation of trade secrets can be enjoined.

§ 6.2.1 STANDARDS FOR THE GRANT OF PRELIMINARY RELIEF

The procedural rules of each jurisdiction where a trade secret case is pending should be consulted to determine how and when to move for preliminary relief. *See, e.g.*, Fed. Rule Civ. Proc. Rule 65 (2008). Usually, the grant of injunctive relief, particularly preliminary relief, is governed by long-standing principles of equity. According to *E.I. DuPont de Nemours and Co. v. Kolon Industries, Inc.,* No. 3:09cv58, 2012 WL4490547, at *12 (E.D. Va. Aug. 30, 2012), these principles have a substantive law dimension and, thus, in diversity cases are to be determined by applicable state law. The court in *Kolon*

noted, however, that "the permissive statutory text
[the use of "may" in the Virginia UTSA injunction
provision] preserves the settled equity principle that
issuance of injunction is a matter of judicial discretion." *Id.* at *12.

As noted *infra* in § 6.3, there are four well-
recognized factors for the grant of permanent injunctive relief. The requirements for preliminary
relief are slightly different, and in many respects
more stringent, because the moving party seeks relief before a full trial on the merits and often before
any discovery has occurred.

Generally, preliminary injunctive relief will not
be granted unless the moving party can establish:
(1) a reasonable likelihood of success on the merits
of its claim; (2) that it has no adequate remedy at
law; and (3) that it will suffer irreparable harm unless preliminary injunctive relief is granted. *See
Clorox Co. v. S.C. Johnson & Son, Inc.*, 627 F. Supp.
2d 954, 970 (citation omitted). *See also, Sega Enterprises Ltd. v. Accolade, Inc.*, 977 F.2d 1510, 1517
(9th Cir. 1992) (describing a different formulation of
the test which, among other things, examines "the
balance of hardships"). Courts also examine the potential harms to the parties and to the public. *See SI
Handling Systems, Inc. v. Heisley*, 753 F.2d 1244,
1254 (3d Cir. 1985) (citations omitted) (listing a
four-factor test for preliminary relief). It is only
when the scales of equity are in favor of the plaintiff
that preliminary relief should be granted.

As noted in the *Restatement of Unfair Competition,* the factors to be considered in determining

whether to grant an injunction in a trade secret case are similar to the factors that are applied in tort cases generally. *See* Restatement (Third) of Unfair Competition § 44(2) (1995) (listing eight factors to be considered). The competitive nature of trade secret claims, however, raises a number of special issues.

In *Clorox*, in addition to considering the asserted irreparable harm of the plaintiff, the court evaluated the harm that the defendant would suffer from "being deprived of a top employee for the near future." 622 F. Supp. 2d at 971. It also considered the effect of preliminary relief on nonparties, including the employee who would be deprived of his livelihood and the ability to pursue his career. The court in *SI Handling* noted that the effect of injunctive relief on employee mobility is an important factor to consider in deciding to grant a preliminary injunction, not only because of the general rule that individuals should be allowed to pursue their callings, but because any limit on employee mobility restrains an employee's bargaining power and diminishes the dissemination of ideas, processes, and methods. 753 F.2d at 1265.

Because injunctions may result in consumers being deprived of goods or services, the effect of injunctive relief on the market and the lives of consumers should also be considered and may tip the balance against the grant of preliminary relief. *See E.I. DuPont de Nemours and Co. v. Kolon Industries, Inc.*, No. 3:09cv58, 2012 WL4490547, at *13 (E.D. Va. Aug. 30, 2012) (*citing eBay, Inc. v. Merc–Exchange, L.L.C.*, 547 U.S. 388). On the other hand, courts often cite the need to enforce contracts, protect trade secrets, and promote business ethics as public interests that justify the grant of injunctive relief. Quoting *ePlus, Inc. v. Lawson Software, Inc.,* No. 3:09cv620, 2011 WL2119410, at *17 (E.D. Va. May 23, 2011), *the co*urt in *Kolon* noted: "the touchstone of the public interest factor is whether an injunction, both in scope and effect, strikes a workable balance between protecting the [trade secret owner]'s rights and protecting the public from the injunction's adverse effects." 2012 WL4490547, at *15.

§ 6.2.2   PRESUMPTION OF IRREPARABLE HARM

An issue that arises in trade secret cases at both the preliminary and permanent injunction stages is whether the equitable factor of "irreparable harm" can be presumed from a finding of trade secret misappropriation. If so, then the burden on the issue of irreparable harm shifts to the defendant to establish that monetary damages are adequate to compensate the plaintiff for any future loss of trade secrets.

Some courts have recognized a presumption of irreparable harm once a sufficient showing of misappropriation is made (*see Faiveley Transport Malmo AB v. Wabtec Corp.*, 559 F. 3d. 110, 118 (2d Cir. 2009)) and others have not. *Campbell Soup Co. v. ConAgra, Inc.*, 977 F. 2d. 86, 92–93 (3d Cir. 1992). The position of the plaintiff in this regard may be strengthened if a confidentiality agreement between the parties states that irreparable harm is to be presumed, but the plaintiff will still have the initial burden of showing misappropriation. *See Veliz v. Cintas Corp.*, 2004 WL 2452851 (N.D. Cal. 2004).

§ 6.2.3   THE SCOPE OF PRELIMINARY INJUNCTIONS

Once the issue of whether a preliminary injunction should be granted is decided, the next challenge for litigants and the court is to determine the proper language, scope, and duration of the injunction. Procedural rules, such as Fed. Rule of Civ. Proc. Rule 65, often specify the basic components of an injunction order but the particulars concerning the restrictions to be placed upon the activities of the defendant are the focus of most of the debates concerning the proper scope of an injunction. *See, e.g., SI Handling Systems, Inc. v. Heisley,* 753 F.2d 1244. "An injunction should not impose unnecessary burdens on lawful activity." *WaldmanPub.Corp. v. Landoll, Inc.,* 43 F.3d 775, 785 (2d Cir.1994).

In keeping with the fear of the loss of trade secrecy, the plaintiff will typically advocate for broad injunctive relief that often extends beyond the actual parties to the litigation. For instance, the plaintiff may request that the injunction apply to all of the defendants and their agents and associates, including their legal counsel. If the defendant is a company, the plaintiff will request that the injunction apply to all officers, employees, and agents of the company. Fearing potential consequences, including contempt proceedings for failing to comply with an injunction, the defendant will typically argue for an injunction that only applies to the parties to the litigation and a few designated individuals.

It is often stated that the purpose of temporary restraining orders and preliminary injunctions is to preserve the *status quo* until a decision on the merits of the plaintiff's claims. Thus, it is generally easier for a plaintiff to obtain a prohibitory injunction rather than a mandatory injunction (*see Tom Doherty Associated, Inc. v. Saban Entertainment, Inc.*, 60 F.3d 27, 34 (2d Cir. 1995) (discussing the differences between a mandatory and prohibitory injunction), although UTSA § 2(c) specifically authorizes courts "in appropriate circumstances" to order affirmative acts to protect trade secrets. In trade secret cases, a prohibitory injunction would be worded to prohibit specified individuals from using or disclosing the alleged trade secrets. A mandatory injunction, in contrast, might require the alleged trade secrets to be returned to the plaintiff or deposited with a third-party for safe keeping until such time as the trade secret litigation is completed.

As a practical matter, because of the reluctance of courts to grant mandatory injunctions (and the higher burden of proof that may apply), particularly at the preliminary relief stage, plaintiffs in trade secret misappropriation cases are well advised to word their proposed injunction orders as prohibitory injunctions. This also helps to reduce potential Fifth Amendment defenses. *See supra* § 5.10.

§ 6.2.4 SECURITY (OR BOND) REQUIREMENT

The rules of many jurisdictions, most notably the federal courts, require that the grant of preliminary injunctive relief be conditioned on the posting of security (also known as a bond or undertaking). *See, e.g.,* Fed. Rule Civ. Proc. Rule 65(c) (2008); Cal. Code Civ. Proc. § 529(a) (2013). The amount of security is within the discretion of the court but should be set at an amount that will compensate the defendant for any harm that is caused by the injunction. As explained in *ABBA Rubber v. Seaquist*, 235 Cal. Ct. App. 3d 1, 14 (citations omitted), "the trial court's function is to estimate the harmful effect which the injunction is likely to have on the restrained party, and to set the undertaking at that sum."

Because of the security requirement and the costs of pre-trial motions, plaintiffs in trade secret misappropriation cases should not move for preliminary relief unless they have sufficient resources to post a bond. Although arguments can be made to keep the amount of the bond as low as possible, the nature of the trade secrets and the scope of the requested injunction may dictate a large bond. Indeed, a defendant who "loses the battle" on the issue of a preliminary injunction may "win the war" by arguing for a bond amount that the plaintiff cannot afford.

§ 6.3   PERMANENT INJUNCTIVE RELIEF

A plaintiff in a trade secret case need not prove actual harm in order to prevail, but it cannot recover monetary damages unless it does. In the absence of monetary harm (and sometimes in addition thereto), the principal remedy is likely to be permanent injunctive relief. According to UTSA § 2(a), such relief may be granted to enjoin actual or threatened trade secret misappropriation.

The label "permanent injunction" is somewhat of a misnomer because most injunctions are limited in time and, in any case, can be dissolved after they are first issued. *See, e.g., MicroStrategy, Inc. v. Business Objects, S.A.*, 369 F. Supp. 2d 725, 734–737 (2005) (motion to dissolve injunction denied but with leave to renew the motion in 9 months). In this regard, the length of permanent injunctive relief in trade secret cases is specifically limited by the UTSA to the period of time during which the subject trade secrets remain secret. *See* Unif. Trade Secrets Act § 2(a) cmt. (amended 1985); *infra* § 6.3.3. Thus, the label "permanent" refers to injunctions that are issued after a decision on the merits of a case, whereas injunctive relief issued before a final decision on the merits is referred to a "preliminary relief."

§ 6.3.1 STANDARDS FOR THE GRANT OF PERMANENT INJUNCTIONS

Although different courts in different jurisdictions may have slightly different formulations of the test, in *eBay, Inc. v. MercExchange, LLC*, 547 U.S. 388, 391 (2006), the United States Supreme Court recognized that there are four well-established factors for the grant of a permanent injunction to a plaintiff: "(1) that it has suffered an irreparable injury; (2) that remedies available at law, such as monetary damages, are inadequate to compensate for that injury; (3) that, considering the balance of hardships between the plaintiff and defendant, a remedy in equity is warranted; and (4) that the public interest would not be disserved by a permanent injunction."

These factors differ slightly from the preliminary injunction factors (*see supra* § 6.2.1) because, whereas a plaintiff on a motion for preliminary injunction must establish "a likelihood of success on the merits," for a permanent injunction, the plaintiff must establish actual success. *See Amoco Productions Co. v. Village of Gambell, AK*, 480 U.S. 531 (1987).

Once a plaintiff in a trade secret case proves misappropriation, particularly in a UTSA jurisdiction, they may argue that they are "automatically" entitled to injunctive relief because such relief is a statutorily prescribed remedy. *See, e.g., E.I. DuPont de Nemours and Co. v. Kolon Industries, Inc.,* 2012 WL4490547. Whether this argument will work depends upon the law of the applicable state. There is nothing in the language of the UTSA § 2(a) that specifically requires courts to apply "principles of equity" as was the case with patent law in the *eBay* case. *See eBay, Inc. v. MercExchange, L.L.C.,* 547 U.S. 388. However, consistent with the common law origins of trade secret law, the grant of permanent injunctive relief is ordinarily subject to principles of equity. Moreover, as the court in *Kolon* noted, the use of the word "may" in UTSA § 2(a) gives courts discretion to grant injunctive relief and by doing so they can consider the equities. 2012 WL4490547, at *12.

Applicable law and the facts of each case will dictate the equitable factors on which courts focus when deciding whether to grant permanent injunctive relief. Sometimes the focus is on the first two *eBay*-factors. Other times, the balance of the hardships and the public interest play a greater role. In cases where there is only an alleged threat of disclosure, injunctive relief is possible but may not be necessary. As the court in *Standard Brands, Inc. v. Zumpe*, 264 F. Supp. 254, 269–70 (E.D. La. 1967). explained, "[a]bsent disclosure or imminent threat of disclosure, injunctive relief should not be granted." *See also, Del Monte Fresh Produce Co. v. Dole Food Co, Inc.*, 148 F. Supp. 2d 1326, 1328 (S.D. Fla. 2001) (noting that California and Florida law require a "substantial threat of impending injury").

§ 6.3.2   THE SCOPE OF PERMANENT INJUNCTIONS

As with preliminary injunctions, the proper scope and wording of a permanent injunction must be carefully considered. *See, e.g., General Electric v. Sung*, 843 F. Supp. 776 (D. Mass 1994). First, injunctions must be sufficiently specific so that the individuals and companies that are subject to them know what they can and cannot do. *See Computek Computer & Office Supplies, Inc. v. Walton*, 156 S.W.3d 217 (Tex. App. 2005). Second, because of the anti-competitive nature of trade secret injunctions, they cannot be overly broad. *Id.*

The nature of permanent injunctive relief can take many forms depending upon the circumstances and the creativity of the plaintiff and the court. Often they are both mandatory and prohibitory, mandating the return of any misappropriated trade secrets and prohibiting the disclosure or use of such secrets. In addition, prohibitory injunctions may range from simple "use injunctions" to more complex injunctions which attempt to prevent the defendant from enjoying the fruits of the misappropriated trade secrets. In *Sung*, for instance, the court granted a "production injunction" which prohibited the defendant from engaging in the business of manufacturing saw-grade diamonds for a period of time. The court explained that production injunctions are used "where a use injunction would be ineffective in eliminating the competitive advantage gained by the misappropriator." *General Electric v. Sung*, 843 F. Supp. 776, 779.

§ 6.3.3   THE LENGTH OF PERMANENT INJUNCTIONS

The drafting history of the UTSA, as well as its commentary, indicates that one of the concerns that motivated the adoption of the UTSA was the tendency of some courts to grant "perpetual injunctions." *See* Unif. Trade Secrets Act § 2 cmt. (amended 1985), reprinted in Appendix A. At the time of the UTSA drafting process, there were three competing common law approaches to the length of injunctions in trade secret cases: (1) the perpetual injunction approach of *Shellmar Products Co. v. Allen Qualley Co.*, 87 F.2d 104 (7th Cir. 1937) (involving disclosures made in issued patents); (2) the no-injunction after disclosure of trade secrets approach of *Conmar Products Corp. v. Universal Slide Fastener Co.*, 172 F.2d 150 (2d Cir. 1949) (involving disclosures made in issued patents); and (3) the "lead-time" or "head-start" approach of *Winston Research Corp. v. Minnesota, Min. & Manuf. Co.*, 350 F.2d

134 (9th Cir. 1965) (involving disclosures made in the marketing and sale of plaintiff's products).

The individuals who drafted the UTSA believed that perpetual injunctions are both anti-competitive and unnecessary. As a result they explicitly adopted the holding and reasoning of *K-2 Ski Co. v. Head Ski Co., Inc.,* 506 F.2d 471 (9th Cir. 1974) (duration of injunctive relief limited to period of time it would have taken the defendant to discover trade secrets through independent development or reverse engineering), opting for the lead-time advantage rule of *Winston Research.* Unif. Trade Secrets Act § 2(a), cmt. (amended 1985), reprinted in Appendix A. Specifically, UTSA § 2(a) provides that: "an injunction shall be terminated when the trade secret has ceased to exist, but the injunction may be continued for an additional reasonable period of time to eliminate the commercial advantage that otherwise would be derived from the misappropriation."

Based upon the foregoing language from the UTSA, the length of permanent injunctive relief depends upon the facts of each case and how the "commercial advantage" is determined. In *General Electric Co. v. Sung,* 843 F. Supp. at 780, the court looked at "the amount of time it would have taken [the defendant] to independently develop or reverse engineer a technology for commercial production of high-grade saw diamonds." Once the proper length of the injunction is determined, then the judge must determine if it should run from the date of the entry of judgment (the approach followed in *Sung*) or from the date of misappropriation. In cases where a preliminary injunction was issued, credit may be given

for the duration of the preliminary injunction. *See,
e.g., K-2 Ski Co. v. Head Ski Co., Inc.,* 506 F.2d at
475.

In non-UTSA jurisdictions, particularly those that
follow the *Restatement of Torts,* long-term injunctions are more likely to be the norm and may explain why some states have not yet adopted the
UTSA. Additionally, not all UTSA jurisdictions
adopted the language of UTSA § 2(a) quoted above
(*see* Ala. Code § 8–27–4 (2012) Colo. Rev. Stat. Ann.
§ 7–74–103 (2012)) and others have modified the
language of § 2 so that longer injunctions are possible. *See, e.g.,* Ga. Code Ann. § 10–1–762 (2012); 765
Ill. Comp. Stat. 1065/3 (2012); Tenn. Code Ann.
§ 47–25–1703 (2001).

Differences in approaches regarding the length of
injunctions have to do, at least in part, with differences of opinion regarding the purpose of injunctive
relief in trade secret cases. When the grant of injunctive relief is seen as a penalty for wrongdoing,
as opposed to a means of preventing a defendant
from benefitting from his wrongdoing, injunctions
tend to be longer and more permanent. When injunctions are seen as a means to quell competition,
they tend to be shorter.

As a practical matter, the duration of a permanent injunction depends upon the status of the
plaintiff's trade secrets at the time the injunction is
issued. If the trade secrets are no longer secret at
that time, then an injunction is not needed to prevent them from being disclosed to the public, but
may be needed to prevent the defendant from bene-

fiting from his wrongdoing. If a plaintiff's trade secrets retain their trade secret status at the time a judgment is about to be ordered, then it may be appropriate to grant injunctive relief without a temporal limit, subject to the right of the defendant to apply to the court to terminate the injunction if and when the trade secrets lose their secrecy. Under either scenario, a court (except in non-UTSA jurisdictions) is likely to limit the length of an injunction to the time that it would take a person who is skilled in the art to reverse engineer or independently develop the trade secrets.

§ 6.4   COMPENSATORY DAMAGES

At common law compensatory damages for torts are ordinarily awarded only for the actual harm suffered by the plaintiff. In the case of business torts, actual harm is often measured by lost profits. This same measure of damages is available to plaintiffs in trade secret cases, but due to the nature of trade secret misappropriation claims and the difficulty of proving actual harm in a competitive environment, the allowable measure of compensatory damages is broader. Damages in trade secret cases can include "actual loss caused by misappropriation and the unjust enrichment that is caused by misappropriation that is not taken into account in computing actual loss." Unif. Trade Secrets Act § 3(a) (amended 1985). As explained in the commentary to the UTSA, "[a]s long as there is no double counting, Section 3(a) adopts the principle of the recent cases allowing recovery of both a complainant's actual losses and a misappropriator's unjust benefit that are caused by misappropriation."

The availability of compensatory damages under the UTSA is not without its limits. As explained in the comments to section 3, "[l]ike injunctive relief, a monetary recovery for trade secret misappropriation is appropriate only for the period in which information is entitled to protection as a trade secret, plus the additional period, if any, in which a misappropriator retains an advantage over good faith competitors because of misappropriation." Additionally, the grant of injunctive relief, either preliminary or permanent, will naturally limit the amount of monetary relief that is available. Unif. Trade Secrets Act § 3, cmt. (amended 1985) ("A claim for actual damages and net profits can be combined with a claim for injunctive relief, but, if both claims are granted, the injunctive relief ordinarily will preclude a monetary award for a period in which the injunction is effective.")

If a plaintiff in a trade secret case acts quickly and is successful in preventing the actual use or disclosure of its trade secrets, then there should be no actual harm, no matter how measured. On the other hand, if there is evidence that the defendant used or disclosed the secrets, an award of compensatory damages is possible. The measure of damages for the wrongful disclosure of trade secrets is likely to be the actual and potential value of the secrets to the plaintiff if there had been no disclosure.

Evidence of damage due to the wrongful use of trade secrets can be established based upon a number of different measures. *See, e.g.*, *In re Jonatzke*, 47 B.R. 846 (Bkrtcy. E.D. Mich. 2012) (identifying lost profits, erosion of market share, and out-of-pocket expenses as possible measures of damages); *University Computing Co. v. Lykes-Youngstown Corp.*, 504 F.2d 518, 536 (citation omitted) (5th Cir. 1974) (identifying the plaintiff's lost profits and the "benefits, profits, and advantages gained by the defendant in the use of the trade secret" as potential measure of damages). In *Roton Barrier, Inc. v. Stanley Works*, 79 F.3d 111 (Fed. Cir. 1996), the plaintiff successfully argued that it should be awarded both lost profits and price erosion damages. The lost profits were measured by the plaintiff's loss of market share while the price erosion damages were measured by the difference in prices charged by plaintiff before and after defendant entered the market with a misappropriated tool.

Often the award of compensatory and other monetary damages comes down to a battle of damage experts and the question of whether their tstimony is plausible and believable.

§ 6.5   REASONABLE ROYALTIES

Reasonable royalties are not generally a form of compensatory damages, but they are available under the UTSA in two separate and distinct situations. First, where proof of the amount of actual harm or defendant's profits is difficult, reasonable royalties may be used as an alternative measure of damages. Section 3(a) of the UTSA states: "In lieu of damages measured by any other methods, the damages caused by misappropriation may be measured by imposition of liability for a reasonable royalty for a misappropriator's unauthorized disclosure or use of a trade secret." Significantly, there must first be a finding of the defendant's actual use or disclosure of misappropriated trade secrets. In other words, the award of reasonable royalties under this first scenario is not a substitute for proof of actual harm; rather, it is an alternative measure of damages.

The second reasonable royalty scenario under the UTSA concerns rare situations where the grant of injunctive relief would ordinarily be called for but is against public policy or principles of equity. Section 2(b) of the UTSA provides that: "in exceptional circumstances, an injunction may condition use upon payment of a reasonable royalty for no longer than the period of time for which use could have been prohibited." In other words, in some circumstances, a reasonable royalty will be granted to the plaintiff instead of enjoining the defendant from using the trade secrets. The grant of royalties in this situation is sometimes called a "royalty injunction" and must be distinguished from the grant of a royalty as a measure of damages.

There is not a lot of case law on what constitutes "exceptional circumstances," but it is clear that the provision was based upon a pre-UTSA case in which the court refused to enjoin the use of trade secrets that were needed for the war effort. *See* Unif. Trade Secrets Act § 2(b), cmt. (*citing* and explaining *Republic Aviation Corp. v. Schenk*, 152 U.S.P.Q. 830 (N.Y. Sup. Ct. 1967).) In *Progressive Products, Inc. v. Swartz*, 292 Kan. 977, 980 (Kan. 2011), the court noted that "[t]here are no set rules for what constitutes 'exceptional circumstances.'" It went on to explain, citing cases from trademark law, that the analysis requires consideration of equitable issues similar to those considered for injunctive relief, including the public interest.

The length of a reasonable royalty under UTSA § 2(b) is limited to the "duration of the competitive advantage." Uniform Trade Secrets Act § 2(b), cmt (amended 1985). Under UTSA § 3(a), the reasonable royalty is an alternative measure of compensatory damages and usually will be stated as a "lump-sum," particularly in cases where the subject information lost its trade secret status before the entry of judgment. In cases where the trade secrets continue to exist, the reasonable royalty measure of damages is usually for the period of defendant's wrongful use of the trade secrets.

The amount of any reasonable royalty will generally be based upon expert testimony concerning industry norms with respect to the type of information involved. In many fields of technology there is a standard range of royalties. However, due to the exclusive (or semi-exclusive) nature of trade secrets, trade secret owners may wish to ask for a premium.

§ 6.6   PUNITIVE DAMAGES

UTSA § 3(b) specifically allows for the grant of punitive (or exemplary) damages, but only in cases of "willful and malicious misappropriation" and only in an amount not to exceed twice the amount of compensatory damages. Unif. Trade Secrets Act, § 3(b) (amended 1985), reprinted in Appendix A.

However, when adopting the UTSA, some states either modified or eliminated this cap. *See, e.g.,* Mich. Stat. Ann. § 445.1901 *et seq.* (2012); Mo. Rev. Stat. § 417.457 (2013). Nebraska did not adopt either the damages or attorney's fees provisions of the UTSA. *See* Neb. Rev. Stat. § 87–501 *et seq.* (2012).

As noted in *Roton Barrier, Inc. v. Stanley Works*, 79 F.3d 1112, 1120 (citations omitted), because punitive damages are not favored in the law, "courts must take caution to see that punitive damages are not improperly or unwisely awarded." This is particularly true in trade secret cases which must be based, in the first instance, on knowing bad acts. *See supra* § 4.4. Thus, willful and malicious behavior means something more than the knowing bad acts required to prove misappropriation. Given the competitive setting in which most trade secret cases arise, the court in *Roton Barrier* noted that a distinction must be made between "motivation by malice" and "motivation by competition." Competition, even aggressive and ruthless competition, is not bad; to justify an award of punitive damages there must be showing of actual malice. *Id.* at 1120–1121.

Note that the same evidence that justifies an award of punitive damages in cases under the UTSA may also justify an award of attorney's fees under the UTSA, and *vice versa. Id; see also Vacco Industries, Inc. v. Van Den Berg*, 5 Cal. App. 4th 34, 54 (Cal. Ct. App. 1992). However, the comments to the UTSA state that courts should take the grant of punitive damages into account in determining whether an award of attorney's fees is also necessary. Unif.

Trade Secrets Act § 4, cmt. (amended 1985), reprinted in Appendix A.

§ 6.7 ATTORNEY'S FEES AND COSTS

The general rule in civil cases in the U.S. (the so-
called American rule) is that attorney's fees are not
available to the prevailing party. Section 4 of the
UTSA modifies this rule for trade secret claims by
stating that attorney's fees "may" be awarded to the
prevailing party if: (1) a claim of misappropriation is
made in bad faith; (2) a motion to terminate an injunction is made or resisted in bad faith; or (3) willful and malicious misappropriation exists. Whether
or not to grant attorney's fees, and how much to
award, is within the discretion of the court. *See, e.g.,
Real-Time Laboratories, Inc. v. Predator Systems,
Inc.*, 757 So.2d 634, 638 (Fla. App. 2000) (noting
that the discretion applies even if there is a finding
of bad faith).

An underlying goal of the UTSA's attorney's fees
provision is to act as a deterrent to specious claims.
Unif. Trade Secrets Act § 4, cmt. (amended 1985)
("Section 4 allows a court to award reasonable attorney fees to a prevailing party in specified circumstances as a deterrent to specious claims of misappropriation, to specious efforts by a misappropriator
to terminate injunctive relief, and to willful and malicious misappropriation.") Consistent with this
goal, attorney's fees may be awarded to the prevailing party (either the plaintiff or defendant) on a motion to terminate an injunction. This provision was
designed to discourage putative trade secret owners

from seeking injunctive relief for anti-competitive purposes.

The "willful and malicious" language of section 4 of the UTSA was apparently borrowed from patent law where attorney's fees can be granted in "exceptional cases." *See* 35 U.S.C. § 285 (2006); Unif. Trade Secrets Act § 4, cmt. (amended 1985), reprinted in Appendix A. Section § 6.6 *supra*, discusses the meaning of willful and malicious as expressed in one trade secret case.

The UTSA does not define "bad faith," but applicable case law in California has held that the conduct must be "more culpable than mere negligence." See *Gemini Aluminum Corp. v. California Custom Shapes, Inc.*, 95 Cal. App. 4th 1249, 1261 (Cal. Ct. App. 2002) (*quoting Stillwell Development, Inc. v. Chen*). Citing *Gemini* with favor, the court in *Flir Systems, Inc. v. Parrish*, 174 Cal. App. 1270, 1275 (Cal. Ct. App. 2009) explained:

> Although the Legislature has not defined "bad faith," our courts have developed a two-prong standard: (1) objective speciousness of the claim, and (2) subjective bad faith in bringing or maintaining the action, i.e., for an improper purpose.

The objective factor looks at the merits of the claims or motion; the subjective factor looks at the motivation of the actor. *See* Elizabeth A. Rowe, *Trade Secret Litigation and Free Speech: Is it Time to Restrain the Plaintiffs?*, 50 Boston College Law Rev. 1425, 1448–49 (2009) (discussing bad faith trade secret claims).

Costs (other than attorney's fees) are generally awarded to prevailing parties at the discretion of the judge and in accordance with applicable procedures. *See, e.g.*, Fed. Rules Civ. Proc. Rule 54(d) (2012). Pursuant to other provisions of law or practice (including procedural rules, case law, and local rules), costs usually include filing and motion fees, deposition costs, jury fees, and expert witness fees.

CHAPTER 7

PROTECTING TRADE SECRETS IN THE EMPLOYMENT CONTEXT

§ 7.1 INTRODUCTION TO TRADE SECRECY ISSUES RELATED TO EMPLOYMENT

Statistically, most trade secret misappropriation cases arise in the employment context. The typical case involves the decision of a valued employee to either start her own business or leave her current employment to start work with a competitor. As noted previously, all too frequently the former employer is caught unawares and may not appreciate that it owns trade secrets until it becomes concerned about what its former employee might disclose. Thus trade secret cases that arise in the employment context often involve after-the-fact efforts to identify trade secrets and to assert implied duties of confidentiality which, depending upon the circumstances, may or may not succeed. Where the former employer is sophisticated and has taken steps to identify and protect its trade secrets, the adequacy and enforceability of those efforts are often called into question.

A very important public policy issue that courts struggle with in trade secret cases involving former employees is the freedom of movement of labor and the extent to which trade secret protection limits this right of mobility. Employees are generally free to work for whomever they wish and to pursue a livelihood. In many ways, trade secret law restricts this fundamental right of employees to move freely from employer to employer. As such, courts usually try to determine where to draw the line between protectable information and an employee's general skill and knowledge. Restrictive covenants that purport to limit employee mobility are carefully evaluated to determine whether they are reasonable. At the same time, other countervailing policy interests such as safeguarding rigorous but fair competition and protecting against breaches of confidence enter into the balance.

§ 7.2   DISGRUNTLED AND MOBILE EMPLOYEES: A PROBLEM FOR EMPLOYERS

The expectation of long-term employment until retirement with any company is a thing of the past. Most full-time employees change jobs (and perhaps careers) several times over the span of their lives. That mobility, in itself, creates more opportunities for employees to transfer trade secrets to new employers or to their own competing ventures. Furthermore, dissatisfied and angry employees are likely to leave their companies quietly without discussing their departure with their employers, fueling the likelihood of trade secret misappropriation in the process.

The following case examples demonstrate the kinds of scenarios that result when employees who are highly mobile and quick to join competitors or start their own competing ventures become dissatisfied with their jobs or changes in corporate ownership.

Employees who feel that they are not paid well enough by their employers can be angry and resentful. In *Lexis-Nexis v. Beer*, 41 F. Supp. 2d 950 (D. Minn. 1999), an employee became dissatisfied with his compensation. After the employer refused several requests for a salary increase, the employee resigned and accepted employment with a competitor. Before he returned all office equipment provided by his former employer, the disgruntled employee copied emails and the customer information database previously stored on a company laptop onto a zip disk. He later transferred this information to a new laptop he received from his new employer.

Layoffs can be a major source of dissatisfaction. In *MicroStrategy, Inc. v. Business Objects, S.A.*, 331 F. Supp. 2d 396 (E.D. Va. 2004), a software company experienced financial instability. When the company began to lay off its employees and shrink its businesses, several employees also planned their departure. In an effort to gain new employment, they disclosed confidential information to the number one competitor in the market, and promised to "swing business" in return. As a result, the company lost a significant amount of trade secrets, including sales techniques, descriptions of software architecture, and competitive intelligence.

Mergers gone badly can also feed discontent. In *Hilb, Rogal & Hamilton Co. of Atlanta v. Holley*, 644 S.E.2d 862 (Ga. Ct. App. 2007), an insurance agent merged his own professional agency with another company and became a shareholder employee. He later became dissatisfied with his new job after he learned that the merged company would no longer focus on his business specialty and he decided to leave. He took with him an electronic organizer containing customer contact information. By using that information, approximately twenty to twenty-five percent of the clients he serviced during his former employment followed him to his new employer.

In *Anadarko Petroleum Corp. v. Davis*, 2006 WL 3837518, at *2 (S.D. Tex. Dec. 28, 2006), a petroleum engineer worked for the predecessor company for approximately twenty years. The predecessor company later merged into another corporation. After the change of ownership, the engineer became dissatisfied with his career ("He felt that he had been passed over for promotions and 'pushed to the side. . . .'"). He also believed that his supervisors knew less about the business than he did and were making "poor decisions." As a result, he joined a competitor and took trade secret information belonging to the former employer.

Employees who form their own competing ventures often capitalize on their former employer's trade secrets to jump-start their businesses. For instance, in *Latuszewski v. Valic Financial Advisors, Inc.*, 2007 WL 4462739, at **5-7 (W.D. Pa. Dec. 19, 2007), several financial advisors formed their own competing business venture while they were still employed with the former employer. In order to move customers who represented millions of dollars in assets to their own business venture, these employees selectively targeted a group of customers and collected their customer data before submitting their resignations. Three months after leaving, they transferred ten million dollars in assets from the former employer.

In *Intellisports L.L.C. v. Fitzgerald*, 2004 WL 794458, at *1 (Kan. Ct. App. Apr. 9, 2004), a departing editor offered to buy one of the divisions owned by his employer publishing company. After his employer refused to sell the division, he resigned and started his own competing publication business. He then obtained the employer's subscriber list from a former coworker and used it to solicit customers of his former employer to his new business.

§ 7.3   DUTY OF LOYALTY VS. DUTY TO MAINTAIN CONFIDENTIALITY

In many respects, the employment relationship is a special relationship under the law with a number of statutory and implied obligations being imposed upon both the employer and the employee. *See, e.g.*, Mark A. Rothstein et al., *Employment Law* 3–4 (4th ed. 2010). As was noted *supra* in § 4.6.4, one of the implied obligations that is generally imposed on employees is a duty of confidentiality with respect to employer-owned trade secrets. Employees are also often subject to either an implied or statutory duty of loyalty. *See* Brian S. Malsberger, *Employee Duty of Loyalty: A State-by-State Survey* (4th ed. 2009 & Supp. 2010).

An issue that frequently arises with respect to both the duty of confidentiality and the duty of loyalty concerns the precise definition and scope of those duties. Understandably, employers assert that the duties of confidentiality and loyalty should be interpreted broadly to prohibit employees from disclosing and using a wide variety of business information. Employers also argue that the duties of confidentiality and loyalty should be interpreted to limit the ability of employees to go to work for a competitor and solicit former clients. As we have seen elsewhere, however (for instance in the discussion of general skill and knowledge *supra* § 2.8.5), there are important public policy reasons why courts are reluctant to restrict the activities of employees too much.

In practice, how the duties of confidentiality and loyalty are defined in a given case will depend on the facts of the case and the applicable state law. Some states, most notably California, are much more solicitous of the rights of employees than others, and thus, are more apt to use public policy arguments to limit restrictions on employee mobility. *See, e.g., Metro Traffic Control, Inc. v. Shadow Traffic Network*, 22 Cal. App. 4th 853, 859–60 (Cal. Ct. App. 1994). Other states, while cognizant of the public policy issues, are more receptive to employer claims, particularly if the subject employee entered into a written confidentiality or non-compete agreement with his employer. *See, e.g., National Reprographics, Inc. v. Strom*, 621 F. Supp. 2d 204, 229 (D. N.J. 2009).

Employers who wish to strengthen their position with respect to current and former employees often attempt to do so contractually through the use of one or more agreements, including a confidentiality or non-disclosure agreement, a non-solicitation agreement, and a non-compete agreement. However, because these agreements create a policy tension between the employer's freedom to contract and the employee's freedom to seek new employment, courts will scrutinize their reasonableness in deciding whether to enforce them. Indeed, in some states, statutes have been adopted which dictate such scrutiny.

No provision of the UTSA defines a duty of confidence. The *Restatement (Third) of Unfair Competition* section 42, subparagraph (b), provides that an implied duty of confidentiality arises when the circumstances justify the conclusion that the person receiving the information knew or had reason to know that the disclosure was intended to be in confidence and the trade secret owner was reasonable in inferring that the recipient of the information consented to an obligation of confidentiality. This definition requires examination of: (1) the circumstances surrounding the disclosure; (2) the recipient's state of mind; and (3) the reasonableness of the trade secret owner's actions.

When discussing the existence of an implied duty of confidentiality, many cases do not carefully differentiate between information that would meet the definition of a trade secret and other proprietary and business information. Technically, however, the nature of the information does matter with respect to available causes of action and remedies. Thus, it is theoretically possible for someone to breach a duty of confidentiality but not be subjected to a successful claim for relief. This could happen where: (1) the information is not a trade secret, and therefore no trade secret claim could be brought successfully;

(2) the duty of confidentiality is not a contractual duty, so no breach of contract claim could be asserted successfully; and (3) where the particular jurisdiction interprets section 7 of the UTSA to preclude tort claims not based upon the misappropriation of a trade secret.

A large number of cases state that there is an implied duty of confidentiality between an employer and its employees. However, whether or not an employment relationship (like any relationship) gives rise to an implied-at-law duty of confidentiality depends upon a number of factors, including: (1) the nature of the employment relationship and the employee's duties; (2) the nature of the alleged trade secrets; (3) whether the employee charged with misappropriation was aware of the existence of trade secrets and of the employer's desire for confidentiality; and (4) who is deemed the owner of the trade secret. *See Zoecon Industries v. American Stockman Tag Co.*, 713 F.2d 1174, 1178 (5th Cir. 1983).

Admittedly, courts are more willing to find an implied duty of confidentiality in an employment relationship than other business relationships, particularly when there is evidence that an employee acted badly. However, defendants in trade secret cases should not concede this point and instead should argue that there was no duty of confidentiality under the circumstances or, if there was, that the duty was narrow.

§ 7.4   NON-DISCLOSURE AGREEMENTS

As discussed previously in Chapter 4, in the absence of a written confidentiality agreement, courts are left to interpret the facts surrounding a given relationship and may or may not find that an implied duty of confidentiality exists. Thus, as a condition of employment, many employees, especially higher level employees, are required to sign agreements acknowledging that the employment creates a relationship of confidence and trust with respect to confidential information.

In the employment context, confidentiality or non-disclosure agreements (NDAs) generally express in writing the common law obligation of an employee to maintain his employer's confidences. On a more practical level, they are helpful for: (1) delineating the confidentiality expectations between the employer and employee, particularly with respect to trade secrets; (2) showing that the employer takes trade secret protection seriously; and (3) demonstrating the employer's reasonable efforts to maintain the secrecy of its confidential information. Typically, particularly if the NDA is acquired at the time employment begins, employers do not need to provide additional consideration for NDAs and, unlike noncompetition agreements, employees should have little hesitation signing them unless the scope of the information to be protected is overly broad.

Confidential information may be broadly defined in NDAs (and other forms of confidentiality agreements) to include all kinds of information such as, processes, formulae, data and know-how, discoveries, developments, designs, improvements, inventions, marketing plans, forecasts, new products, software, budgets, costs, and customer and supplier lists. However, a confidentiality agreement cannot transform information that does not otherwise meet the legal definition of a trade secret into a trade secret. This raises the practical issue whether broadly worded confidentiality agreements can be enforced to protect the non-trade secret information of an employer. Employees who are concerned about the overbreadth of a NDA should attempt to limit the subject information to trade secrets or other information that is not generally known or readily ascertainable.

In a typical NDA, an employee acknowledges that the confidential information (as defined in the agreement) is the sole property of the employer. The employee also promises that during and after her employment she will not disclose the information to anyone outside the company or use it for her own benefit or for the benefit of others without the company's prior written permission. In well-written NDAs, the employee will further promise to return to the company all documents or other materials relating to her work upon termination of the employment relationship.

§ 7.5   NON-COMPETITION AGREEMENTS

When employers wish to restrict employees from working for competitors they should enter into written restrictive covenants (often labeled "Noncompetition Agreement" or "Noncompete Agreement") that are designed to protect their legitimate business interests. By entering into a noncompetition agreement, the employee usually agrees that for a specified period of time after the end of his employment he will not work for any company that is a competitor of the employer.

Noncompetition agreements (or clauses) are generally more controversial than confidentiality agreements because they interfere more directly with employee mobility. There is an obvious tension between competing policies: the employer's freedom to contract to avoid the challenge and uncertainty of litigation versus society's interest in an individual's freedom to seek new employment. Because of this tension, states vary on the enforceability of noncompetition agreements.

Many states recognize and enforce noncompetition agreements as long as the restrictions are reasonable in view of the totality of the circumstances, including the scope of geographical, temporal, and competitive activity restrictions. *See Campbell Soup Co. v. Desatnick*, 58 F. Supp. 2d 477, 489 (D. N.J. 1999). Even in these jurisdictions, however, courts often will take into consideration the financial hardship to the employee if the noncompetition agreement is enforced. Some states will recognize and enforce noncompetition agreements under narrow and specified circumstances, with the presumption being against enforceability. *See Paramount Termite Control Co., Inc. v. Rector*, 380 S.E.2d 922, 924 (Va. 1989). California is notable for declaring noncompetition agreements void and unenforceable except in very limited situations. *See* Calif. Bus. & Prof. Code

§ 16600; *Edwards v. Arthur Anderson, LLP*, 44 Cal. 4th 937 (Cal. Sup. Ct. 2008).

While states differ in how they approach the enforceablility of noncompetition agreements, some general rules apply. First, while noncompetition agreements are disfavored because of their anti-competitive effect, when they are designed to protect some legitimate interest (such as a trade secret or good will) they will be enforced if "reasonable." Specific questions most often addressed with respect to the reasonableness of the restrictions are: (1) the duration of the restrictions; (2) the geographic scope of the restrictions; (3) the nature of the interest to be protected; and (4) how quickly the trade secret may diminish (generally 1–2 years is the maximum courts will enforce). As for the territory covered, courts often examine the area in which the employee operated, which is likely to be the area in which the employee would have some opportunity to affect the employer's goodwill.

Second, when a noncompetition agreement appears overbroad but the transaction is not otherwise tainted with unfairness, some courts will modify the restrictions to make them reasonable. *See, e.g., Proudfoot Consulting Co. v. Gordon*, 576 F.3d 1223, 1231 (11th Cir. 2009); *Simpson v. C & R Supply, Inc.*, 598 N.W.2d 914, 920 (S.D. 1999). This is often referred to as "blue-penciling." In jurisdictions that follow this practice, courts will strike and replace provisions of the agreement deemed to be unreasonable, but they will not add terms and conditions that were not originally part of the parties' agreement. *See Williston on Contracts*, § 13:25 (2012).

Third, noncompetition agreements require consideration for the employee's promise. If signed at the beginning of the relationship, the employment itself provides the consideration. If signed after the employee begins work, it might be okay if it was understood from the beginning that such an agreement would be a condition of the job. Some courts have held, however, that mere continuation of at-will employment is not enough consideration for a noncompetition agreement signed during the term of employment. *See Guercio v. Production Automation Corp.*, 664 N.W.2d 379, 386–87 (Minn. Ct. App. 2003). Thus, the employer would need to provide fresh consideration such as a salary increase.

Fourth, when the employer changes through merger or acquisition, the existing non-competition agreement might not continue without the employee's consent, unless there was an assignment clause in the agreement. *See OfficeMax Inc. v. County Qwick Print, Inc.*, 709 F. Supp. 2d 100, 110 (D. Me. 2010). Some courts have held that an assignment clause itself needs separate consideration, especially if the new employer inherited the noncompetition agreement from an asset purchase agreement rather than through a merger. *See Traffic Control Serv., Inc. v. United Rentals Northwest, Inc.*, 87 P.3d 1054, 1057 (Nev. 2004).

§ 7.6   NON-SOLICITATION AGREEMENTS

Non-solicitation agreements (or clauses) are another type of restrictive covenant. These are generally less controversial than noncompetition agreements because they do not preclude competition but simply limit the customers that can be solicited by a former employee. *See Digitel Corp. v. Deltacom, Inc.*, 953 F. Supp. 1486, 1495 (M.D. Ala. 1996). However, courts often draw a distinction between solicitation of customers, which directly affects a company's legitimate interest in its good will, and solicitation of employees (offering less protection). In some cases, the fact finder needs to dig into the circumstances to determine whether a former employee was merely announcing a job change to the former employer's customers or actively soliciting them. *See, e.g., USI Ins. Services v. Miner*, 801 F.Supp.2d 175, 191–92 (S.D. N.Y. 2011).

§ 7.7   THE INEVITABLE DISCLOSURE DOCTRINE

The inevitable disclosure doctrine allows a court to enjoin an employee from working for a company where that employment will result in the disclosure of a former employer's trade secret information. *See PepsiCo, Inc. v. Redmond*, 54 F.3d 1262 (7th Cir. 1995), discussed *infra*. When it is applied, it provides a powerful weapon under trade secret law because it permits an employer to do that which it would not otherwise be entitled to do under the auspices of employment law: restrict an employee without a noncompetition agreement. Indeed, it appears to go against the at-will doctrine, an important tenet of employment law. The employment at-will doctrine provides that without an agreement to the contrary an employee may leave his or her employer at any time, or for any reason. *See, e.g., McCrady v. Oklahoma Dept. of Public Safety*, 122 P.3d 473, 474–

75 (Okla. 2005). Similarly, an employer may terminate an employee at any time, for any reason.

The inevitable disclosure doctrine is one of the most controversial areas of trade secret law. Although the doctrine can be used in cases where a noncompetition agreement was executed, its use in these cases is not as controversial as in cases where the employer did not obtain an explicit noncompetition agreement from the employee. In those cases, application of the doctrine amounts to an implied restriction on competition and gives rise to a policy tension between the employee's right to move freely and pursue his or her livelihood and the employer's right to protect its trade secrets.

Because of the social importance of employee mobility, courts tend to approach inevitable disclosure cases with great care. Thus, application of the doctrine, and its acceptance by states, is mired in variations and inconsistencies. Whether or not a particular court will accept the inevitable disclosure doctrine is often tied to the state's policies regarding noncompetition agreements. Many states have applied the doctrine, others recognize it in only very limited circumstances, and some (like California) have rejected it outright. *See Whyte v. Schlage Lock Co.*, 101 Cal. App. 4th 1443 (Cal. Ct. App. 2002) ("The chief ill in the covenant not to compete imposed by the inevitable disclosure doctrine is its after-the-fact nature . . . .").

In *PepsiCo, Inc. v. Redmond,* the Seventh Circuit affirmed a district court's grant of a preliminary injunction enjoining William Redmond, Jr., a former employee of PepsiCo, from divulging trade secrets in his new job with a competitor, Quaker, and temporarily preventing him from assuming his duties with Quaker. Because his new position at Quaker was so closely related to his former position at PepsiCo, the court reasoned that "unless Redmond possessed an uncanny ability to compartmentalize information, he would necessarily be making decisions about Gatorade and Snapple by relying on his knowledge of [PepsiCo's] trade secrets." The court rejected Quaker's argument that the information would be useless to it, and found that "Quaker, unfairly armed with PepsiCo's plans, would be able to anticipate its distribution, packaging, pricing and marketing moves . . . ." *PepsiCo, Inc.,* 54 F.3d at 1269–70.

In jurisdictions that accept the inevitable disclosure doctrine, plaintiffs often try to map the narratives and legal arguments of their case as close to *PepsiCo* as possible in order to increase the likelihood of prevailing. The critical facts of the case being: (1) the intense competition between Redmond's former and new employer; (2) the closeness of Redmond's old and new job responsibilities; (3) the high-level position of Redmond; and (4) the time-sensitive nature and competitive value of the alleged trade secrets.

Fortunately for plaintiffs, the inevitable disclosure doctrine need not be utilized in all cases. Typically, it is used as a form of circumstantial evidence to prove the threatened misappropriation that is necessary for the issuance of an injunction. Where there is direct or other circumstantial evidence of threatened misappropriation, or evidence of actual misappropriation, the plaintiff in a trade secret case need not argue that the threatened use or disclosure of the information is "inevitable."

§ 7.8 OWNERSHIP ISSUES AND INVENTION ASSIGNMENT AGREEMENTS

The UTSA and the *Restatement of Torts* do not directly address the question of trade secret ownership. This is due to the fact that most trade secret cases involve the transfer of information from the putative trade secret owner (like the company-employer) to another (like a company-employee). Sometimes, however, the person who is being accused of trade secret misappropriation claims to be the one who actually created the trade secret (e.g., an employee of the company asserting the trade secret rights).

In the absence of an express "Invention Assignment Agreement" or similar agreement, the issue of trade secret ownership is generally resolved by application of common law principles, many of which were developed with respect to disputes concerning patent ownership. *See Banks v. Unisys Corp.*, 228 F.3d 1357, 1359 (Fed. Cir. 2000). As such, the case law and statutes of individual states should be consulted to determine the rules regarding trade secret ownership in each state. In most states, the general rule is that the inventor/creator owns the trade secrets. However, there are three important and well-established exceptions. *See* Restatement (Third) of Unfair Competition § 42, cmt. e (1995); Restatement (Second) of Agency § 397, cmts. a and g (1958).

The first exception to the general rule of inventor/creator ownership involves contract law. Savvy employers who engage in research and development efforts will require their employees to execute "Invention Assignment Agreements," transferring all rights and ownership in employee inventions to the employer. These agreements are generally enforceable if they are reasonable. Some states, like California, have specific statutes that define the acceptable parameters of such agreements. *See* Calif. Labor Code §§ 2870–2872.

Second, whether the employer owns an employee's invention depends primarily on whether inventing is part of the employee's job. This is often phrased as whether she was "hired to invent." If an invention results from work done by the employee within the scope of her assigned duties, then the employer owns it. *See United States v. Dubilier Condenser Corp.*, 289 U.S. 178 (1933). The *Restatement of Unfair Competition* § 42, cmt. e indicates that this rule applies even when the end result is the product of the employee's skill and knowledge.

The hired to invent concept, while similar to the "within the scope of employment" concept of *respondeat superior*, is not usually as broad. Thus, an employee may be working within her scope of employment but not be hired to invent. Also, an employee may be hired to invent one type of invention, but actually invent another type of invention.

Based upon the foregoing, if an employee is not hired to invent and the invention did not result from the employee's assigned work, then the employee owns the invention. If, however, the employer's trade secrets were used without authorization in creating the invention, then the employee may be liable to the employer for misappropriation.

A third exception to the general rule provides that if the invention was created using resources of the employer, then the employer may have a "shop right" in the invention. A shop right is an equitable doctrine meant to enforce an implied agreement that the employer can use an invention, or can receive fair compensation for its contribution to the invention. *See United States v. Dubilier Condenser Corp.*, 289 U.S. at 188–89. Generally, such rights are not transferrable. (This rule applies to independent contractors as well).

§ 7.9   THE THREAT FROM TECHNOLOGY

The wide use of computer technology in the workplace poses a grave threat to employers' trade secrets because the trade secrets can be easily and quickly taken and disseminated to others. Accordingly, the opportunity created by computers combined with the motivation to be unfaithful to an employer has led to the prevalence of employees using technology to misappropriate trade secrets. A sampling of cases show how e-mail, laptops, zip drives, and flash drives, can be hazards to trade secrets, even by those without high-tech training.

It has become a familiar story that employees download, with little effort, large amounts of a company's electronically stored trade secrets onto CDs or flash drives. For instance, in *LeJeune v. Coin Ac-*

ceptors, Inc., 849 A.2d 451, 455–56 (Md. 2004), an employee who worked from his home and regularly received company documents gained employment with a primary competitor. Prior to his departure, he transferred digital copies of sensitive information, including budgeting software and pricing information, from his company laptop to a CD. He then erased the information to hide the downloading activity before he returned the company laptop. In *DuCom v. State*, 654 S.E.2d 670, 672 (Ga. Ct. App. 2007), an employee planned to start her own business after she left her employer. On the day she resigned, she "copied a 'massive' amount of information" from her employer's hard drive onto a disk, including computer software programs and the entire associated business database.

With the advent of the Internet, e-mail systems, and cloud computing services, employees do not even have to go to the time, trouble, and expense of downloading trade secrets onto a tangible storage device. They can simply e-mail trade secrets to themselves and to competitors. In one case, *MicroStrategy, Inc. v. Business Objects, S.A.*, 331 F. Supp. 2d 396, 404 (E.D. Va. 2004), several employees e-mailed their employer's trade secrets to a competitor for whom they wished to work.

Sometimes the very employees trusted with overseeing and implementing the company's technology and security can use their knowledge and access to misappropriate their employer's trade secrets. Employees within information technology departments, for example, have been known to sell their employer's trade secrets to competitors. Those in high-level managerial positions may also try to recruit other key employees, who also had access to trade secrets, to leave and join a competitor. However, such conduct could be a breach of loyalty to the former employer. In *Augat, Inc. v. Aegis, Inc.*, 409 Mass. 165 (1991), a managerial employee secretly solicited and successfully convinced several other senior managers to join a competing start-up. The court held that the former employee breached his duty of loyalty by not protecting his employer's interests against the loss of key employees.

The above illustrates the premise that the biggest threat to a company's trade secrets is from its own employees. Many employees have legal access to trade secret information by virtue of their employment status and can take advantage of that access to misappropriate trade secrets. The motivation to do so need not be a desire to start a competitive business, but can be the act of a disgruntled current or former employee who wants a measure of revenge against his former employer. Thus, a corporate security program cannot overlook the threat posed by employees. *See infra* § 7.10. Granted, it is often a delicate balance to view employees both as valued members of the corporate family and as threats to the company's trade secrets. However, in addition to the high risks associated with blind trust, arguably the employer would not be taking "reasonable steps" to protect its trade secrets if the employee threat is ignored or not effectively addressed.

§ 7.10   PLANNING TO PROTECT TRADE SECRETS

We learned in § 3.4 that a company's reasonable efforts to protect trade secrets are critical. Ideally, no company wants to be in the position of having to prove that it engaged in reasonable efforts because it would mean that the company is in litigation and that its trade secrets may already have been misappropriated. However, the safest and most conservative approach for any company that owns trade secrets is to be prepared for the day when it may have to prove its efforts to a court. This means that trade secret protection should not be an afterthought. Instead, the protection of trade secrets requires a conscious risk assessment approach that anticipates and ultimately stems the inappropriate dissemination or disclosure of trade secrets.

As you have seen from the examples earlier in this chapter, the widespread availability and use of computers together with an apparent decline in employee loyalty provides fertile ground for the dissemination of trade secrets. Losses due to theft of proprietary information can potentially cost companies millions of dollars annually, but the non-financial costs are more significant and harder to quantify. The misappropriation of a trade secret is particularly devastating when it results in public disclosure because a trade secret, once lost, is lost forever.

§ 7.10.1   VIGILANCE IS REQUIRED

The lesson for trade secret owners is that they must be vigilant and proactive in maintaining and protecting their trade secrets. Not only should companies be mindful of protecting trade secrets against internal and external threats, they should also be cautious about circumstances when they share their trade secrets with outside parties.

Vigilance is an ongoing process that requires comprehensive security measures. Employers should consider establishing and implementing trade secret protection programs tailored to their specific needs. The first part of any such program is to identify the specific information considered to be trade secrets. It is important that companies do not take the position that every bit of information that they utilize in their business is a trade secret because such a claim is untrue and, more importantly, it fails to put employees on notice of the actual information that can qualify for trade secret protection. Moreover, courts are reluctant to sanction the overbroad assertion of trade secret rights when to do so would limit the mobility of employees.

The second component of a reasonable trade secret protection program requires efforts that are designed to secure the secrecy of trade secret information. It is within this component that the threats posed by employees should be identified and addressed. *See* Elizabeth A. Rowe, *A Sociological Approach to Misappropriation*, 58 Kansas L. Rev. 1 (2009). The options available to employers are varied and will depend on the organization and the nature and form of its trade secrets. For instance, the strategies that are used to maintain the secrecy of a recipe that only needs to be known by a few people will be different from those that should be used to protect computer code that is embedded in mass-distributed software.

§ 7.10.2 TECHNOLOGY ALONE MAY BE INSUFFICIENT

The use of technological tools will be an important component of any security plan to protect trade secrets. However, such tools alone, divorced from consideration of human behavior, are not sufficient. While the use of firewalls, passwords and encryption are widely used to protect data that is stored on computers, reliance on these tools alone is not optimal. Among other reasons, technological tools tend to be reactive and are not capable of the intelligence and risk assessments that could avoid inappropriate access to trade secret information in the first instance. The question is not simply whether a company has used technology to secure its information, it is whether a company has used tools (both technological and non-technological) that address the actual risks that are posed to its trade secrets.

Beyond careless or accidental disclosures, companies need to protect against those who maliciously or intentionally set out to acquire trade secrets. These include, but are not limited to, hackers and crackers who often outsmart the technological barriers because their motivation is so strong or because they enjoy a challenge. (Chapter 10, *infra*, discusses possible criminal remedies for such intrusions, but these are after-the-fact and cannot replace before-hand protective measures). Companies must be mindful of the interaction and influence of human behavior in a comprehensive data protection scheme. They should identify sensitive data, monitor where it goes, audit who has access to it, and restrict access in order to better assess risks.

Planning for trade secret security must be done in a proactive rather than a reactive framework. The trade secret owner needs an infrastructure in place to protect its secrets; one that includes specific processes and technological measures. Conducting a risk analysis of potential threats to the company's trade secrets should be comprehensive, paying attention to people, processes, and technology.

§ 7.10.3 PRACTICAL MEASURES TO CONSIDER

There is no one-size-fits-all trade secret protection program. Each organization must decide what measures are the best fit for its culture, business needs, and the nature of the trade secrets to be protected. Ultimately, as a practical matter, which strategies a company chooses to employ will depend on how important the secrets are to the organization and how expensive it is to institute the recommended security measures.

While certainly not exhaustive, the list below identifies some of the typical safeguards that many companies consider.

a) Restricting access to buildings and areas that contain trade secret information. These restrictions should apply to employees and visitors.

b) Securing spaces where trade secrets are used, developed, or exposed with locks, guards, surveillance cameras, or intrusion detection devices.

c) Segmenting trade secrets so that those with access, including employees or subcontractors, only have part of the trade secret necessary to their task, rather than access to its entirety.

d) Labeling confidential materials and posting visible warnings.

e) Requiring secure technological measures such as passwords, encryption, and firewalls, for electronically-stored trade secret information.

f) Auditing trade secrets and access to them and designating persons who are responsible for the overall maintenance of trade secret protection programs.

g) Notifying and reminding employees of the importance of protecting company confidential and trade secret information. This may be done through entrance and exit interviews, and well as through periodic meetings and written notices.

h) Requiring employees, and all others who have access to company trade secrets, to sign confidentiality and non-disclosure agreements.

i) Instituting policies to govern employees who work at home or outside of the office, particularly with respect to their use of the

Internet and technological devices while commuting or traveling.

j) Requiring third-parties and consultants who have access to trade secrets to sign non-disclosure agreements and to observe appropriate safeguards while using trade secrets.

§ 7.10.4 RELATIONSHIP TO DATA SECURITY GENERALLY

Too often, companies do not proactively track, monitor, and protect their trade secrets until there has been a misappropriation incident, and at that point it may be too late. Thus, the challenge of protecting trade secrets should be reviewed as part of the larger issue of data security generally, where preventing the loss of sensitive data is of critical importance. There are many parallels in the evolution and modern approach to data security that can be instructive to trade secret protection and management. Since many companies conduct enterprise risk assessments of their security strategy, trade secrets ought to be included as part of their security risk assessments. Trade secrets should be treated as a subset of the sensitive commercial data that must be protected, in addition to the private consumer information, and thus should not be left out of risk assessments.

The use of technological tools such as firewalls, user monitoring, and encryption are now more widely used to protect data. Having these tools already in place and available in the workplace means that they could be implemented in a program to secure trade secrets without too much difficulty. However, reliance on the tools alone is not optimal, as technological tools tend to be reactive and are not capable of the intelligence and risk assessments that could avoid inappropriate access to trade secrets in the first instance. It is also important to consider the people and processes that may affect trade secret protection. *See supra* § 7.10.2.

Because the most likely culprit in a data security incident is not a hacker, but an employee, reasonable efforts to protect trade secrets requires a comprehensive approach that takes into consideration a trade secret owner's measures to protect its secrets against outside threats, as well as the often overlooked inside threats from employees. Accordingly, the use of traditional security measures, which are generally facilities-based approaches, are likely to be insufficient when used in isolation.

While it is recommended that trade secret protection be made a part of data security procedures generally, a trade secret owner's compliance with applicable data security laws and norms will not necessarily satisfy the reasonable efforts requirement of trade secret law. In some cases, such efforts may be deemed to be reasonable because such a conclusion depends upon what is reasonable "under the circumstances." Conversely, evidence that a trade secret owner's efforts to protect its data do not meet the requirements of data security laws or industry norms may be used as evidence of a lack of reasonable efforts.

CHAPTER 8

PROTECTING TRADE SECRETS IN THE GOVERNMENTAL CONTEXT

§ 8.1 INTRODUCTION

There are a number of ways that trade secret issues arise in the governmental context. The first involves the sharing of trade secrets or other information with the government because of regulatory oversight. *See infra* § 8.2. This includes, for instance, the voluntary inclusion of potential trade secrets in patent applications. *See infra* § 8.3. Sometimes, however, companies are reluctant or refuse to share trade secrets and other confidential information with governmental officials and this raises a host of public-policy concerns. *See infra* § 8.4.

A second set of issues involve the Freedom of Information Act (FOIA) (and equivalent state laws) and the risks that governmental officials' compliance with such open-government laws pose to trade secrets and other data that are submitted to the government. *See infra* §§ 8.5–8.7. Related to this issue are federal and state laws which prohibit government employees from disclosing confidential information and the Constitutional prohibition on the taking of private property without just compensation. *See infra* §§ 8.8 and 8.9.

Finally, there are issues having to do with government claims of trade secret ownership. *See infra* § 8.10. Although it may seem incongruous for governmental entities to own trade secrets, in certain situations they will assert such rights. This is particularly true where the governmental entity is engaged in commerce. There is nothing in the UTSA or at common law that prevents governments from owning trade secrets provided that the requirements for protection are met.

§ 8.2   PROTECTING TRADE SECRETS IN DEALINGS WITH THE GOVERNMENT

Federal and state governments collect and store large amounts of commercially useful data from businesses. While some of this information is self-generated, some of it is obtained from individuals and companies. This might happen, for instance, where a company submits a bid for a government contract or where an individual files his tax return. It can also occur in industries that are regulated by state or federal authorities, such as the banking and aviation industries.

To the extent companies are required to disclose their trade secrets to the government, they should be concerned whether and how those trade secrets will be protected. *See* Elizabeth A. Rowe, *Striking a Balance: When Should Trade-Secret Law Shield Disclosures to the Government?*, 96 Iowa L. Rev. 791 (2011). Although a company may choose not to do business with the government, it cannot choose to avoid applicable regulations. This creates a tension between trade secret rights and the many public interests served by a regulated society. *See* David S. Levine, *Secrecy and Unaccountability: Trade Secrets in our Public Infrastructure*, 59 Florida L. Rev. 135 (2007).

Generally, the ability of a trade secret owner to maintain the secrecy of information that is submitted to a governmental entity depends upon the laws and regulations of that governmental entity. The presumptive rule, as expressed in state and federal freedom of information acts (discussed *infra*), is that information in the hands of the government is open to public disclosure. Where exceptions to this rule exist under applicable law or regulations, the information owner is typically required to label the information that it claims to be trade secret or proprietary information.

The regulations of the Securities and Exchange Commission provide an illustration. They provide for nondisclosure of confidential business information. However, no specific definition of "trade secret" or "confidential information" appears to be included in the SEC regulations, even though mention is made of trade secrets in a few areas. Rather, the regulations appear to incorporate FOIA and a catch-all of "other reason[s] permitted by Federal law," which would encapsulate trade secrets. Nevertheless, the fact that confidential business information comprises a broader group of information of which trade secrets are a subset leaves no doubt that the rules would cover trade secrets.

For the SEC to treat information as confidential, the submitter must omit from the material filed that portion that it wishes to remain confidential and must mark the omitted material as "confidential material" before filing it with the SEC. However, a determination on whether the material will indeed be treated as confidential is not made until a

FOIA request has been received by a member of the public for the materials. The regulation lists nine factors that one requesting confidential treatment may address to substantiate the request. *See* 17 C.F.R. § 200.83(d)(2) (2010). Among them are the "measures taken by the business to protect the confidentiality" of the materials and the "ease or difficulty of a competitor's obtaining or compiling" the information.

It is critical to remember that each agency has its own regulations and practices governing the protection of confidential or trade secret information and there can be wide variations between and among them. Accordingly, the relevant regulations for each applicable agency should be consulted to determine when and how trade secrets can be protected. At a minimum, individuals and companies that do business with the government or that operate in regulated industries are well-advised to carefully identify and properly mark all submitted information that they wish to protect from public disclosure.

Because the categories of information that may be exempt from government disclosure (discussed *infra*) are different and arguably broader than the definition of a trade secret under the UTSA, the information that a company wishes to protect may include confidential and proprietary information that would not otherwise qualify for trade secret protection. Where special data exclusivity laws apply, it may also include wide-swaths of submitted data, such as the data that must accompany applications for Food and Drug Administration approval of new drugs. *See, e.g.,* 21 U.S.C. § 355 (2006). *See also, e.g.,*

AstraZeneca Pharmaceuticals, LP v. Food & Drug Admin., 872 F. Supp. 2d 60 (D. D.C. 2012) (finding no market exclusivity for certain safety information related to the drug Seroquel).

§ 8.3   TRADE SECRETS IN PATENT APPLICATIONS

As discussed earlier, when an issued patent (or patent application) is published by the United States Patent and Trademark Office (the USPTO), any trade secrets disclosed in the patent are lost. *See supra* § 2.8.3. This can be a potential trap for a trade secret holder who has filed a patent application but does not receive the patent. That is because, even if a patent is not ultimately issued, publication of a patent application that contains a trade secret will also destroy trade secrecy status.

According to applicable law, patent applications in the United States are published eighteen months after they are filed. 35 U.S.C. § 122 (2006). Therefore, even if a patent is not ultimately granted, the contents of the patent application become public knowledge when the patent application is published in the *Official Gazette*. While there are some limited exemptions to publication, most U.S. patent applications filed by large entities are published. To the extent those applications disclose information that is not protected by an issued patent, others are entitled to use the information without liability. *See Bondpro Corp. v. Siemens Power Generation, Inc.*, 463 F.3d 702, 706–07 (7th Cir. 2006).

Prior to the prescribed time for publication, pending applications remain confidential, 37 C.F. R. § 1.14, preserving whatever trade secrecy exists in the information that is contained in the application. If the patent applicant chooses to abandon the application before 18 months from filing, it may maintain that protected status. However, once published, even rejected applications will result in the loss of any trade secrets contained in the application.

§ 8.4   THE PUBLIC POLICY OF GOVERNMENT OPENNESS

There is a general public policy that the public has a "right to know" about the dealings of the government; indeed, the functioning of democracy depends upon it. While, there has been a move by the Obama Administration to have agencies move toward a policy of greater disclosure to the public, many agency regulations appear to be based on a culture of keeping company-submitted information secret. At the Food and Drug Administration, for instance, questions have arisen about the propriety of keeping information about FDA decisions and data about drugs and devices under study confidential. Similarly, at the Environmental Protection Agency, the Toxic Substances Control Act exempts trade secrets from the information that manufacturers are required to report to the federal government about new chemicals that they intend to market.

To the extent secrecy provisions in agency regulations make it difficult to control potential dangers or for consumers to have information about potential health and safety risks, the public appeal against secrecy is understandable. Moreover, the public interest in the details of government is particularly strong when the activities of the government involve important Constitutional values such as the right to vote or freedom of speech and the press. Activities that may harm the environment are also of great public concern. The need to ensure the integrity and quality of important data and processes that support these values weigh in favor of the public interest in disclosure and transparency.

While the default policy position may be that the public has a right to obtain information from the government unless the information is specially exempted from disclosure, in practice, trade secret protection has often trumped public access and transparency, especially when they involve contracts between the government and a private entity. For example, the private companies that provide electronic voting machines to states have refused to permit or have restricted access to the internal mechanisms by which the machines work. *See, e.g.*, *Diebold Election Sys., Inc. v. N.C. State Bd. of Elections*, No. 05–CVS–15474 (N.C. Super. Ct. Nov. 16, 2005). (*See infra* § 8.10 for a discussion of government owned trade secrets.)

§ 8.5   THE FREEDOM OF INFORMATION ACT

With the foregoing public policy in mind, it is not surprising that about the same time that the Civil Rights Act of 1964 was adopted, efforts were underway to improve government openness through the enactment of the Freedom of Information Act of 1966 (FOIA), 5 U.S.C. § 552 (2009). In the advent of the Watergate scandal in the early 1970s, there were calls for even more openness in government and the Privacy Act of 1974 was enacted to strengthen and expand FOIA. 5 U.S.C. § 552a (2010). Similar state laws also exist. *See, e.g.*, Conn. Gen. Stat. Ann. § 1–210(5) (West 2011); W. Va. Code Ann. § 29B–1–4 (West 2012); Mich. Comp. Laws. Ann. 15.243 (West 2012); S.C. Code Ann. § 30–4–40 (West 2012).

Under FOIA, anyone may request copies of documents that form the records of agencies of the Executive Branch. One does not need to show standing, legitimate interest, or any other threshold requirement to be entitled to the information. *See Wearly v. FTC*, 462 F. Supp. 589, 600 (D. N.J. 1978), *vacated on other grounds*, 616 F.2d 662 (3d. Cir. 1980). Many FOIA requests are filed by members of the media, but they are also used by businesses seeking information about competitors. Thus, to the extent that trade secret information is on file with governmental authorities, a FOIA request poses a considerable risk of loss to trade secret owners.

Pursuant to FOIA (and similar state laws), federal employees are required to disclose information in response to a request unless an applicable exemption applies. While the presumptive rule under FOIA favors the disclosure of information, FOIA contains a number of exemptions that government officials can invoke in appropriate circumstances to refuse to disclose information held by the federal government. *See* 5 U.S.C. § 552(b) (2009). Most litigation concerning FOIA focuses on the meaning and scope of these exemptions.

There are two exemptions that may implicate trade secret or other proprietary information submitted to the government by a company. Subsection 3 of 5 U.S.C. § 552(b)(3) ("Exemption 3"), exempts information that is "specifically exempted from disclosure by statute." It is questionable when and whether Exemption 3 applies to protect trade secrets, mostly because courts differ on whether there is a statute that specifically exempts trade secrets from disclosure within the meaning of Exemption 3. *Compare Westinghouse Elec. Corp. v. Schlesinger*, 542 F.2d 1190, 1199–203 (4th Cir. 1976) (finding the Trade Secrets Act to be an Exemption 3 withholding statute), abrogated by *Gen. Motors Corp. v. Marshall*, 654 F.2d 294 (4th Cir. 1981), *with Anderson v. Dep't of Health & Human Servs.*, 907 F.2d 936, 948–49 (10th Cir. 1990) (finding the Trade Secrets Act is not an Exemption 3 withholding statute), and *Gen. Elec. Co. v. U.S. Nuclear Regulatory Comm'n*, 750 F.2d 1394, 1401–02 (7th Cir. 1984).

Exemption 4 is the category most applicable and most often used in FOIA litigation to protect trade secrets and confidential information. Exemption 4 provides that "trade secrets and commercial or financial information obtained from a person and privileged or confidential" need not be disclosed. 5 U.S.C. § 552(b)(4) (2009). It is significant to note, however, that the Supreme Court has found these exemptions to be permissive, not mandatory. *See Chrysler Corp. v. Brown,* 441 U.S. 281, 292–94 (1979). Thus, while FOIA permits federal agencies

to withhold company records containing trade secrets, it does not require them to do so.

Because FOIA and the later Privacy Act of 1974
were both adopted before the UTSA, its language is
not based upon the UTSA's definition of a trade secret. In fact, Exemption 4 applies to a wider category of information beyond trade secrets because it
includes "commercial or financial information"
which is privileged or confidential. This would pre-
sumably include information that is confidential
and proprietary to a company, but that would not
meet the UTSA's definition of a trade secret.

Litigation that has addressed the scope and
meaning of Exemption 4 has held that information
submitted to the government is deemed confidential
when the "disclosure of that information could cause
substantial harm to the competitive position of the
person from whom the information was obtained."
Lion Raisins v. U.S. Dept. of Agric., 354 F.3d 1072,
1079 (9th Cir. 2004). With respect to the definition
of "trade secrets" in Exemption 4, the agencies and
courts typically look to the Trade Secrets Act (a federal criminal law applicable to federal employees),
rather than the UTSA, for guidance. *See* 18 U.S.C
§ 1905 (2008); Dep't of Justice, Freedom of Information Act Guide, 2009 WL 8545461 (D.O.J.)
(2009).

To a great extent, companies and individuals who
submit trade secrets to the government must rely
upon government officials to protect their interests
by invoking a FOIA exemption. Often, FOIA laws do
not require governmental agencies that receive

FOIA requests to notify the provider of the information that a request has been made (*but see* discussion of Executive Order 12,600, *infra* § 8.6). However, particularly when there is doubt about the applicability of an exemption, the agencies, pursuant to their own regulations, may notify a trade secret owner of a pending request. When this happens, trade secret owners may wish to file an action to block the disclosure or otherwise intervene in the FOIA proceedings.

When a submitter of trade secrets to an agency seeks to prevent the agency from disclosing the trade secrets to a third-party FOIA requester, the mechanism for doing so within the courts is known as a reverse-FOIA action. *See supra* § 8.6. The process of a reverse-FOIA action occurs in two major sequential stages. In the first stage the submitter objects to the prospective disclosure directly to the agency, and in the second stage the submitter can appeal an unfavorable determination by the agency in federal court.

While Exemption 4 is the category most applicable and most often used in FOIA litigation to protect trade secrets and confidential information, the FOIA exemptions do not apply to Congress. *See* 5 U.S.C. § 552(d) (2009) ("This section is not authority to withhold information from Congress."). Thus, if Congress obtains trade secret information, either directly or through a request to an agency, there is a risk that information could be leaked, thereby destroying the trade secret status of the information.

§ 8.6   REVERSE-FOIA ACTIONS

The procedural steps of the first stage of a reverse-FOIA action typically begin when a requester submits a request to an agency for agency records. If, after receiving and reviewing the FOIA request the agency determines that it may disclose the requested information, it must give notice to the submitter of the information pursuant to Executive Order 12,600. When the submitter receives notice that the agency has determined that the submitter's information must be disclosed under FOIA, the submitter may begin the first stage of a reverse-FOIA action by objecting to the disclosure to the agency. In situations involving potential disclosure of the submitter's trade secrets, the submitter will object to disclosure on grounds that the information falls within Exemption 4 of FOIA. If the agency agrees that the information requested falls within FOIA's Exemption 4, the agency must not disclose the information because it is barred from doing so. *See CNA Fin. Corp. v. Donovan*, 830 F.2d 1132, 1133 n.1 (D.C. Cir. 1987).

If the agency makes a final determination that the information does not fall within Exemption 4 and thus must be disclosed, the submitter may proceed to the second stage of a reverse-FOIA action by suing the agency in federal court under the Administrative Procedure Act (APA). 5 U.S.C. § 704 (2011). In reviewing agency action under the APA, the court will examine the record developed by the agency to determine whether the agency's actions were arbitrary and capricious. *See Mallinckrodt Inc. v. West*, 140 F. Supp. 2d 1, 4 (D.D.C. 2000).

A reviewing court must first establish that the threshold requirements of Exemption 4 are present by determining that the information was obtained from a person and that the information falls within the definition of information defined in Exemption 4. *See, e.g., Buffalo Evening News, Inc. v. Small Bus. Admin.*, 666 F. Supp. 467, 469 (W.D.N.Y. 1987); *Am. Airlines, Inc. v. Nat'l Mediation Bd.*, 588 F.2d 863, 870 (2d Cir. 1978). If these threshold requirements are met, the court must next determine whether the information was required or voluntarily submitted. *See Critical Mass Energy Project v. Nuclear Regulatory Comm'n*, 975 F.2d 871 (D.C. Cir. 1992) (en banc) (holding that voluntarily submitted information to the government will be treated as confidential if it is not ordinarily public).

The determination whether information was voluntarily submitted is the most important analytical step in a reverse-FOIA case. The required voluntary finding establishes which test will be applied for the finding of confidentiality under Exemption 4. *See Parker v. Bureau of Land Mgmt.*, 141 F. Supp. 2d 71, 77 (D.D.C. 2001). There are no clear rules for distinguishing what was voluntary from what was required. A court order to compel production would seem to fall under the "required" category. *See McDonnell Douglas Corp. v. EEOC*, 922 F. Supp. 235, 242 (E.D. Mo. 1996). However, submissions in response to an agency subpoena are not necessarily compulsory. Court enforcement of the subpoena, if granted, would make it required. Some regulations of some agencies define a voluntary submission.

If the court determines that the information was required, the court applies the *National Parks* analysis to determine whether the information is confidential. *See Nat. Parks & Conservation Ass'n v. Morton*, 498 F.2d 765 (D.C. Cir. 1974). This test provides that material is only protected by Exemption 4 from disclosure if either (1) disclosure would "impair the Government's ability to obtain necessary information in the future," or (2) disclosure would "cause substantial harm to the competitive position of the person from whom the information was obtained." *Id.* at 770.

If the court determines that the information was voluntarily submitted, then it applies the *Critical Mass* analysis to determine whether the information is confidential. *Critical Mass Energy Project v. Nuclear Regulatory Comm'n*, 975 F.2d 871 (D.C. Cir. 1992). This is an easier standard that calls for protection from disclosure under Exemption 4 as long as the information is (1) commercial or financial and (2) "not customarily [made] available to the public." *Id.* at 872. If the court determines that the information is confidential under *Critical Mass*, it does not disclose the information. *See McDonnell Douglas,* 922 F. Supp. at 241.

Note that neither test requires proof of trade secrecy. Confidentiality is enough. The *National Parks* test, however, has a substantial competitive-harm requirement, which has some semblance of a trade secret test. However, the precise contours of that test are not entirely clear, and a party opposing disclosure need not show actual competitive harm; instead, only a likelihood of such harm would be sufficient. *See Pub. Citizen Health Research Grp. v. Food & Drug Admin.*, 704 F.2d 1280, 1291 (D.C. Cir. 1983).

The voluntary vs. required test reflects certain policy choices and values that seek to balance the governmental interests with business' proprietary interests. When the government obtains information by force, it needs to ensure that the information is nonetheless reliable; when, however, the information is voluntarily provided, the government needs to ensure its continued availability. As the court noted in *Critical Mass*, "the disclosure of information the Government has secured from voluntary sources on a confidential basis will both jeopardize its continuing ability to secure such data on a cooperative basis and injure the provider's interest in preventing its unauthorized release." *Critical Mass Energy Project*, 975 F.2d at 879.

§ 8.7   PRODUCTION OF TRADE SECRETS IN NON-FOIA DISPUTES

This section addresses cases involving discovery-type disputes between the government and a company that arise outside of a FOIA request. These cases often occur in a regulatory context where a governmental entity seeks information from a business that it deems necessary for proper regulation.

Courts in these cases tend to focus more on relevance than on the trade secret status of the information sought and almost always rule in favor of disclosure. For example, in *Kleinerman v. United States Postal Service*, 100 F.R.D. 66 (D. Mass. 1983), the court granted a government contractor's motion to compel production of documents that included confidential technical reports and proposals. Without actually engaging in an analysis of whether these documents are trade secrets, the court collapsed the trade secret analysis into the determination of relevancy. Additionally, the court stated that the defendants had not provided adequate proof of harm from disclosure.

In another case where the government sought an order to allow it to inspect defendant's business premises, the court engaged in balancing between the government-plaintiff's need for information and the harms that could come from disclosure of defendant's trade secrets. *United States v. Nat'l Steel Corp.*, 26 F.R.D. 603 (S.D. Tex. 1960). The court allowed inspection of the process but did not analyze whether a trade secret existed. It was satisfied that the government's stipulation not to reveal the trade secrets was adequate protection.

Other cases recognize the importance of a threshold determination of trade secrecy in analyzing whether to permit disclosure. In *Chevron Chem. Co. v. Costle*, 443 F. Supp. 1024, 1032 (N.D. Cal. 1978), the plaintiff sued for declaratory and injunctive relief against the threatened disclosure of test data on fungicides and insecticides submitted to the EPA. Chevron claimed that the test data constituted trade secrets. In deciding to release the data, the EPA had not made a determination of whether the information qualified for trade secret protection. The court held that the EPA should have determined the trade secret status of the data and the agency's failure to do so was an arbitrary and capricious exercise of its judgment. Similarly, in *Mobay Chemical Corp. v. Costle*, the court remanded the case back to the EPA to determine whether the environmental safety data submitted by the plaintiff is a "trade secret" according to the *Restatement of Torts* definition. 447 F. Supp. 811, 835 (W.D. Mo. 1978).

§ 8.8   THE TRADE SECRETS ACT

The Freedom of Information Act governs situations where non-government individuals and companies request information from the government. The federal Trade Secrets Act is a criminal statute which sets forth the duties of government employees in the absence of a FOIA request. 18 U.S.C. § 1905 (2008). It prohibits the disclosure of certain confidential information by government employees. It was based on a predecessor statute that sought to protect citizens from "reckless or corrupt revenue agents." *See Chrysler Corp. v. Brown*, 441 U.S. 281, 296–97 (1979). It provides that:

> Whoever, being an officer or employee of the United States or of any department or agency thereof . . . publishes, divulges, discloses, or makes known in any manner or to any extent not authorized by law any information coming to him in the course of his employment or official duties or by reason of any examination or investigation made by, or return, report or record made to or filed with, such department or agency or officer or employee thereof, which information concerns or relates to the trade se-

crets, . . . shall be fined under this title, or imprisoned not more than one year, or both; and shall be removed from office or employment.

18 U.S.C. § 1905 (2008). The statute does not provide a private right of action. A claim under the Act could only be against an individual, and any fine may not exceed $1000. It therefore provides virtually no compensation to a company that may have suffered a multimillion dollar loss as a result of an inappropriate disclosure of trade secrets by government officials. Accordingly, the more feasible option for a company, with a better chance of damages, is a takings claim. *See infra* § 8.9.

§ 8.9   PRIVATE RECOURSE FOR GOVERNMENT DISCLOSURES

If a company submitted trade secret information to the government and that information was disclosed by the government to the public, it is the trade secret owner who ultimately bears the costs of the government's misguided actions. This is in part because when a trade secret is revealed, it loses all of its value, the loss is irreparable, and the company may not be made whole by monetary damages.

Generally, a trade secret owner cannot sue the government for the wrongful disclosure of its trade secrets unless applicable government tort liability rules allow it to do so. However, there may be a trade secret misappropriation claim against the requesting party, particularly if it used misrepresentations to obtain the information from the government. *See Hirel Connectors, Inc. v. United States,*

No. CV 01–11069 DSF (VBKx), 2004 WL 5639770, at * 22 (C.D. Cal. Jan. 23, 2004). Also, in the right case, an aggrieved trade secret owner may have a constitutional-takings claim against the government. *See Ruckelshaus v. Monsanto Co.*, 467 U.S. 986 (1984), discussed *infra*. There may also be a possible criminal action under the Trade Secrets Act against an individual government employee who disclosed the trade secrets. *See Acumenics Research & Tech. v. U.S. Dept. of Justice*, 843 F.2d 800, 806 (4th Cir. 1988) (*citing* 18 U.S.C.A. § 1905 (West 2008)).

In *Ruckelshaus v. Monsanto Co.*, the U.S. Supreme Court held that a federal pesticide statute constituted a taking of trade secrets in some circumstances when the EPA used studies submitted by one pesticide manufacturer in evaluating similar pesticides by the manufacturer's competitors. In the circumstances where it found a taking, the Court focused on statutory language that seemed to guarantee the manufacturer confidentiality for its trade secrets, noting that "[t]his explicit governmental guarantee formed the basis of a reasonable investment-backed expectation." For information submitted by Monsanto during another period, however, the Court found that the government had made no guarantee of confidentiality. Rather, Monsanto chose to enter a U.S. market "that long has been the focus of great public concern and significant government regulation," and should not have reasonably expected that the trade secrets would remain confidential. Accordingly, the Court ruled there was no taking with respect to that information.

Although often cited for the proposition that trade secrets are a form of property, *Monsanto* is a mixed bag for trade secret owners whose trade secrets have been inappropriately used or disclosed by the government. There is a real risk that when a company submits business information to an agency and it falls into the hands of a competitor, a court could find there was no promise of confidentiality, and thus no taking.

The states' power to compel disclosure of trade secret ingredients from a company was addressed in *Phillip Morris, Inc. v. Reilly*, 312 F.3d 24 (1st Cir. 2002). It contains a very thorough analysis of why the Takings Clause may prevent certain regulations. It also shows how the takings principles introduced in *Ruckelshaus* are often used by powerful interests to avoid disclosing information that is arguably needed to ensure public health and safety. Massachusetts required disclosure of all additives in cigarettes in order to publish them. Significantly, the required disclosures were not simply for regulatory purposes but were designed to provide information to consumers so they could make more informed choices about the cigarettes they purchase. Tobacco companies objected claiming that the disclosure would constitute an unconstitutional taking of trade secret information. The Commonwealth argued that it can require public disclosure of trade secrets to advance public health and safety, and that the tobacco companies have no property interest in their trade secrets.

§ 8.10   GOVERNMENT OWNERSHIP OF TRADE SECRETS

The government and public agencies are entitled to trade secret protection for information that they create in the much the same way as private entities are protected. The UTSA does not distinguish between public and private entities or for-profit and not-for-profit entities in trade secret ownership. The definition under the UTSA of "persons" who may have trade secrets includes the government. Unif. Trade Secrets Act § 1(3) (amended 1985), reprinted in Appendix A. Similarly, the *Restatement of Unfair Competition* also includes governments among the organizations that can own trade secrets. *See* Restatement (Third) of Unfair Competition § 39 cmt. d (1995).

The foregoing principle was recently upheld in a case involving various databases at the University of Connecticut. In *University of Connecticut v. Freedom of Information Commission,* 303 Conn. 724 (2012), Jonathan Pelto submitted a freedom-of-information request to the University of Connecticut seeking information from several of the university's databases. Among the information requested were names, addresses, telephone numbers, and email addresses from (1) the athletics department's database of season ticket purchasers, (2) the Center for Continuing Studies' database of people having an interest in its programs and course offerings, and (3) the university library's database of donors and friends.

The university refused to disclose the information claiming that they were trade secrets. The Connecticut Supreme Court agreed, finding that the Connecticut Trade Secrets Act expressly applies to both public and private entities, and that the status of the university as a public institution did not negate its ability to claim trade secret protection for information that it created and maintained as a trade secret. The fact that the university was not an entity engaged in trade was irrelevant.

CHAPTER 9

PROTECTING TRADE SECRETS INTERNATIONALLY

§ 9.1   INTRODUCTION

With the practice of outsourcing has come the need for U.S.-based and other companies to protect trade secrets throughout the world. Due to principles of national sovereignty and territoriality, whether this is possible ultimately depends upon the laws and enforcement mechanisms of the other countries. Fortunately, all members of the World Trade Organization (WTO) (now most countries of the world) are required to adopt laws to protect trade secrets (referred to internationally as "undisclosed information"). *See* Agreement on Trade-Related Aspects of Intellectual Property Rights, art. 39, Apr. 15, 1994, 1869 U.N.T.S. 299, 33 I.L.M. 1197 (hereinafter the TRIPS Agreement).

Whether trade secrets are protected to the same extent in other countries as they are in the United States is an open question. This is not necessarily because countries are not committed to protecting trade secrets, but may be due to the fact that other countries apply the applicable legal concepts differently. Additionally, other countries may not have the same enforcement procedures as the United States and may not have the resources that are needed to consider trade secret claims in a timely manner.

As a practical matter, U.S. companies are advised to think very carefully before disclosing or using their trade secrets in other countries. If they decide to do so, they should carefully identify and mark all of their trade secrets and obtain a written agreement of confidentiality from the person(s) to whom the information will be disclosed. This is particularly true in countries that require contracts as a predicate to trade secret misappropriation claims. In keeping with the reasonable efforts requirement of the UTSA, which is part of the TRIPS Agreement, they should also institute other security measures as appropriate.

§ 9.2   ARTICLE 39 OF THE TRIPS AGREEMENT

For the first time in a multi-national agreement, the obligation of countries to protect trade secrets is directly addressed in Article 39 of the TRIPS Agreement. Modeled after the UTSA, but not nearly as detailed, Article 39.2 requires countries to provide a means for natural and legal persons to prevent information from "being disclosed to, acquired by, or used by others without their consent in a manner contrary to honest commercial practices." In keeping with the UTSA, the information that must be protected must be secret, have commercial value because of its secrecy, and be subject to reasonable steps under the circumstances to keep it secret. Footnote 10 to Article 39 defines "a manner contrary to honest commercial practices" in much the same way that misappropriation is defined under the

UTSA, and specifically lists "breach of contract" as a form of dishonest commercial practices.

Significantly, and for political reasons having to do with the challenge of obtaining approval for Article 39, Article 39 does not contain all of the provisions of the UTSA. For instance, it does not contain the remedies provisions or, arguably, even a requirement that the protection for trade secrets be provided under the civil or tort laws of a country. Thus, it is up to each WTO-member country to determine how to protect trade secrets. The most that can be said about Article 39 is that it defines what a trade secret is and some acts of misappropriation. It also frames an act of trade secret misappropriation as an act of unfair competition. *See* TRIPS Agreement, art. 39.1.

Although Article 39 is criticized in some circles for extending IP protection too far, it is arguably subject to the same limits on trade secret protection that are part of the UTSA. *See* Sharon K. Sandeen, *The Limits of Trade Secret Law: Article 39 of the TRIPS Agreement and the Uniform Trade Secrets Act on which it is Based*, in The Law and Theory of Trade Secrecy 537 (Edward Elgar 2011). In particular, it is not designed to protect all business information; only trade secrets that meet the three requirements of Article 39.2. For this reason, among others, the laws of other countries may actually provide greater protection for proprietary business information than is available in the United States. Obviously, the laws of each country where a company intends to conduct business must be evaluated to determine if this is the case and what is required for such protection.

In order to comply with Article 39, many countries adopted trade-secret protection statutes, copies of which can be found through the WTO website. However, as noted in Article 39.1, the obligation of WTO-member countries to protect trade secrets is specifically tied to a pre- existing obligation under Article 10*bis* the Paris Convention that requires countries to "assure . . . effective protection against unfair competition." Thus, in some countries, particularly countries with a common law tradition (like the United Kingdom and India), trade secret law may be governed by general principles of unfair competition, much like the historic origins of trade secret law in the United States.

While the existence of Article 39.2 may give U.S. trade secret owners hope that Article 39 enhanced trade secret protection abroad, this may not be the case in all countries. Some countries (including the United States) have taken the position that their pre-TRIPS laws are sufficient to meet the obligations of Article 39. This reality is ameliorated somewhat by the efforts of the United States to strengthen protection for trade secrets and other forms of intellectual property rights. *See, e.g.*, Exec. Office of the President, Administration Strategy on Mitigating the Theft of U.S. Trade Secrets (Feb. 20, 2013).

§ 9.3   ENFORCEMENT OBLIGATIONS UNDER THE TRIPS AGREEMENT

Article 39 of the TRIPS Agreement specifies that WTO-member countries are required to provide protection for "undisclosed information," but it does not specify how. Part III of the TRIPS Agreement deals with the enforcement obligations of WTO-members. Specifically, Article 41.1 provides:

> Members shall ensure that enforcement procedures as specified in this Part are available under the law so as to permit effective action against any act of infringement of intellectual property rights covered by this Agreement, including expeditious remedies to prevent infringements and remedies which constitute a deterrent to further infringements.

Article 41 then proceeds to describe in general terms the required features of an enforcement process, but does not prescribe whether it must entail administrative, civil, or criminal enforcement. Under the TRIPS Agreement, criminal enforcement is only required for "trademark counterfeiting or copyright piracy on a commercial scale." *See* TRIPS Agreement, art. 61.

Based upon the foregoing, countries that institute enforcement processes to meet their obligations under Article 39 can utilize a variety of different approaches that may differ significantly from what trade secret owners enjoy in the United States. In particular, although Article 50 of the TRIPS Agreement requires that "judicial authorities" have "authority to order prompt and effective provisional measures . . . to prevent an infringement of any intellectual property rights from occurring," the grant of provisional relief may not be as swift as the temporary restraining order and preliminary relief processes that are in place in the United States. This, of course, puts trade secrets at greater risk of becoming "generally known" and counsels against sending trade secrets abroad in the first instance. (*See supra* § 2.8.2)

§ 9.4   SAMPLING OF FOREIGN PROTECTIONS

In order to comply with their obligations under the TRIPS Agreement to protect undisclosed information, many WTO-member countries have enacted trade secrecy provisions. Other countries rely upon their common law traditions to provide a civil remedy for trade secret misappropriation. Still others recognize claims for breaches of express promises of confidentiality. Thus, there are wide variations in these laws and it is best to consult each country's laws to fully understand the nature of such protections and exclusions, and to ascertain how they compare to the United States.

The subsections that follow provide a flavor of the approaches used in a few countries:

§ 9.4.1   CANADA

When considering the laws of Canada, one must always account for the fact that Canada is divided into different Provinces with different sets of procedural and substantive laws and different legal traditions. However, as with the United States, Canada has adopted a number of federal laws. The federal law that concerns trade secrets is titled the "Security of Information Act, Economic Espionage." *See* R.S.C. 1985, c. O–5, § 19. It is a criminal law that is similar to the U.S. Economic Espionage Act, discussed *infra* § 10.2.

The civil enforcement of trade secrecy in Canada is determined by the laws of each Province. Generally, in keeping with its common-law heritage, the Provinces of Canada (with the exception of the Province of Quebec which is a civil law jurisdiction) have no uniform statutes governing the civil enforcement of trade secret rights. Rather, a claim for trade secret infringement must be brought under principles of common law, including principles of unfair competition.

§ 9.4.2   CHINA

China is primarily a civil law country. Accordingly, in an effort to comply with its TRIPS obligations it has adopted an unfair competition statute that covers trade secrets and its claim for trade secret misappropriation appears similar to the conceptual application in the United States. However, the available remedies are comparatively low. Article 25 of China's competition law, as translated, provides that: "If any party . . . infringes the business secret of another . . . the relevant control and inspection authority shall order that party to desist from the illegal act and may, according to circumstances, [impose on the party a fine of more than approxi-

mately U.S. $1,665 and less than approximately
U.S. $33,300.]" There is also a scheme for criminal
enforcement of trade secret rights. Breach of contract actions to enforce express promises of confidentiality are often the preferable course of action in
China.

§ 9.4.3   EUROPEAN UNION

Broadly speaking, the European Union, like Canada and the United States, is a collection of individual states, each with their own sets of laws. However, the European Union (through prescribed legislative processes) is authorized to adopt directives and
regulations to require EU-member countries to
adopt specific laws. In the case of EU Directives,
each EU-member country has flexibility to comply
with each Directive as it sees fit. Thus, the laws of
each individual EU-member country must be consulted to determine applicable law.

To date, the European Union has not adopted a
Directive with respect to trade secrets, but some
individual countries within the E.U. have adopted
trade secret laws. Others rely upon common law or
general principles of unfair competition. *See* Study
on Trade Secrets and Parasitic Copying (Look-a-
likes), MARKT/2010/20/D, Report on Trade Secrets
for the European Commission, (Hogan Lovells Intern'l, LLP 2011) (noting that "[a]ll Member States
offer some form of protection although in one or two
Member States protection is extremely limited").
For instance, in the United Kingdom, trade secrets
are protected by contract law and principles of unfair competition. In Norway, section 25 in the Fair

Marketing Practices Act of 2009 prohibits all acts that are against "fair business practices" and has been deemed to apply to trade secret misappropriation claims.

§ 9.4.4   INDIA

In keeping with its common law tradition, India has not adopted a statute concerning either the civil or criminal enforcement of trade secret rights. Instead, trade secrets are protected in India either through contract law or based upon a tort or equitable claim of breach of confidentiality. However, this may change in the future as India and other countries are asked to consider (by the U.S. and various International IP organizations) the adoption of greater protection schemes.

§ 9.4.5   MEXICO

Since becoming a member of the North American Free Trade Agreement (NAFTA), Mexico has enacted statutes for the protection of intellectual property which include provisions for the protection for trade secrets. *See* Ley de Proteccion a la Propiedad Industricl [LPPI] [Industrial Property Law], as amended, Title III, Diario Oficial de law Federacion [DO], June 29, 2010 (Mex.).

§ 9.5   THE PRINCIPLE OF TERRITORIALITY

When a foreign individual or company misappropriates the trade secrets of an American company, and the acts of misappropriation occur entirely outside of the United States, the trade secret laws of the United States generally will not apply. This is consistent with the principle of territoriality and identifies a major vulnerability for companies that choose to conduct operations or engage in other business abroad. In such situations, the substantive and procedural laws of another country are likely to define whether the allegedly misappropriated information is protected and has been misappropriated (unless there is an enforceable contract between the parties that contains a contractual obligation of confidentiality and specifies the law to be applied to the relationship).

The civil trade secret jurisprudence in the U.S. currently lacks a specific framework for determining when U.S. trade secret law will apply to misappropriation that occurs on foreign soil. Unlike U.S. patent law that includes specific provisions with "extraterritorial" affect, neither the UTSA nor the *Restatements* address this issue. If a trade secret owner wants to sue another in United States courts for trade secret misappropriation occurring in another country, it will have to rely upon general principles of extraterritoriality. Furthermore, under general principles of personal jurisdiction, ordinarily a foreign defendant must have a sufficient "presence" in the United States or the tort or consequent injury must occur in the United States before it can be sued in courts within the United States.

§ 9.6   ACTIONS BEFORE THE INTERNATIONAL TRADE COMMISSION

The International Trade Commission (ITC) is an independent, quasi-judicial federal agency that is comprised of six commissioners appointed by the President. The ITC is an optional venue for American trade secret owners dealing with trade secret misappropriation abroad. This is because the ITC has the power to grant an order to seal the U.S. border against the entry of products that have been created as a result of trade secret misappropriation.

There are several advantages to choosing the ITC over a court for trade secret misappropriation. The speed with which investigations are completed is a top factor. Most investigations are completed in about a year, with more complicated cases completed within eighteen months. Furthermore, because ITC proceedings are *in rem* actions, personal jurisdiction over misappropriators is not necessary, thus eliminating one of the most difficult challenges in bringing a court action against a foreign defendant. The exclusion order issued by the ITC is enforced at all ports of entry in the United States by the Customs Service. The discovery process carries advantages as well, including nationwide service of process for subpoenas for documents and depositions, and virtually unlimited discovery.

Developments in a relatively recent case before the ITC appear to provide an avenue for American trade secret owners to redress trade secret misappropriation that has occurred entirely on foreign soil. Using section 337 of the Tariff Act of 1930 (a trade statute that protects United States industry from unfair foreign competition) the Federal Circuit upheld the ITC's decision to apply U.S. trade secret law to misappropriation that occurred in China.

In *TianRui Grp. v. ITC*, 661 F.3d 1322 (Fed. Cir. 2011), the Federal Circuit determined that the Congressional presumption against extraterritorial application of legislation did not apply to the case for three reasons. First, Section 337 is specifically directed to importation of articles into the United States, an inherently international transaction, and thus "it is reasonable to assume that Congress was aware, and intended, that the statute would apply to conduct . . . that may have occurred abroad." Second, the Court points out that the ITC "does not purport to regulate purely foreign conduct." Rather, the "unfair" activity is only prohibited to the extent that it results in importing goods into the United States and causing domestic injury. Finally, the Court determined that the legislative history of section 337 supports interpreting the statute as permitting the ITC to evaluate conduct that occurs extraterritorially since "Congress intended a . . . broad and flexible meaning."

CHAPTER 10

TRADE SECRET RELATED CRIMES

§ 10.1 CRIMINAL CONSEQUENCES FOR TRADE SECRET MISAPPROPRIATION

In addition to each state recognizing a claim for civil trade secret misappropriation under either the UTSA or common law, many states (about half) have enacted criminal statutes that are specifically directed at trade secret theft. *See, e.g.*, Ala. Code § 13A–8–10.4(b) (2013); Ark. Code Ann. § 5–36–107 (West 2012); Calif. Penal Code § 499c (West 2013); Colo. Rev. Stat. Ann. § 18–4–408(1) (West 2013); Ga. Code Ann. § 16–8–13 (West 2012); Tex. Penal Code Ann. § 31.05(b) (West 2011). In these jurisdictions it is therefore possible for a defendant in a civil trade secret misappropriation case to also face state criminal charges for the same alleged misappropriation.

In states that do not have specific criminal trade secret statutes, other laws which prohibit larceny, property theft, or the receipt of stolen property may cover trade secret misappropriation, particularly if the alleged trade secrets are embodied in a tangible form. *See, e.g.*, Del. Code Ann. tit. 11, § 857(6), (9) (West 2013) (including trade secrets in definition of property for theft crimes); *Hancock v. State*, 402 S.W.2d 906 (Tex. Crim. App. 1966) (involving prosecution for theft of confidential computer programs before Texas adopted a criminal trade secret statute). Criminal defendants in trade secret cases may also be charged with other related statutory provisions such as violation of state or federal computer access statutes, including the federal Computer Fraud and Abuse Act (18 U.S.C. § 1030 (2013)), discussed *infra* § 10.3.

While an individual who misappropriates trade secrets may also be subject to criminal prosecution, state criminal actions for trade secret theft are not very common. Among other reasons, state prosecutors are unlikely to use their limited resources to prosecute an economic crime where the victim-company has a readily available, and perhaps better suited, civil cause of action and remedy. When criminal actions are brought by state and federal prosecutors they tend to involve egregious (or apparently egregious) instances of corporate or foreign espionage. *See, e.g., Weightman v. State*, 975 S.W.2d 621 (Tex. Crim. App. 1998) (affirming conviction of buyer and seller of misappropriated trade secrets related to machine manufacturing industry); *United States v. Chung*, 659 F.3d 815 (9th Cir. 2011) (affirming conviction of a former Boeing engineer who provided trade secrets to China); *see also* Economic Espionage Act, 18 U.S.C. § 1831 (2013), discussed *infra*.

Generally, when a criminal trade secret action is brought, the prosecutors must prove that the information in question is a trade secret in much the same way as would be required in a civil action (unless the language of the criminal statute suggests otherwise). Accordingly, the same kinds of evidence, such as efforts to preserve secrecy, are required. Unlike civil cases, however, one important additional requirement under the criminal statutes is the *mens rea* (or intent) requirement. Usually, the defendant must have "knowingly" or "intentionally" misappropriated the trade secret. *See, e.g.,* Tex. Penal Code Ann. § 31.05(b) (West 2011) ("A person commits an offense if, without the owner's effective consent, he knowingly" steals, copies, or communicates trade secrets); Colo. Rev. Stat. Ann. § 18–4–408(1) (West 2013) (requiring "intent to deprive or withhold from the owner" or "intent to appropriate. . . for [the wrongdoer's] own use or the use of another" for the crime of trade secret theft); Ala. Code § 13A–8–10.4(b) (2013) (requiring that a person "knowingly" steal, copy, or communicate trade secrets in order for the statute to apply). This is considered to be a higher standard than the civil requirement that the defendant "know or have reason to know" that the trade secrets were misappropriated. *See supra* § 4.4.

There may also be significant definitional differences between the applicable civil trade secret statute and the criminal trade secret statute with respect to both the definition of a trade secret and the meaning of misappropriation. In *Restatement of Torts* jurisdictions, where trade secret law is based upon common law principles that were developed before the criminal statutes, the civil definitions of a trade secret and misappropriation tend to differ from the state criminal statute (especially if the state's criminal statute is modeled after the federal Economic Espionage Act or the UTSA). Conversely, in a civil UTSA jurisdiction, the criminal statute may define a trade secret to include only scientific or technical information, thus narrowing the scope of subject matter that can be prosecuted under the statute. This appears to be the case in Alabama,

Arkansas, New Hampshire, and Utah. *See* Ala. Code § 13A–8–10.4(a)(4) (2013); Ark. Code Ann. § 5–36–101(11) (West 2012); N.H. Rev. Stat. Ann. § 637:2(I) (2013); Utah Code Ann. § 76–6–401(1) (West 2012).

Based upon the foregoing, each criminal statute which may apply to an alleged misappropriation of trade secrets should be carefully evaluated to determine the applicable definition of a trade secret and whether that definition differs from the UTSA norm. Additionally, the proscribed activity must be identified to determine what acts constitute criminal wrongdoing. Typically, criminal trade secret statutes involve a different definition of misappropriation, principally with respect to the knowledge or *mens rea* requirement of the crime. The federal Economic Espionage Act, discussed *infra*, is one example.

§ 10.2 THE ECONOMIC ESPIONAGE ACT

Before the Economic Espionage Act of 1996 ("the EEA"), 18 U.S.C. §§1831, et seq. (2013), no trade secret specific statute existed under which the federal government could prosecute the theft of trade secrets. Rather, federal authorities had to rely on other statutes to prosecute alleged trade secret misappropriators, such as the federal laws that (i) prohibit wire and mail fraud (*see* 18 U.S.C. §§ 1341, 1343 (2013); *Carpenter v. United States*, 484 U.S. 19, 28 (1987) (holding that the conspiracy to trade an employer's confidential information is within the reach of the mail and wire fraud statutes) and (ii) prohibit the transportation of stolen property across state lines (*see* 18 U.S.C. § 2314 (2013); *United*

States v. Brown, 925 F.2d 1301, 1307–08 (10ᵗʰ Cir. 1991) (holding that stolen computer program and source code did not fit under the Transportation of Stolen Property Act because it did not constitute physical, tangible property).

To date, the EEA is the only federal law on trade secret misappropriation. Although there have been repeated calls for a federal civil law on trade secret misappropriation, there is currently no civil counterpart to the EEA. Additionally, unlike the Computer Fraud and Abuse Act ("the CFAA," discussed *supra* at § 4.14 and *infra* at § 10.3), the EEA does not create a private right of action. Generally, the EEA gives federal authorities, under the auspices of the U.S. Department of Justice and local federal prosecutors, the power to investigate and prosecute individuals or companies that buy or receive trade secrets improperly obtained from third parties.

EEA prosecutions can involve acts of corporate espionage by outsiders. However, employees, former employees, and other company "insiders," are the primary wrongdoers in the vast majority of EEA prosecutions. The prototypical EEA case involves employees who violate their duty of loyalty by using or disclosing their employer's confidential business information. For example, in July 2010, two individuals were indicted for stealing and selling $40 million worth of trade secret information related to General Motor's hybrid automobile plans. *See United States v. Qin*, 10–cr–20454, U.S. District Court, Eastern District of Michigan (Detroit). The allegations were that the employees downloaded and saved confidential General Motor documents and then gave the information to a Chinese automaker.

Foreign governments have also been known to engage in acts of corporate economic espionage. *See* Indictment, *United States v. Fei Ye*, CR 02–20145 JW, 2002 WL 32153617 (N.D. Cal. 2002) (charging Fei Ye and Ming Zhong with economic espionage for the benefit of China under the EEA. Ye and Zhong pled guilty to the charge of economic espionage to benefit a foreign government); Indictment, *United States v. Hanssen*, 01–188–A (E.D. Va. 2001) *available at* http://www.fas.org/irp/ops/ci/hanssen_ indict.html (last visited Mar. 27, 2013) (charging Hanssen with economic espionage for the benefit of Russia under the EEA. Hanssen pled guilty to the charges). Indeed, it was the fear of such activities that was behind the enactment of the EEA in the first-place, and helps to explain why the EEA, while similar to the UTSA, has a slightly different focus. *See* S. Rep. No. 104–359, at 6–7 (1996) ("[T]here is considerable evidence that foreign governments are using their espionage capabilities against American companies.").

§ 10.2.1 PROHIBITED CONDUCT UNDER THE EEA

Sections 1831 and 1832 of the EEA define the prohibited conduct under the Act. 18 U.S.C. §§ 1831–1832 (2013). As stated in both sections, the criminal wrongdoing can take five basic forms:

Whoever, intending or . . . knowingly—

(1) steals, or without authorization appropriates, takes, carries away, or conceals, or by fraud, artifice, or deception obtains a trade secret;

(2) without authorization copies, duplicates, sketches, draws, photographs, downloads, uploads, alters, destroys, photocopies, replicates, transmits, delivers, sends, mails, communicates, or conveys a trade secret;

(3) receives, buys, or possesses a trade secret, knowing the same to have been stolen or appropriated, obtained, or converted without authorization;

(4) attempts to commit any offense described in any of paragraphs (1) through (3); or

(5) conspires with one or more other persons to commit any offense described in any of paragraphs (1) through (3), and one or more of such persons do any act to effect the object of the conspiracy . . .

18 U.S.C. §§ 1831(a) and 1832(a). Of particular relevance, and in comparison to a civil misappropriation claim, are the *mens rea* ("intending or knowing," "knowingly," and "with intent to convert") and *actus rea* requirements of each section.

The decision of which of the two sections to apply turns on whether the theft was intended to benefit a foreign government. If so, the conduct falls under section 1831. Section 1832 is similar to a UTSA claim except that it includes additional elements. First, it applies only when there is intent to "convert a trade secret . . . related to a product or service used in or intended for use in interstate or foreign commerce." 18 U.S.C. § 1832(a) (2013). Second, the actor must intend or know that the conversion will harm the trade secret owner. *Id.; see also United States v. Howley*, 707 F.3d 575, 580 (6th Cir. 2013). These requirements are not elements of a civil misappropriation claim and, therefore, are important distinctions between EEA prosecutions and civil misappropriation claims. Moreover, because the "in commerce" requirement is the reason Congress can enact the EEA under its Commerce Clause powers, it is not an element that can or should be ignored, particularly since trade secrets that are only used internally within a company may not meet the statutory in commerce requirement. *See United States v. Aleynikov*, 676 F.3d 71 (2d Cir. 2012).

In *United States v. Aleynikov*, (also discussed *infra* § 10.2.4), the court reversed the conviction of the defendant based upon a finding that the subject trade secrets were not "produced for" or "placed in" interstate commerce as was then required by section 1832(a). 676 F.3d at 82. In response to this decision, Congress passed legislation to amend the EEA with the apparent intent to broaden the activities to which it applies. *See* Theft of Trade Secrets Clarification Act of 2012, Pub. L. No. 112–236, 126 Stat. 1627 (2012). The legislation was signed by President Obama on December 28, 2012 and amended the prior language of section 1832(a). As amended, section 1832(a) now covers theft of a trade secret "that is related to a product or service used in or intended for use in interstate or foreign commerce, to the economic benefit of anyone other than the owner thereof." 18 U.S.C. § 1832(a)(2013).

Significantly, both sections 1831 and 1832 make an attempt to steal trade secrets and a conspiracy to steal trade secrets a crime. *See* §§ 1831(a)(4)–(5) and 1832(a)(4)–(5) (2013). Thus, it is conceivable that someone may be prosecuted under the EEA even though no trade secrets were, in fact, stolen. As explained in *United States v. Martin*, "to find a defendant guilty of conspiracy, the prosecution must prove (1) that an agreement existed, (2) that it had an unlawful purpose, and (3) that the defendant was a voluntary participant." 228 F.3d 1, 10–11 (1st Cir. 2000).

§ 10.2.2   KEY DEFINITIONS UNDER THE EEA

Section 1839 of the EEA, defines trade secrets broadly, using a variation on the wording of the UTSA. A "trade secret" is information that "the owner thereof has taken reasonable measures to keep . . . secret," and that "derives independent economic value, actual or potential, from not being generally known to, and not being readily ascertainable through proper means by, the public." 18 U.S.C. § 1839(3) (2013). Thus, federal government prosecutors must prove three elements: (1) that the information is actually secret because it is neither known to, nor readily ascertainable by, the public; (2) that the owner took reasonable measures to maintain that secrecy; and (3) that independent economic value was derived from that secrecy. *See*

United States v. Chung, 659 F.3d 815, 824–25 (9th Cir. 2011). The language of section 1839(3) further provides that information is to be protected regardless of its form.

The secrecy requirement is part of the EEA's definition of a trade secret, and like the UTSA, is defined by what it is not; secret information is neither known nor readily ascertainable. However, the EEA defines the relevant group, the members of which may not have knowledge of the information, in a slightly different way. In the UTSA, "trade secret" is defined as that which is "not . . . generally known to, and not . . . readily ascertainable by proper means by, other persons who can obtain economic value from its disclosure or use." Unif. Trade Secrets Act § 1(4) (amended 1985). Under the UTSA, this has been interpreted to include a sub-part of the general public, such as members of a particular industry group or technical discipline. *See supra* § 3.1. In other words, information need not be known by the public at large in order to be generally known under the UTSA. The EEA changes the last clause of the secrecy requirement to read "by the public."

There appears to be some conflict between the circuits as to whether the difference in the definition of a trade secret under the EEA modifies the analysis of secrecy. In *United States v. Lange*, 312 F.3d 263, 267 (7th Cir. 2002) the court interpreted "the public" as not necessarily meaning the "general public," but potentially "the economically relevant public." In contrast, the court in *United States v. Hsu*, 155 F.3d 189, 196 (3d Cir. 1998), noted that "the EEA alters the relevant party from whom proprietary information must be kept confidential" to be the public at large, a narrower group than provided under the UTSA. However, in adopting the EEA there is no indication that Congress intended to alter the UTSA's definition of a trade secret. *See* S. Rep. No. 104–359, at 14 (1996) ("This definition is closely modeled on the definition of a 'trade secret' used in the Uniform Trade Secrets Act."). More importantly, as a practical matter, the narrower definition applied in *Hsu* appears to raise greater due process and evidentiary concerns since it may be difficult for individuals to "know" what is claimed as a trade secret if the alleged secrets are known and widely-distributed within an industry.

§ 10.2.3 EXTRATERRITORIAL REACH OF THE EEA

A concern that was at the heart of the debates leading to the enactment of the EEA was the fear that foreign governments and foreign entities were attempting to steal U.S. trade secrets. For this reason, the reach of the EEA extends well outside the boundaries of the United States. If a theft of trade secret occurs in a foreign country, jurisdiction may be asserted if: (a) the defendant is a U.S. citizen or corporation, or (b) any "act in furtherance of the offense" was committed within the United States. 18 U.S.C. § 1837 (2013). Accordingly, the EEA, unlike the UTSA, has some explicit extra-territorial reach.

§ 10.2.4 LEGAL CHALLENGES TO THE EEA

The constitutionality of the EEA has been challenged in a handful of cases, but it has so far withstood such attacks. To date, the principal attack made against the EEA is that it violates due process because it is unconstitutionally vague. In *United Sates v. Hsu*, 40 F. Supp. 2d 623 (E.D. Pa. 1999), the first case to be prosecuted under the EEA, the defendant challenged the statute as unconstitutionally vague, arguing that it fails to define the term "related to or included in" and that the statute's definitions of "trade secret" fails to define either "reasonable measures" to keep the information secret or what is meant by information that is not "generally known" or "readily ascertainable." *Hsu*, 40 F. Supp. 2d at 626. Hsu's motion to dismiss was unsuccessful and the case was affirmed on appeal. 155 F.3d 189, 196 (3d Cir. 1998).

In a later case, *United States v. Krumrei*, 258 F. 3d 535 (6th Cir. 2001), the Sixth Circuit court applied *United States v. Hsu* to address the defendant's vagueness argument. Like the defendant in *Hsu*, Krumrei argued that the definition of a trade secret (specifically the term "reasonable measures") in the EEA was unconstitutionally vague. The indictment arose from a meeting between Krumrei and a private investigator (whom the defendant thought to be a competitor) at which the defendant conveyed information that he knew was a trade secret of his employer. The court explains that the defendant bears the burden of establishing that the statute is vague as applied to his case. In other words, vagueness is considered in context and not with respect to some other hypothetical person or situation.

As noted previously, the Second Circuit interpreted the phrases "produced for" or "placed in" interstate commerce of old section 1832(a) quite narrowly. In *United States v. Aleynikov*, 676 F.3d 71 (2d Cir. 2012), the defendant was a computer programmer for Goldman Sachs where he worked on developing the firm's high-frequency trading system. When offered the opportunity to develop a similar system for a competitor, he copied hundreds of thousands of lines of source code related to the trading system and transferred the information to an outside server located in Germany. He then downloaded the source code material from the outside server onto his personal computers and a portable flash drive. The defendant was convicted of violating the Economic Espionage Act.

On appeal, the circuit court determined that the high-frequency trading system was neither "produced for" nor "placed in" interstate or foreign commerce because the firm had no intention of selling the system or licensing it to anyone. *United States v. Aleynikov*, 676 F.3d at 82. Because the trading system was not designed to enter or pass into commerce, or to make something that does, the court concluded that the defendant's theft of source code relating to that system was not an offense under the EEA.

In response to the *Aleynikov* decision, Congress passed legislation to amend the relevant language of the EEA. *See* Theft of Trade Secrets Clarification Act of 2012, Pub. L. No. 112–236, 126 Stat. 1627 (2012). The amended section 1832(a) now covers theft of a trade secret "that is related to a product or service used in or intended for use in interstate or foreign commerce, to the economic benefit of anyone other than the owner thereof." 18 U.S.C. § 1832(a) (2013). Whether this solves the *Aleynikov* problem remains to be seen as it is still unclear what "used in or intended for use" means. The amendment may not necessarily change the outcome in another *Aleynikov*-type scenario if, as in *Aleynikov*, the court defines "use" narrowly.

To date, none of the cases that have challenged the constitutionality of the EEA have reached the U.S. Supreme Court, but in keeping with the constitutional rights of criminal defendants, it is likely that such issues will continue to be raised until the Court speaks on the issues. As a practical matter, however, and consistent with the holding in *Krumrei,* the more employees and others are put on actual notice of the existence of trade secrets, the more difficult vagueness challenges will be.

§ 10.2.5 PENALTIES UNDER THE EEA

On January 14, 2013 the EEA was amended by the Foreign and Economic Espionage Penalty Enhancement Act of 2012 to increase the penalties provided under the EEA for those intending to benefit a foreign government, instrumentality, or agent. *See* Pub. L. No. 112–269, 126 Stat. 2442 (2013). For offenses committed by individuals under section 1831(a), the upper limit of the potential fine was increased from $500,000 to $5,000,000. For those offenses committed by organizations under section 1831(b) (the section covering domestic acts), the upper limit of the fine was increased from $10,000,000 to the greater of $10,000,000 or three times the value of the stolen trade secret. The term of imprisonment remains at not more than fifteen years.

The penalties under section 1832, the broader and more widely used section, remain unchanged. The maximum fine for an individual violating the section is not specified (unlike in § 1831), and the prison term is up to ten years. Having not provided a specified fine, the maximum fine of $250,000 set in 18 U.S.C. § 3571(b)(3) for felony offenses is likely to serve as the ceiling. This is significantly less than the $5,000,000 fine for section 1831 offenses and reflects the fear of industrial espionage by foreign governments. For an organization violating section 1832, the specified fine is up to $5,000,000 (half of that provided under § 1831 by the new amendment.).

§ 10.3　THE COMPUTER FRAUD AND ABUSE ACT

The Computer Fraud and Abuse Act (the CFAA) was adopted to address the problem of computer hacking and does not directly address trade secret misappropriation. 18 U.S.C. §1030 (2013). Unlike the EEA, however, it includes a private right of action (discussed in § 4.14 *supra*) that some plaintiffs use to turn a state trade secret claim into a federal case. With respect to potential criminal liability, the CFAA makes it a crime for anyone to intentionally access a computer without authorization or exceeding authorization in order to access "information from any protected computer." 18 U.S.C. § 1030(2)(c) (2013).

Because the principal wrongdoing as defined by the CFAA is "accessing a protected computer," its provisions conceptually overlap with the improper acquisition provisions of trade secret law. *See supra* § 4.3. Generally, if the facts of a trade secret case involve the acquisition of trade secrets that are stored on a computer, the defendant in a civil trade secret case should also be concerned about potential criminal prosecution under the CFAA.

§ 10.3.1 WHAT CONSTITUTES UNAUTHORIZED ACCESS?

As previously discussed in § 4.14 *supra*, whether the defendant's access to the subject computer was unauthorized or exceeded existing authorization is at the heart of a CFAA claim. In some ways, CFAA claims are analogous to the improper means requirement for misappropriation under the UTSA. It is unclear, however, whether they mean the same thing, or whether the CFAA requirement is broader or narrower than the UTSA. Of particular concern to individuals who regularly use the Internet is whether a violation of ubiquitous "Terms of Use Agreements" can make some activities "unauthorized" for purposes of the CFAA. Similar concerns are raised with respect to common provisions of employment agreements and confidentiality agreements that limit computer access.

There is currently a split in authority among jurisdictions about how to define "unauthorized access" in employment relationships that, depending on the eventual outcome of the split, may expose more alleged trade secret misappropriators to criminal prosecution under the CFAA. The specific issue is whether employees who have permission to access their employer's computers can ever be deemed to have accessed these computers "without authorization." The answer depends on whether the interpretation of the statute is broad or narrow. It might also depend upon legislative efforts to narrow the definition of "without authorization." *See supra* § 4.14.

Some courts reason that a breach of loyalty or other break in the agency relationship resulting from a purpose that is contrary to the interests of the employer is an unauthorized access. *See Int'l Airport Ctrs., LLC v. Citrin*, 440 F.3d 418, 420–21 (7th Cir. 2006) (finding that former employee who destroyed data on former employer's computer prior to resigning to join competitor exceeded authorization to access). According to Judge Posner in *Citrin*, when an employee accesses a computer or information on a computer to further interests that are adverse to his employer, he violates his duty of loyalty, thereby terminating his agency relationship and losing any authority he has to access the computer or any information on it. *Id.* at 420–21.

Other courts look to the employers' specific employment policies delineating the kinds of computer access that are permissible for employees and which are prohibited. *See, e.g., EF Cultural Travel B.V. v. Zefer Corp*, 318 F.3d 58, 63 (1st Cir. 2003); *United States v. John*, 597 F.3d 263, 272 (5th Cir. 2010). Still, some courts find unauthorized access without regard to company policies, where the employee used the computer for an improper or non-business related purpose. *See United States v. Tolliver*, No. 10–3439, 2011 WL 4090472 *5 (3d Cir. Sept. 15, 2011)(former bank teller provided confidential customer account information to others for criminal purpose); *United States v. Teague*, 646 F.3d 1119, 1122 (8th Cir. 2011) (employee of Department of Education government contractor viewed President Obama's student loan records without a business purpose).

The narrowest view looks to whether the defendant has circumvented any technological barriers to access the information. Thus, under this view, mere violations of company policies or unauthorized use of information obtained from a computer are not enough to trigger the statute. Rather, the focus is more on computer hacking-type behavior; the manner of access, not the use of the information after it has been accessed is critical. *See United States v. Nosal*, 676 F.3d 854, 863 (9th Cir. 2012) ("the phrase 'exceeds authorized access' in the CFAA does not extend to violations of use restrictions.") The court in *Nosal* reasoned that the CFAA only applies to outsiders who have no authorized access to the computer at all or those insiders or employees whose initial access to a computer is authorized but who access unauthorized information.

Similarly, in *WEC Carolina Energy Solutions LLC v. Miller*, 687 F.3d 199, 207 (4th Cir. 2012) the court held that the CFAA applies only to "individuals who access computers without authorization or who obtain or alter information beyond the bounds of their authorized access." The defendants in *WEC* were former employees who allegedly downloaded

proprietary company information and used it to solicit a new customer in competition with WEC. In
pleading its CFAA claim, the company alleged that
their conduct was in violation of its policies "prohibiting the use of any confidential information and
trade secrets unless authorized" and prohibiting the
"download[ing] [of] confidential and proprietary information to a personal computer." *Id.* at 206–07.
Because the defendants had legitimate access to
this information as employees, the court found that
while they may have misappropriated information,
they did not access a computer without authorization or exceed their authorized access in violation of
the CFAA.

The courts that have adopted a narrow interpretation of the CFAA generally express concern about
the policy and fairness ramifications of a broad interpretation which are particularly applicable to
criminal prosecutions. To put it simply, a broad definition of "unauthorized access" may make numerous relatively "innocent" activities criminal under
circumstances where, in the past, such activities
would not even give rise to a claim for civil relief.
For instance, the fear is that, "any employee who
checked the latest Facebook posting or sporting
event scores in contravention of his employer's use
policy . . . would be left without any authorization to
access his employer's computer systems." *WEC Carolina Energy Solutions LLC v. Miller,* 687 F.3d at
206. While at first blush it may seem that a broad
interpretation of the CFAA would benefit most employers, arguably it would create an environment
where it is difficult for employees to differentiate

between trade secrets that they should handle with care and other business information.

§ 10.4 THE NATIONAL STOLEN PROPERTY ACT AND OTHER PROPERTY CRIMES

Although the property/not property debate of trade secret law continues (*see supra* § 1.4), there is no question that trade secrets will be treated as a form of property for some purposes. Whether this is true for property crimes depends upon the wording of the applicable criminal statute and whether intangible property rights are covered. Sometimes, statutes involving property crimes are worded or interpreted to cover intangible property, like trade secrets. *See, e.g.*, Del. Code Ann. tit. 11, § 857(6), (9) (West 2013) (including trade secrets in definition of property for theft crimes); Minn. Stat. Ann. § 609.52 (West 2013) (defining property subject to theft as including trade secrets). For purposes of potential criminal liability, however, it is also important to recognize that trade secrets may be embodied (or fixed) in a tangible form, the theft of which may be a crime.

The National Stolen Property Act (the NSPA) is an example of a criminal statute that makes it a crime to receive stolen property. 18 USCS § 2311 et seq. (2013). Similar statutes have been adopted in most states. *See, e.g.*, Cal. Penal Code § 496 (West 2013). Among other things, the NSPA makes it a federal crime if anyone "transports, transmits, or transfers in interstate or foreign commerce any goods, wares, merchandise, securities or money, of the value of $ 5,000 or more, knowing the same to have been stolen, converted or taken by fraud." 18 U.S.C. § 2314 (2013). The obvious question that this language (and similar language in analogous state statutes) raises is whether trade secrets are goods or wares.

In *United States v. Aleynikov*, 676 F.3d 71 (2d Cir. 2012) the court considered whether the NSPA covered intangible trade secrets. The defendant, Sergey Aleynikov, a computer programmer at Goldman Sachs & Co., developed source code for the company's high-frequency trading system. Aleynikov later accepted an offer to work at a Chicago-based startup that was planning to develop its own high-frequency trading system. On his last day at Goldman Sachs, Aleynikov uploaded over 500,000 lines of the source code to a server in Germany and later downloaded the source code to his home computer. After taking a flash drive containing the source code to a meeting with his new employer in Chicago, Aleynikov was arrested by the FBI. A jury convicted him of violating the National Stolen Property Act and the Economic Espionage Act of 1996. *See supra* § 10.2.4 for discussion of the EEA claim in that case.

Aleynikov appealed his conviction, arguing that the source code is not a "good" that was stolen within the meaning of the NSPA. The court found that the NSPA requires the taking of a physical thing and that source code does not meet this requirement. "Because Aleynikov did not 'assume physical control' over anything when he took the source code, and because he did not thereby 'deprive [Goldman] of its use,' Aleynikov did not violate the NSPA. *Aleynikov*, 676 F.3d at 78–79. The fact that the source code was later downloaded onto a flash drive did not change the analysis. "The later storage of intangible property on a tangible medium does not transform the intangible property into a stolen good." *Id.* at 78.

§ 10.5   POTENTIAL RICO OFFENSES

The Racketeer Influenced and Corrupt Organizations Act, commonly referred to as "RICO," is a federal law that provides criminal penalties and civil remedies for crimes committed as part of a criminal enterprise. 18 U.S.C. §§ 1961–1968 (2013). Since it requires the commission of an underlying predicate crime, the commission of both federal and state crimes (including trade secret related crimes) may give rise to a prosecution or claim under RICO. *See, e.g., R.E. Davis Chem. Corp. v. Nalco Chem. Co.*, 757 F. Supp. 1499 (N.D. Ill 1990) (involving an alleged pattern of trade secret theft).

APPENDIX A

UNIFORM TRADE SECRETS ACT WITH 1985 AMENDMENT

Drafted by the

NATIONAL CONFERENCE OF COMMISSIONERS
ON UNIFORM STATE LAWS

and by it

Approved and Recommended for Enactment
in All the States

At its

ANNUAL CONFERENCE
MEETING IN ITS NINETY-FOURTH YEAR
IN MINNEAPOLIS, MINNESOTA
AUGUST 2–9, 1985

With Prefatory Note and Comments

Approved by the American Bar Association
Baltimore, Maryland, February 11, 1986

The Committee that acted for the National Conference of Commissioners on Uniform State Laws in preparing the Uniform Trade Secrets Act with 1985 Amendments was as follows:

LINDSEY COWEN, 24 Ridgewood Drive, Cartersville, GA 30120, *Chairman*

THOMAS E. CAVENDISH, 31st Floor, 41 South High Street, Columbus, OH 43215

ROBERT H. CORNELL, 25th Floor, 50 California Street, San Francisco, CA 94111

RICHARD COSWAY, University of Washington, School of Law, Seattle, WA 98105

RICHARD F. DOLE, JR., University of Houston, Law Center, 4800 Calhoun, Houston, TX 77004

CARLYLE C. RING, JR., Room 322–D, 5390 Cherokee Avenue, Alexandria, VA 22312, *President (Member Ex Officio)*

WILLIAM J. PIERCE, University of Michigan, School of Law, Ann Arbor, MI 48109, *Executive Director*

Final, approved copies of all Uniform and Model Acts and other printed matter issued by the Conference may be obtained from:

NATIONAL CONFERENCE OF COMMISSIONERS

ON UNIFORM STATE LAWS

645 North Michigan Avenue, Suite 510

Chicago, Illinois 60611

(312) 321–9710

UNIFORM TRADE SECRETS ACT WITH 1985 AMENDMENTS

TABLE OF CONTENTS

PREFATORY NOTE
SECTION

UNIFORM TRADE SECRETS ACT
WITH 1985 AMENDMENTS

(The 1985 Amendments are Indicated
by Underscore and Strikeout)

PREFATORY NOTE

A valid patent provides a legal monopoly for seventeen years in exchange for public disclosure of an invention. If, however, the courts ultimately decide that the Patent Office improperly issued a patent, an invention will have been disclosed to competitors with no corresponding benefit. In view of the substantial number of patents that are invalidated by the courts, many businesses now elect to protect commercially valuable information through reliance upon the state law of trade secret protection. *Kewanee Oil Co. v. Bicron Corp.*, 416 U.S. 470 (1974), which establishes that neither the Patent Clause of the United States Constitution nor the federal patent laws pre-empt state trade secret protection for patentable or unpatentable information, may well have increased the extent of this reliance.

The recent decision in *Aronson v. Quick Point Pencil Co.*, 99 S.Ct. 1096, 201 USPQ 1 (1979) reaffirmed *Kewanee* and held that federal patent law is not a barrier to a contract in which someone agrees to pay a continuing royalty in exchange for the disclosure of trade secrets concerning a product.

Notwithstanding the commercial importance of state trade secret law to interstate business, this law has not developed satisfactorily. In the first place, its development is uneven. Although there typically are a substantial number of reported decisions in states that are commercial centers, this is not the case in less populous and more agricultural jurisdictions. Secondly, even in states in which there has been significant litigation, there is undue uncertainty concerning the parameters of trade secret protection, and the appropriate remedies for misappropriation of a trade secret. One commentator observed:

> "Under technological and economic pressures, industry continues to rely on trade secret protection despite the doubtful and confused status of both common law and statutory remedies. Clear, uniform trade secret protection is urgently needed. . . ."

> Comment, "Theft of Trade Secrets: The Need for a Statutory Solution", 120 U.Pa.L.Rev. 378, 380–81 (1971).

In spite of this need, the most widely accepted rules of trade secret law, § 757 of the Restatement of Torts, were among the sections omitted from the Restatement of Torts, 2d (1978).

The Uniform Act codifies the basic principles of common law trade secret protection, preserving its essential distinctions from patent law. Under both the Act and common law principles, for example, more than one person can be entitled to trade secret protection with respect to the same information, and analysis involving the "reverse engineering" of a lawfully obtained product in order to discover a trade secret is permissible. *Compare* Uniform Act, Section 1(2) (misappropriation means acquisition of a trade secret by means that should be known to be improper and unauthorized disclosure or use of information that one should know is the trade secret of another) *with Miller v. Owens-Illinois, Inc.,* 187 USPQ 47, 48 (D.Md.1975) (alternative holding) (prior, independent discovery a complete defense to liability for misappropriation) *and Wesley-Jessen, Inc., v. Reynolds,* 182 USPQ 135, 144–45, (N.D.Ill.1974) (alternative holding) (unrestricted sale and lease of camera that could be reversed engineered in several days to reveal alleged trade secrets preclude relief for misappropriation).

For liability to exist under this Act, a Section 1(4) trade secret must exist and either a person's acquisition of the trade secret, disclosure of the trade secret to others, or use of the trade secret must be improper under Section 1(2). The mere copying of an unpatented item is not actionable.

Like traditional trade secret law, the Uniform Act contains general concepts. The contribution of the Uniform Act is substitution of unitary definitions of trade secret and trade secret misappropriation, and a single statute of limitations for the various property, quasi-contractual, and violation of fiduciary relationship theories of noncontractual liability utilized at common law. The Uniform Act also codifies the results of the better reasoned cases concerning the remedies for trade secret misappropriation.

The History of the Special Committee on the Uniform Trade Secrets Act

On February 17, 1968, the Conference's subcommittee on Scope and Program reported to the Conference's Executive Committee as follows:

"14. Uniform Trade Secrets Protection Act.

This matter came to the subcommittee from the Patent Law Section of the American Bar Association from President Pierce, Commissioner Joiner and Allison Dunham. It appears that in 1966 the Patent Section of the American Bar Association extensively discussed a resolution to the effect that 'the ABA favors the enactment of a uniform state law to protect against the wrongful disclosure or wrongful appropriation of trade secrets, know-how or other information maintained in confidence by another.' It was decided, however, not to put such a resolution to a vote at that time but that the appropriate Patent Section Committee would further consider the problem. In determining what would be appropriate for the Conference to do at this juncture, the following points should be considered:

(1) At the present much is going on by way of statutory development, both federally and in the states.

(2) There is a fundamental policy conflict still unresolved in that the current state statutes that protect trade secrets tend to keep innovations secret, while our federal patent policy is generally designed to encourage public disclo-

sure of innovations. It may be possible to devise a sensible compromise between these two basic policies that will work, but to do so demands co-ordination of the statutory reform efforts of both the federal government and the states.

(3) The Section on Patents, the ABA group that is closest to this problem, is not yet ready to take a definite position.

It is recommended that a special committee be appointed to investigate the question of the drafting of a uniform act relating to trade secret protection and to establish liaison with the Patent Law Section, the Corporation, Banking and Business Law Section, and the Antitrust Law Section of the American Bar Association."

The Executive Committee, at its Midyear Meeting held February 17 and 18, 1968, in Chicago, Illinois, "voted to authorize the appointment of a Special Committee on Uniform Trade Secrets Protection Act to investigate the question of drafting an act on the subject with instructions to establish liaison with the Patent Law Section, the Corporation, Banking and Business Law Section, and the Antitrust Law Section of the American Bar Association." Pursuant to that action, a Special Committee was appointed, which included Professor Richard Cosway of Seattle, Washington, who is the only original Committee member to serve to the present day. The following year saw substantial changes in the membership of the Committee. Professor Richard F. Dole, Jr., of Iowa City, Iowa, became a member then and has served as a member ever since.

The work of the Committee went before the Conference first on Thursday afternoon, August 10, 1972, when it was one of three Acts considered on first reading. Thereafter, for a variety of reasons, the Committee became inactive, and, regrettably, its original Chairman died on December 7, 1974. In 1976, the Committee became active again and presented a Fifth Tentative Draft of its proposed bill at the 1978 Annual Meeting of the National Conference of Commissioners on Uniform State Laws.

Despite the fact that there had previously been a first reading, the Committee was of the opinion that, because of the lapse of time, the 1978 presentation should also be considered a first reading. The Conference concurred, and the bill was proposed for final reading and adoption at the 1979 Annual Meeting.

On August 9, 1979, the Act was approved and recommended for enactment in all the states. Following discussions with members of the bar and bench, the Special Committee proposed amendments to Sections 2(b), 3(a), 7 and 11 that clarified the intent of the 1979 Official Text. On August 8, 1985, these four clarifying amendments were approved and recommended for enactment in all the states.

UNIFORM TRADE SECRETS ACT
WITH 1985 AMENDMENTS

SECTION 1. DEFINITIONS.

As used in this [Act], unless the context requires otherwise:

(1) "Improper means" includes theft, bribery, misrepresentation, breach or inducement of a breach of a duty to maintain secrecy, or espionage through electronic or other means;

(2) "Misappropriation" means:

(i) acquisition of a trade secret of another by a person who knows or has reason to know that the trade secret was acquired by improper means; or

(ii) disclosure or use of a trade secret of another without express or implied consent by a person who

(A) used improper means to acquire knowledge of the trade secret; or

(B) at the time of disclosure or use, knew or had reason to know that his knowledge of the trade secret was

(I) derived from or through a person who had utilized improper means to acquire it;

(II) acquired under circumstances giving rise to a duty to maintain its secrecy or limit its use; or

(III) derived from or through a person who owed a duty to the person seeking relief to maintain its secrecy or limit its use; or

(C) before a material change of his [or her] position, knew or had reason to know that it was a trade secret and that knowledge of it had been acquired by accident or mistake.

(3) "Person" means a natural person, corporation, business trust, estate, trust, partnership, association, joint venture, government, governmental subdivision or agency, or any other legal or commercial entity.

(4) "Trade secret" means information, including a formula, pattern, compilation, program, device, method, technique, or process, that:

(i) derives independent economic value, actual or potential, from not being generally known to, and not being readily ascertainable by proper means by, other persons who can obtain economic value from its disclosure or use, and

(ii) is the subject of efforts that are reasonable under the circumstances to maintain its secrecy.

COMMENT

One of the broadly stated policies behind trade secret law is "the maintenance of standards of commercial ethics." *Kewanee Oil Co. v. Bicron Corp.,* 416 U.S. 470 (1974). The Restatement of Torts, Section 757, Comment (f), notes: "A complete catalogue of improper means is not possible," but Section 1(1) includes a partial listing.

Proper means include:

1. Discovery by independent invention;

2. Discovery by "reverse engineering", that is, by starting with the known product and working backward to find the method by which it was developed. The acquisition of the known product must, of course, also be by a fair and honest means, such as purchase of the item on the open market for reverse engineering to be lawful;

3. Discovery under a license from the owner of the trade secret;

4. Observation of the item in public use or on public display;

5. Obtaining the trade secret from published literature.

Improper means could include otherwise lawful conduct which is improper under the circumstances; *e.g.,* an airplane overflight used as aerial reconnaissance to determine the competitor's plant layout during construction of the plant. *E. I. du Pont de Nemours & Co., Inc. v. Christopher*, 431 F.2d 1012 (CA5, 1970), cert. den. 400 U.S. 1024 (1970). Because the trade secret can be destroyed through public knowledge, the unauthorized disclosure of a trade secret is also a misappropriation.

The type of accident or mistake that can result in a misappropriation under Section 1(2)(ii)(C) involves conduct by a person seeking relief that does not constitute a failure of efforts that are reasonable under the circumstances to maintain its secrecy under Section 1(4)(ii).

The definition of "trade secret" contains a reasonable departure from the Restatement of Torts (First) definition which required that a trade secret be "continuously used in one's business." The broader definition in the proposed Act extends protection to a plaintiff who has not yet had an opportunity or acquired the means to put a trade secret to use. The definition includes information that has commercial value from a negative viewpoint, for example the results of lengthy and expensive research which proves that a certain process will *not* work could be of great value to a competitor.

Cf. Telex Corp. v. IBM Corp., 510 F.2d 894 (CA10, 1975) per curiam, cert. dismissed 423 U.S. 802 (1975) (liability imposed for developmental cost savings with respect to product not marketed). Because a trade secret need not be exclusive to confer a competitive advantage, different independent developers can acquire rights in the same trade secret.

The words "method, technique" are intended to include the concept of "know-how."

The language "not being generally known to and not being readily ascertainable by proper means by other persons" does not require that information be generally known to the public for trade secret rights to be lost. If the principal ~~person~~ persons who can obtain economic benefit from information ~~is~~ are aware of it, there is no trade secret. A method of casting metal, for example, may be unknown to the general public but readily known within the foundry industry.

Information is readily ascertainable if it is available in trade journals, reference books, or published materials. Often, the nature of a product lends itself to being readily copied as soon as it is available on the market. On the other hand, if reverse engineering is lengthy and expensive, a person who discovers the trade secret through reverse engineering can have a trade secret in the information obtained from reverse engineering.

Finally, reasonable efforts to maintain secrecy have been held to include advising employees of the existence of a trade secret, limiting access to a trade secret on "need to know basis", and controlling plant access. On the other hand, public disclosure of information through display, trade journal publications, advertising, or other carelessness can preclude protection.

The efforts required to maintain secrecy are those "reasonable under the circumstances." The courts do not require that extreme and unduly expensive procedures be taken to protect trade secrets against flagrant industrial espionage. See *E. I. du Pont de Nemours & Co., Inc. v. Christopher, supra.* It follows that reasonable use of a trade secret including controlled disclosure to employees and licensees is consistent with the requirement of relative secrecy.

SECTION 2. INJUNCTIVE RELIEF.

(a) Actual or threatened misappropriation may be enjoined. Upon application to the court, an in-

junction shall be terminated when the trade secret
has ceased to exist, but the injunction may be continued for an additional reasonable period of time in
order to eliminate commercial advantage that otherwise would be derived from the misappropriation.

(b)   ~~If the court determines that it would be unreasonable to prohibit future use~~ In exceptional circumstances, an injunction may condition future use
upon payment of a reasonable royalty for no longer
than the period of time ~~the~~ for which use could have
been prohibited. Exceptional circumstances include,
but are not limited to, a material and prejudicial
change of position prior to acquiring knowledge or
reason to know of misappropriation that renders a
prohibitive injunction inequitable.

(c)   In appropriate circumstances, affirmative acts
to protect a trade secret may be compelled by court
order.

COMMENT

Injunctions restraining future use and disclosure
of misappropriated trade secrets frequently are
sought. Although punitive perpetual injunctions
have been granted, *e.g., Elcor Chemical Corp. v.
Agri-Sul, Inc.,* 494 S.W.2d 204 (Tex.Civ.App.1973),
Section 2(a) of this Act adopts the position of the
trend of authority limiting the duration of injunctive
relief to the extent of the temporal advantage over
good faith competitors gained by a misappropriator.
See, *e.g., K-2 Ski Co. v. Head Ski Co., Inc.,* 506 F.2d
471 (CA9, 1974) (maximum appropriate duration of
both temporary and permanent injunctive relief is

period of time it would have taken defendant to discover trade secrets lawfully through either independent development or reverse engineering of plaintiff's products).

The general principle of Section 2(a) and (b) is that an injunction should last for as long as is necessary, but no longer than is necessary, to eliminate the commercial advantage or "lead time" with respect to good faith competitors that a person has obtained through misappropriation. Subject to any additional period of restraint necessary to negate lead time, an injunction accordingly should terminate when a former trade secret becomes either generally known to good faith competitors or generally knowable to them because of the lawful availability of products that can be reverse engineered to reveal a trade secret.

For example, assume that A has a valuable trade secret of which B and C, the other industry members, are originally unaware. If B subsequently misappropriates the trade secret and is enjoined from use, but C later lawfully reverse engineers the trade secret, the injunction restraining B is subject to termination as soon as B's lead time has been dissipated. All of the persons who could derive economic value from use of the information are now aware of it, and there is no longer a trade secret under Section 1(4). It would be anti-competitive to continue to restrain B after any lead time that B had derived from misappropriation had been removed.

If a misappropriator either has not taken advantage of lead time or good faith competitors already have caught up with a misappropriator at the time that a case is decided, future disclosure and use of a former trade secret by a misappropriator will not damage a trade secret owner and no injunctive restraint of future disclosure and use is appropriate. See, *e.g., Northern Petrochemical Co. v. Tomlinson*, 484 F.2d 1057 (CA7, 1973) (affirming trial court's denial of preliminary injunction in part because an explosion at its plant prevented an alleged misappropriator from taking advantage of lead time); *Kubik, Inc. v. Hull*, 185 USPQ 391 (Mich.App.1974) (discoverability of trade secret by lawful reverse engineering made injunctive relief punitive rather than compensatory).

Section 2(b) deals with a distinguishable the special situation in which future use by a misappropriator will damage a trade secret owner but an injunction against future use nevertheless is unreasonable under the particular inappropriate due to exceptional circumstances of a case. Situations in which this unreasonableness can exist Exceptional circumstances include the existence of an overriding public interest which requires the denial of a prohibitory injunction against future damaging use and a person's reasonable reliance upon acquisition of a misappropriated trade secret in good faith and without reason to know of its prior misappropriation that would be prejudiced by a prohibitory injunction against future damaging use. *Republic Aviation Corp. v. Schenk*, 152 USPQ 830 (N.Y.Sup.Ct.1967) illustrates the public interest justification for withholding prohibitory injunctive relief. The court considered that enjoining a misappropriator from supplying the U.S. with an aircraft weapons control system would have endangered military personnel in Viet Nam. The prejudice to a good faith third party justification for withholding prohibitory injunctive relief can arise upon a trade secret owner's notification to a good faith third party that the third party has knowledge of a trade secret as a result of misappropriation by another. This notice suffices to make the third party a misappropriator thereafter under Section 1(2)(ii)(B)(I). In weighing an aggrieved person's interests and the interests of a third party who has relied in good faith upon his or her ability to utilize information, a court may conclude that restraining future use of the information by the third party is unwarranted. With respect to innocent acquirers of misappropriated trade secrets, Section 2(b) is consistent with the principle of 4 Restatement Torts (First) § 758(b) (1939), but rejects the Restatement's literal conferral of absolute immunity upon all third parties who have paid value in good faith for a trade secret misappropriated by another. The position taken by the Uniform Act is supported by *Forest Laboratories, Inc. v. Pillsbury Co.,* 452 F.2d 621 (CA7, 1971) in which a defendant's purchase of assets of a corporation to which a trade secret had been disclosed in confidence was not considered to confer immunity upon the defendant.

When Section 2(b) applies, a court is given has discretion to substitute an injunction conditioning future use upon payment of a reasonable royalty for an injunction prohibiting future use. Like all injunctive relief for misappropriation, a royalty order in-

junction is appropriate only if a misappropriator has
obtained a competitive advantage through misappropriation and only for the duration of that competitive advantage. In some situations, typically those
involving good faith acquirers of trade secrets misappropriated by others, a court may conclude that
the same considerations that render a prohibitory
injunction against future use inappropriate also
render a royalty order injunction inappropriate. See,
generally, *Prince Manufacturing, Inc. v. Automatic
Partner, Inc.,* 198 USPQ 618 (N.J.Super.Ct.1976)
(purchaser of misappropriator's assets from receiver
after trade secret disclosed to public through sale of
product not subject to liability for misappropriation).

A royalty order injunction under Section 2(b)
should be distinguished from a reasonable royalty
alternative measure of damages under Section 3(a).
See the Comment to Section 3 for discussion of the
differences in the remedies.

Section 2(c) authorizes mandatory injunctions requiring that a misappropriator return the fruits of
misappropriation to an aggrieved person, *e.g.,* the
return of stolen blueprints or the surrender of sur-
reptitious photographs or recordings.

Where more than one person is entitled to trade
secret protection with respect to the same information, only that one from whom misappropriation
occurred is entitled to a remedy.

SECTION 3. DAMAGES.

(a) ~~In addition to or in lieu of injunctive relief~~ <u>Except to the extent that a material and prejudicial change of position prior to acquiring knowledge or reason to know of misappropriation renders a monetary recovery inequitable</u>, a complainant ~~may~~ <u>is entitled to</u> recover damages for ~~the actual loss caused by~~ misappropriation. ~~A complainant also may recover for~~ <u>Damages can include both the actual loss caused by misappropriation and</u> the unjust enrichment caused by misappropriation that is not taken into account in computing ~~damages for~~ actual loss. <u>In lieu of damages measured by any other methods, the damages caused by misappropriation may be measured by imposition of liability for a reasonable royalty for a misappropriator's unauthorized disclosure or use of a trade secret.</u>

(b) If willful and malicious misappropriation exists, the court may award exemplary damages in an amount not exceeding twice any award made under subsection (a).

COMMENT

Like injunctive relief, a monetary recovery for trade secret misappropriation is appropriate only for the period in which information is entitled to protection as a trade secret, plus the additional period, if any, in which a misappropriator retains an advantage over good faith competitors because of misappropriation. Actual damage to a complainant and unjust benefit to a misappropriator are caused by misappropriation during this time alone. See

Conmar Products Corp. v. Universal Slide Fastener Co., 172 F.2d 150 (CA2, 1949) (no remedy for period subsequent to disclosure of trade secret by issued patent); *Carboline Co. v. Jarboe,* 454 S.W.2d 540 (Mo.1970) (recoverable monetary relief limited to period that it would have taken misappropriator to discover trade secret without misappropriation). A claim for actual damages and net profits can be combined with a claim for injunctive relief, but, if both claims are granted, the injunctive relief ordinarily will preclude a monetary award for a period in which the injunction is effective.

As long as there is no double counting, Section 3(a) adopts the principle of the recent cases allowing recovery of both a complainant's actual losses and a misappropriator's unjust benefit that are caused by misappropriation. *E.g., Tri-Tron International v. Velto,* 525 F.2d 432 (CA9, 1975) (complainant's loss and misappropriator's benefit can be combined). Because certain cases may have sanctioned double counting in a combined award of losses and unjust benefit, *e.g., Telex Corp. v. IBM Corp.,* 510 F.2d 894 (CA10, 1975) (per curiam), cert. dismissed, 423 U.S. 802 (1975) (IBM recovered rentals lost due to displacement by misappropriator's products without deduction for expenses saved by displacement; as a result of rough approximations adopted by the trial judge, IBM also may have recovered developmental costs saved by misappropriator through misappropriation with respect to the same customers), the Act adopts an express prohibition upon the counting of the same item as both a loss to a complainant and an unjust benefit to a misappropriator.

As an alternative to all other methods of measuring damages caused by a misappropriator's past conduct, a complainant can request that damages be based upon a demonstrably reasonable royalty for a misappropriator's unauthorized disclosure or use of a trade secret. In order to justify this alternative measure of damages, there must be competent evidence of the amount of a reasonable royalty.

The reasonable royalty alternative measure of damages for a misappropriator's past conduct under Section 3(a) is readily distinguishable from a Section 2(b) royalty order injunction, which conditions a misappropriator's future ability to use a trade secret upon payment of a reasonable royalty. A Section 2(b) royalty order injunction is appropriate only in exceptional circumstances; whereas a reasonable royalty measure of damages is a general option. Because Section 3(a) damages are awarded for a misappropriator's past conduct and a Section 2(b) royalty order injunction regulates a misappropriator's future conduct, both remedies cannot be awarded for the same conduct. If a royalty order injunction is appropriate because of a person's material and prejudicial change of position prior to having reason to know that a trade secret has been acquired from a misappropriator, damages, moreover, should not be awarded for past conduct that occurred prior to notice that a misappropriated trade secret has been acquired.

Monetary relief can be appropriate whether or not injunctive relief is granted under Section 2. If a person charged with misappropriation has ~~acquired~~ materially and prejudicially changed position in reliance upon knowledge of a trade secret acquired in good faith and without reason to know of its misappropriation by another, however, the same considerations that can justify denial of all injunctive relief also can justify denial of all monetary relief. See *Conmar Products Corp. v. Universal Slide Fastener Co.*, 172 F.2d 1950 (CA2, 1949) (no relief against new employer of employee subject to contractual obligation not to disclose former employer's trade secrets where new employer innocently had committed $40,000 to develop the trade secrets prior to notice of misappropriation).

If willful and malicious misappropriation is found to exist, Section 3(b) authorizes the court to award a complainant exemplary damages in addition to the actual recovery under Section 3(a) an amount not exceeding twice that recovery. This provision follows federal patent law in leaving discretionary trebling to the judge even though there may be a jury, *compare* 35 U.S.C. Section 284 (1976).

Whenever more than one person is entitled to trade secret protection with respect to the same information, only that one from whom misappropriation occurred is entitled to a remedy.

SECTION 4. ATTORNEY'S FEES.

If (i) a claim of misappropriation is made in bad faith, (ii) a motion to terminate an injunction is made or resisted in bad faith, or (iii) willful and malicious misappropriation exists, the court may award reasonable attorney's fees to the prevailing party.

COMMENT

Section 4 allows a court to award reasonable attorney fees to a prevailing party in specified circumstances as a deterrent to specious claims of misappropriation, to specious efforts by a misappropriator to terminate injunctive relief, and to willful and malicious misappropriation. In the latter situation, the court should take into consideration the extent to which a complainant will recover exemplary damages in determining whether additional attorney's fees should be awarded. Again, patent law is followed in allowing the judge to determine whether attorney's fees should be awarded even if there is a jury, *compare* 35 U.S.C. Section 285 (1976).

SECTION 5. PRESERVATION OF SECRECY.

In an action under this [Act], a court shall preserve the secrecy of an alleged trade secret by reasonable means, which may include granting protective orders in connection with discovery proceedings, holding in-camera hearings, sealing the records of the action, and ordering any person involved in the litigation not to disclose an alleged trade secret without prior court approval.

COMMENT

If reasonable assurances of maintenance of secrecy could not be given, meritorious trade secret litigation would be chilled. In fashioning safeguards of confidentiality, a court must ensure that a respondent is provided sufficient information to present a defense and a trier of fact sufficient information to resolve the merits. In addition to the illustrative techniques specified in the statute, courts have protected secrecy in these cases by restricting disclosures to a party's counsel and his or her assistants and by appointing a disinterested expert as a special master to hear secret information and report conclusions to the court.

SECTION 6. STATUTE OF LIMITATIONS.

An action for misappropriation must be brought within 3 years after the misappropriation is discovered or by the exercise of reasonable diligence should have been discovered.

For the purposes of this section, a continuing misappropriation constitutes a single claim.

COMMENT

There presently is a conflict of authority as to whether trade secret misappropriation is a continuing wrong. *Compare Monolith Portland Midwest Co. v. Kaiser Aluminum & Chemical Corp.,* 407 F.2d 288 (CA9, 1969) (~~no~~ not a continuing wrong under California law—limitation period upon all recovery begins upon initial misappropriation) with *Underwater Storage, Inc. v. U.S. Rubber Co.,* 371 F.2d 950 (CADC, 1966), cert. den., 386 U.S. 911 (1967) (continuing wrong under general principles—limitation period with respect to a specific act of misappropriation begins at the time that the act of misappropriation occurs).

This Act rejects a continuing wrong approach to the statute of limitations but delays the commencement of the limitation period until an aggrieved person discovers or reasonably should have discovered the existence of misappropriation. If objectively reasonable notice of misappropriation exists, three years is sufficient time to vindicate one's legal rights.

SECTION 7. EFFECT ON OTHER LAW.

(a) ~~This~~ Except as provided in subsection (b), this [Act] displaces conflicting tort, restitutionary, and other law of this State ~~pertaining to~~ providing civil ~~liability~~ remedies for misappropriation of a trade secret.

(b) This [Act] does not affect:

(1) contractual ~~or other civil liability or relief that is~~ remedies, whether or not based upon misappropriation of a trade secret; ~~or~~

(2) ~~criminal liability for~~ other civil remedies that are not based upon misappropriation of a trade secret; or

(3) criminal remedies, whether or not based upon misappropriation of a trade secret.

COMMENT

This Act ~~is not a comprehensive remedy~~ does not deal with criminal remedies for trade secret misappropriation and is not a comprehensive statement of civil remedies. It applies to ~~duties imposed by law in order~~ a duty to protect competitively significant secret information that is imposed by law. It does not apply to ~~duties~~ a duty voluntarily assumed through an express or an implied-in-fact contract. The enforceability of covenants not to disclose trade secrets and covenants not to compete that are intended to protect trade secrets, for example, ~~are~~ is governed by other law. The Act also does not apply to ~~duties~~ a duty imposed by law that ~~are~~ is not dependent upon the existence of competitively significant secret information, like an agent's duty of loyalty to his or her principal.

SECTION 8. UNIFORMITY OF APPLICATION AND CONSTRUCTION.

This [Act] shall be applied and construed to effectuate its general purpose to make uniform the law with respect to the subject of this [Act] among states enacting it.

SECTION 9. SHORT TITLE.

This [Act] may be cited as the Uniform Trade Secrets Act.

SECTION 10. SEVERABILITY.

If any provision of this [Act] or its application to any person or circumstances is held invalid, the invalidity does not affect other provisions or applications of the [Act] which can be given effect without the invalid provision or application, and to this end the provisions of this [Act] are severable.

SECTION 11. TIME OF TAKING EFFECT.

This [Act] takes effect on _____, and does not apply to misappropriation occurring prior to the effective date. With respect to a continuing misappropriation that began prior to the effective date, the [Act] also does not apply to the continuing misappropriation that occurs after the effective date.

COMMENT

The Act applies exclusively to misappropriation that begins after its effective date. Neither misappropriation that began and ended before the effective date nor misappropriation that began before the effective date and continued thereafter is subject to the Act.

SECTION 12. REPEAL.

The following Acts and parts of Acts are repealed:

(1)

(2)

(3)

INDEX

References are to Pages. The bolded page numbers indicate principal treatment of the term.